AN ATTEMPT TO UNTANGLE REVISIONISM

Hawaiian Sovereignty: Do the Facts Matter?

THURSTON TWIGG-SMITH

Hawaiian Sovereignty

DO THE FACTS MATTER?

By Thurston Twigg-Smith

GOODALE PUBLISHING
Honolulu, Hawai'i

© 1998 by Goodale Publishing. All rights reserved

Printed in the United States of America

Library of Congress Cataloging in Publication Data

Twigg-Smith, Thurston, 1921-
  Hawaiian Sovereignty: Do the Facts Matter?

  Bibliography: p.
  Includes index.
  1. History—Hawaii. 2. Politics—Hawaii.

  Hardcover   ISBN 0-9662945-0-5
  Softcover   ISBN 0-9662945-1-3

This book is dedicated to the continued pursuit of the Hawaiian language.

Why the interest in Hawaiian? The first three generations of my grandfather's side of the family in these Islands were fluent in it: Asa Thurston, the missionary, spoke it, preached in it and translated books of the Bible into Hawaiian. His son, speaker of the Kingdom's House of Representatives before his death at age 32, learned it in Kona as a boy and was as fluent in it as in English. His son, Lorrin A., the Revolutionist, was the same. He could catch the detailed nuances of other speakers in the Legislature when he was in it, especially if they thought they could get away with a wisecrack to their colleagues about him.

And on my great-grandmother's side of the family, her father, Lorrin Andrews, put together the first Hawaiian dictionary in 1836 and followed it with an expanded edition in 1865. It was an unsophisticated product compared with the outstanding works of Mary Pukui and Samuel Elbert, but they saluted it for its pioneering thoroughness. They quoted H.W. Williams, a critic of Hawaiian dictionaries, as saying in 1926: "In 1865, it was the most important work of its kind....No other Polynesian dialect had received such thorough treatment...[it] remains a noble production."

In a salute to the missionaries who saved the language by reducing it to a written form in the 1820s, the ultimate dictionary writers quoted the Reverend Lorenzo Lyons, who wrote in 1878:

"I've studied Hawaiian for 46 years but am by no means perfect...it is an interminable language...it is one of the oldest living languages of the earth, as some conjecture, and may well be classed among the best...the thought to displace it, or to doom it to oblivion by substituting the English language, ought not for a moment to be indulged. Long live the grand old, sonorous, poetical Hawaiian language."

If this book should happen to bring in revenue in excess of expenses, that profit will be donated to further support of the Hawaiian language.

Table of Contents

$\mathcal{I}$llustrations

Introduction

s Will and Ariel Durant state in *The Lessons of History,* "Our knowledge of any past event is always incomplete, probably inaccurate, beclouded by ambivalent evidence and biased historians, and perhaps distorted by our own patriotic or religious partisanship."

Sovereignists' knowledge of past incomplete

So it is with Hawai'i's 1893 Revolution and the subsequent events that continue to reverberate today. History is being ignored or rewritten to serve the perceived needs of those partisans of the sovereignty movement in Hawai'i. One of the unfortunate aspects of this is that many tend to accept the revised history without question and with no attempt to revisit the scene in 1893 to examine the events leading up to and following the confrontations that took place.

That 1893 Revolution ended the Hawaiian Monarchy, opened the door to Annexation of Hawai'i by the United States five years later and led to Statehood for the Island territory in 1959.

One might think . . . all is well . . .

One might think that the political process had run its course a century later, and all is well in paradise today. But for the past decade our fiftieth state has been experiencing a difficult, often divisive, argument, whose roots lie in the history of the 1893

Revolution. All Native Hawaiians became U.S. citizens at Annexation, but some Native Hawaiians today are denying their American citizenship and its values. Instead, they are laying claim to sovereignty rights, reparations, state-owned government lands and possible independence from the United States, all based on an interpretation of the history of the revolutionary period that calls what happened a coup by the United States instead of a revolution by a volunteer army of Hawai'i residents. This is a major difference!

Major difference in interpretation

Almost everything about the Revolution is controversial, even what to call it. The men who took over the Kingdom called their action a counter-revolution, claiming Queen Lili'uokalani herself was in revolt. She called their action treason. Sovereignty activists today call it an overthrow.

Such distinctions are more than mere semantics, particularly in view of how current activists attempt to defend their positions on the basis of revised history. As John Clive notes in his book *Not by Fact Alone*, "Let us then come to a preliminary finding, to the effect that the past lends itself all too readily to use by those who have a political axe to grind. Nothing works better to further a cause—good or bad—than to lend it legitimacy by supplying it with a long heritage."

Past can be used for political ends

Caught up in today's nationwide swirl of political correctness, many residents of the Islands are reluctant to speak up against the extravagant claims of some Native Hawaiian leaders. This is the first attempt in book form to question the claims of sovereignty activists, and to dispute the accuracy and interpretations of the historical basis for their goals.

The author, Thurston Twigg-Smith, is uniquely entitled to raise these questions. He is a fifth-generation resident of Hawai'i, a descendant of missionaries who arrived on the first mission vessel, the Brig *Thaddeus,* in 1820.

For the past fifty years he has been intimately associated with *The Honolulu Advertiser*, Hawai'i's leading newspaper—from 1961 to 1993 as its publisher and chief executive officer. His grandfather, Lorrin A. Thurston, was the leader of the revolutionary movement. Thurston's *Memoirs of the Hawaiian Revolution* contains a detailed and documented record of the Revolutionists' viewpoint of the events before, during and after the confrontation.

Five years ago Twigg-Smith jumped into what had been largely a one-sided discourse by writing an article that began: "The overthrow of Queen Lili'uokalani and subsequent annexation to the United States were the best things that ever happened to Hawai'i and its people."

The statement was ridiculed by sovereignty activists, but it got others, including some Hawaiians, to thinking: "It isn't so bad being an American citizen, and maybe some of the other claims and demands being made by sovereignty activists are questionable, too."

The continuing flood of pro-sovereignty articles and letters, particularly in his former newspaper, *The Advertiser* (he relinquished his leadership role in 1993 when the newspaper was sold), made Twigg-Smith realize that the other side of the sovereignty story was not being told.

This book, which might be called "the case against sovereignty," is the result. Based on books and research not easily available, it presents a concerned journalist's viewpoint of what actually took place at that crucial time. Many of the findings are surprising, and the evidence rebuts many current

Twigg-Smith is a fifth-generation resident

Other side not being told

claims, including the one that no Hawaiians were happy with Annexation or came to the Annexation Day ceremonies at 'Iolani Palace. Even the Queen is quoted in 1900 as approving Annexation and the book contains photographs showing there were some Hawaiians present on Annexation Day, both on the dais with President Dole and in the audience on the Palace grounds.

Some Hawaiians wanted Annexation

Twigg-Smith obviously hopes that facts like those and others will give Hawaiians an awareness that the community, somewhat divided now, was not torn apart at Annexation. There was disagreement at the time, but many Hawaiian politicians supported Annexation and capitalized on the new voting power U.S. citizenship gave Native Hawaiians. They dominated Hawai'i politics until World War II.

Moving to the present day, Twigg-Smith describes how the community can come together and how Hawaiian concerns can be addressed without further splintering our society. He believes this understanding will help defuse the potential violence he fears may lie ahead when—or if—key sovereignty goals are not achieved.

Credit the author with digging

This book will be read by different people for different purposes, and this is as it should be. I hope that those who dispute the findings of the book will do so on the basis of historical fact rather than emotion or wishful thinking. Obviously, all history is subject to interpretation, but credit the author with digging deeply into the record of the past, and with making his biases as objective as possible.

Historian Herbert J. Muller, in *The Uses of the Past,* points out that "...historians can never attain the impersonal exactitude to which they must always aspire. There can be no 'pure history'—history in itself, recorded from nobody's point of view, for nobody's sake. The most objective history conceivable is still a selection and an interpretation, necessarily governed by some special interests and based on some particular beliefs. It can be more nearly objective if these interests are explicit, out in the open, where they can be freely examined and criticized."

In this book Twigg-Smith questions whether anything as important as independence or sovereignty for Hawai'i should be based on a one-sided view of history, and he clearly shows that there are at least two sides to this segment of the record of these Islands. Coming at this time, it is an important reference source for anyone interested in the sovereignty movement—either for or against.

Book is important reference source

In 1993 historian David McCullough gave a speech at Punahou School with the provocative title, "Why History?" This book answers that question.

Roderick F. McPhee
President Emeritus
Punahou School

November 1997

$\mathcal{P}$rologue

The little boy tugged at my shirt and looked up with innocent eyes. "Why did your grandpa steal my land?" he asked. "Yeah, and why did he steal our culture, too?" his big sister added.

Children learn untruths

I couldn't believe my ears. Kids usually don't talk that way. Their mother was standing there beaming and you could tell she liked what her kids were doing. The sovereignty line is that the *haole* (foreigners) cheated the Hawaiians, and the kids were talking as though it were a fact. She'd brought them with her to the picket line that was protesting my presence on her island of Maui for an art show during the 100th anniversary year of the Hawaiian Revolution.

Around her another hundred or so people with varying levels of Hawaiian ancestry added comments reflecting their views of *haole* and the problems of Hawaiians.

Revolution of '93 didn't steal land, culture

The comments from the protest group that day also reflected some of the other goals associated with the sovereignty movement. These include taking over government lands and restoring the culture of ancient Native Hawaiians. They're wrong, but sovereignists believe the Revolution in 1893 that overthrew Queen Lili'uokalani's regime also took both land and culture from the Hawaiian people.

The Maui protesters weren't threatening, but I got the message: They wanted me to feel as though my grandfather and others involved in the Revolution and subsequent Annexation to the United States had taken advantage of them.

Comments that day and by sovereignty enthusiasts on many other occasions seem to be elements of an orchestrated program to paint Native Hawaiians as victims and build up guilt among non-Hawaiians in a strategy to advance sovereignty.

It made me want to do something to show Hawaiians that they are not victims, that the revisionist histories they are being fed these days are wrongheaded and can only lead to dangerous division within our community, that we can all work together to keep this divisiveness from happening.

This book is the result. I hope it will help set the record straight.

Acknowledgments

If errors have crept into this book, it is my fault. The many good people who helped me pull it together have set me straight on numerous occasions, whether my deviations involved conceptual errors, errors of fact, repetition (they couldn't get it all out because I believe in repetition when revisionism is being debunked!), excess stridency or just plain misstatements. Agnes Conrad, knowledgeable historian, was an early steersman; Barbara Hastings has been a prime mover of the entire project as well as an invaluable critic, editor and layout artist. In no measure of importance or order, these other friends did their part to keep me on course: Bob Midkiff, whose files got me started; John Strobel, whose able editor's eye worked overtime; Kelvin Taketa, Jeff Watanabe and David Cole, who forewent precious ski time to read and critique the midcourse manuscript; Rubellite Johnson; Rod McPhee, whose flattering introduction means a great deal more than he can ever realize; Mary Judd, the Punahou archivist; Michael Thurston Pfeffer; David McCullough, whose counsel and advice were a strong and calming force; George Chaplin, who took time out from his own book to read and critique this one; Robert Van Dyke, a mother lode of source books; John Goemans; Jolene Taga; Pat Fong; Randy Roth, constantly casting light on the subject; Marilyn Reppun of the Hawaiian Mission Children's Society library and Barbara Dunn of the Hawaiian Historical Society library, both of whom went out of their way to be helpful; and mostly Sharon, who became Mrs. Twigg-Smith midway through the project, remained a loyal critic and put up untiringly with the foibles of an embryonic writer. There were countless unnamed others along the way who helped turn every gathering, every party, into an information session. It couldn't have been done without all of you.

$\mathscr{F}$oreword

Annexation to the United States was "the best thing that could happen for Hawai'i, both for the native and foreign population . . . I rejoice heartily that it has come."

—*John L. Kaulukou, speaker of the House of Representatives of the Republic of Hawai'i, earlier longtime ally of Kalākaua and his sister, Lili'uokalani; former judge, legislator, marshal under the Monarchy. San Francisco Chronicle, July 28, 1898.*

Respected Hawaiian spoke for Annexation

"As you well know, the best thing that has happened for Hawai'i is the foolish and ill-advised move that was made by Royalists on the 6th of January (1895) (Ed.—the unsuccessful counter-revolution)....For myself I am in for Annexation and will use my best endeavors . . . to bring it about as soon as possible, the sooner the better . . . . Lili'uokalani has abdicated and my hands are untied. Annexation now is the goal for me. You will find more of us, Samuel Parker for one . . ."

—*John F. Colburn, Hawaiian member with Sam Parker of Lili'uokalani's last Cabinet. He and Parker were key planners in the move by that Cabinet the first day of the 1893 Revolution to depose the Queen if she did not withdraw her notion of a new Constitution; in a letter to Lorrin A. Thurston dated January 30, 1895. Archives of Hawai'i.*

Two ministers came to favor U.S. tie

"Be it Resolved, by the Senate and House of Representatives of the Territory of Hawai'i, that the Congress of the United States . . . is hereby respectfully requested to pass . . . an Act enabling the people of this Territory . . . to meet in convention and frame and . . . adopt a State Constitution where under . . . this Territory may be admitted as a State into the Union."

—First action of the 1903 Hawai'i Legislature, adopted unanimously by the Senate and the Native Hawaiian-dominated House and delivered to Congress by Hawai'i's Native Hawaiian delegate to Congress, Prince Kūhiō Kalaniana'ole.

Lili'uokalani saw hope in Annexation

"Tho' for a moment it [the overthrow] cost me a pang of pain for my people it was only momentary, for the present has a hope for the future of my people."

—Former Queen Lili'uokalani in her diary on Sunday, September 2, 1900.

"The question of the restoration of the Monarchy is gone from us forever. We are now a people, however, who can vote. You all know we have two-thirds of the votes in this country. . . . If you want to rule, it is for you to decide."

". . . a people who can vote."

—Robert W. Wilcox in 1900, from The Unconquerable Rebel, University Press of Colorado, 1996.

These and other comments of the time paint a picture of Hawaiian satisfaction with American citizenship, American law, American benefits, quite different from the picture painted by sovereignty proponents today.

Sovereignty activists are saying Native Hawaiians did not have a voice in our present alliance with America, that therefore some sort of sovereignty must be restored, reparations must be paid, lands must be turned over to Native Hawaiians, even though most by this time have a minority of Hawaiian blood in their veins.

Charging toward division?

What's happened? Does the quest for sovereignty represent the will of the people or the desire of a minority for power? What are its goals? Are we charging down the road toward a divided society for no particularly good reason?

This book attempts to answer some of the questions, present some of the facts that need to be considered before a valid and balanced judgment can be made.

The viewpoint of the majority of Hawai'i's population needs to be expressed. Its approval is essential for anything involving state lands or monies to be achieved from sovereignty efforts. Even the non-monetary but no less valuable goals of developing cultural awareness, ethnic pride and social and economic improvement would benefit from majority approval. Will the majority let its legislative representatives give away state land or allocate major segments of overall tax monies for the benefit of only one of Hawai'i's ethnic groups? Without agreement of the majority of the people of Hawai'i, it is hard to see how anything significant can be put into law.

What does majority say?

A plebiscite within the Hawaiian community on the question: "Shall the Nation of Hawaiian people elect delegates to propose a Native Hawaiian government?" brought inconclusive results as to how even that community feels about sovereignty. (Put aside for the moment that at the time the question was asked, there was no "Nation of Hawaiian people" nor any widely accepted definition of what constitutes a "Native Hawaiian.")

Plebiscite inconclusive

Interpretation of the actual plebiscite vote, announced in September 1996, was clouded by a very low level of voter participation. Only some 28 percent of the seventy-nine thousand four hundred ballots sent to eligible Hawaiian voters were cast in favor of the proposal. More than forty-six thousand ballots were returned unmarked or not returned at all. Of the thirty-three thousand ballots that were returned, twenty-two thousand were marked "yes" and eleven thousand "no". Combining the "no" votes with those not returned or returned blank means some 72 percent of Hawaiians eligible to vote chose not to vote at all or voted against the convention.

Are revisions the basis of movement?

So who wants sovereignty, and how much and what kind do they want? Are the claims of sovereignty activists based on fact or are they based on erroneous revisions of Hawaiian history?

This book takes the position that much of the sovereignty argument is based on rewritten Island history. For example, Lili'uokalani today is pictured as a good Queen, beloved by all her people. In actuality, while she was a charming and erudite lady, she was an ineffectual ruler. The historian William Adam Russ, Jr., in his "Summing Up" at the conclusion of his definitive history of the period, *The Hawaiian Revolution,* called her government "inefficient, corrupt, and undependable." Her own hand-picked Cabinet, as we'll see in Chapter Four, came close to deposing her at the start of the Revolution of 1893. Today, the focus of admiration is on her musical ability, her charm as a person, the memory of a Queen with royal bearing. Forgotten are her weaknesses, her arrogance, her duplicity, her failures as a leader of the Kingdom.

Queen was ineffectual

History does involve interpretation, and

interpreters can look at the same facts and come up with different stories. But there are some absolutes in Hawaiian history.

Understanding shouldn't be limited

The Hawaiian Kingdom took foreigners under its wing from the time of first Western contact. Once sworn in as subjects of the Kingdom, as the majority of the Revolution's leaders were, their input into the history of Hawai'i should have validity even for a native historian. Our understanding of what happened at the time of the Revolution in 1893 should not be limited to a Hawaiian activist view or a *haole* view. If the Kingdom was corrupt and inefficient in the eyes of many of its subjects—native-born and naturalized alike—it was not an evil act on its face for those subjects to seek change.

It is a fact that the Kingdom was in dire condition by any measure of its financial strength, its dwindling population or its standing in the view of other nations. Its monarch, Queen Lili'uokalani, had prepared and was trying to promulgate a new Constitution that included a half-dozen moves backward toward a more absolute Monarchy. Among other things it would have disenfranchised her foreign-born subjects, taken away the right of her native-born subjects to elect the upper house of the Legislature by giving her the power to appoint it and emasculated the strong Cabinet system that had been put in place as a check against King Kalākaua's extravagances. These facts are irrefutable whether a historian is looking at the era through Hawaiian eyes or foreign eyes. As the quotations at the start of this foreword show, Hawaiian eyes themselves saw Annexation in different ways. The viewpoints of those leaders of the period, which belie the notion of "stolen," are not mentioned by new-age Hawaiian sovereignty writers in their newly written histories.

Kingdom was in dire condition

Some facts irrefutable

I am aware that charges will be made that this account is merely an attempt to defend the revolutionary actions of my grandfather, Lorrin A. Thurston. Thurston needs no defending. He was passionate in his belief that the removal of the Monarchy and the achievement of Annexation to the United States were goals that would benefit all of the people of Hawai'i. Sensing a mood thirty years after the Revolution to romanticize the Queen and her rule, he and President Sanford B. Dole in the 1920s wrote their personal memoirs of the tumultuous events of 1893, supplementing them with considerable documentary evidence. Their love for Hawai'i is apparent.

Thurston needs no defense

Enough facts exist to enable one to argue that much of the current version of Hawaiian history of the revolutionary period is wrong, revisionist and politically motivated. This book attempts to point out where activists attempting to write history one hundred years after the events have ignored facts and strayed away from established reports to create a bias that is being used erroneously and divisively to support the cause of sovereignty. It is time to find out what *really* happened in Hawai'i at the end of the 19th century.

TT-S
Kona
January 1998

Hawaiian Sovereignty:

Do the Facts Matter?

$\mathcal{J}$overeignty — The Claims Are Flawed

n the 1970s, at a time when they feared their culture was facing oblivion and their language was being left to history, Native Hawaiians began the long struggle back toward pride and self-esteem in what came to be called the sovereignty movement.

Struggle for pride and self-esteem

In one sense, future historians are likely to look on this preservation and perpetuation of the Hawaiian culture as a model for the globe. The program already deserves applause and support. But maybe because it's easier to rally the troops when there's an enemy, the sovereignty people felt they had to blame someone else for their problems—the Revolutionists, the *haole*, the United States, the missionaries—anyone but themselves or their *ali'i* (rulers). Their leadership began this process as the centennial of the 1893 Revolution grew nearer, and by 1991 a revisionist view of Hawaiian history was in full swing. Facts get in the way of such an approach, however, and dangers for all of us lie ahead.

Distorting facts bodes ill for future

Characterizing the Revolutionists as villains engaged in an illegal act and building up expectations in the next generation by setting forth extravagant claims appear to be key parts of the game plan. Whether it is part of the plan or not, divisiveness is a result. Sovereignty leaders hope to justify claims against the U.S. government and they need to rewrite history to make the claims stick.

Within this approach, however, lies the potential for a huge problem. Blame someone else for the failures, make the kids think something was stolen from them, make everyone with any amount of Native Hawaiian blood think he or she is one of the aggrieved, a victim. Then you have the ingredients for possible violence on the part of those whose expectations have been stretched beyond any rational dimension, and thus can't be fulfilled.

Victimization is dangerous

At the moment the various Hawaiian groups are making their claims in a peaceful if occasionally strident manner. They are slowed by the fact they are far apart on defining many of their goals and methods of reaching them. But the next generation, or hot-headed members of the current generation, easily could lash out in a quick and violent manner if lands they erroneously believe are theirs are not turned over to them or if other of their unrealistic goals are not achieved.

One vital part of the Hawai'i economy is clearly vulnerable: tourism. Our economic future, at least in the near term, depends on visitors. More than 30 percent of Hawai'i's people derive their income directly from the visitor industry and more than that gain their income indirectly from visitors. Success of tourism is tied to the Aloha Spirit, a blending of all races in a place of rare beauty. This peaceful and productive combination distinguishes Hawai'i from the world's other scenic spots. The feeling, the spirit, needs to be protected—and kept from misuse and commercialization. Divisive tactics could severely damage it.

Vulnerability of tourism

To help stop the divisiveness, we in Hawai'i must lay to rest unfounded claims regarding land ownership and expose the falsity of the myth that the Monarchy, particularly in the Kingdom's last decade, was a benevolent and widely loved institution. We must explore the reasons for current Hawaiian social conditions and clarify other sovereignty positions that are based on false accounts of Hawaiian history.

Revisionism can lead to insupportable claims

How can we do this? Certainly one way is to expose the revisionism that has been used to lead sovereignty groups to insupportable demands. Once the revisionism is recognized, I believe the good judgment and common sense possessed by the majority of Hawaiians and part-Hawaiians will bring people together again. We can help shift the focus of sovereignty efforts from unachievable, damaging and widely varied goals to worthy goals that could be achieved without harming Hawai'i or dividing its people.

Many false claims need to be discussed and facts set forth. The distorted story of the Revolution espoused by the activists and their exaggerated lists of grievances have been publicized so well that hardly a soul today knows what is fact and what is fiction. In a sense the leaders of the various sovereignty movements are doing to the Hawaiians what some of the kings and their chiefs of old did for centuries: rallying them to warfare and pointing them toward goals that might benefit the leadership but not the masses.

Goal might benefit leadership, not people

The question of ancestry is a good place to begin to set the record straight. Statistics are critical to measuring progress. But what is the definition of a Hawaiian? More than 80 percent of Hawai'i residents said in a *Honolulu Advertiser* poll in November 1995 that they didn't want sovereignty if it meant isolating and separating Hawaiians from the rest of the community. One of the reasons for that is under-

Community doesn't want to be split

standable: Hawaiians, for the most part, are so woven with the rest of us by intermarriage and family relationships that they are themselves the "rest of the community."

So what is a Hawaiian? Before Kamehameha I, natives living on the Big Island may have called themselves Hawaiians. Those on Maui or Oʻahu would have been called Mauians or Oahuans. Anyone from another island usually was viewed as an enemy. Today, anyone living in the state is, in one sense, a Hawaiian—a resident of Hawaiʻi just as an Oregonian or New Yorker is a resident of those states. But the term has been adopted to refer only to those residents with Native Hawaiian blood, no matter how small may be their percentage of it.

Defining "Hawaiian" isn't easy

The failure to define "Hawaiian" in terms of a reasonable level of blood quantum already creates a statistical nightmare in analyzing matters related to race. It's a failure that renders suspect many generalizations involving groups of Hawaiʻi residents, such as measures of social welfare, crime and prison records, susceptibility to illnesses, and so forth.

A clear definition is needed

Except for those comparatively few who have 50 percent or more of Hawaiian blood, most of those we label Hawaiians are predominantly something other than Hawaiian. They have love and aloha for their parents and grandparents of other ethnic backgrounds.

Many Islanders, of course, "feel Hawaiian." It is hard for anyone living in these Islands not to have this feeling, including most of us who have no Hawaiian blood at all. As a fifth-generation resident, this writer considers himself every bit as much a "Hawaiian" as anyone whose family roots here can be traced back ten generations but who might at this distance from his native ancestor possess only one-thirty-second Hawaiian blood.

Quite aside from how it could cast a different and more accurate light on sovereignty portrayals of Hawaiians as victims, a widely accepted, clear quantum-level definition of "Hawaiian" would be helpful to everyone. To be assured of wide acceptance, such a definition probably should be set forth by the Legislature or the courts. Fifty percent already is required for purposes of the Hawaiian Homes Commission, an agency created by the U.S. Congress in 1920 to provide homesteads for Native Hawaiians. And much of the trust money administered by the Office of Hawaiian Affairs, created in 1980 by the Hawai'i Legislature to direct support for Native Hawaiians, comes to OHA with the restriction it be used only for those with 50 percent or more native blood. But that high standard may not be necessary for the evaluation and administration of social welfare programs that are needed to help residents in distress, be they Hawaiian or otherwise. At the other end of the scale, a reduction to one-sixteenth, say, seems low. In practice, the standard is often lower. In 1997, Kamehameha Schools, recognized as being available only to children of Hawaiian descent, had no fixed blood quantum as an admissions requirement. The school says a trace is sufficient, although it must be documented.

Who's a Hawaiian beneficiary?

Kamehameha Schools has loose qualification for "Hawaiian"

Past census practice, where the government accepted from a master list whatever label one put on one's self, also seems of questionable value. In mid-1997, Congress ruled out "Native American" as a designation for Hawaiians, staying with "Pacific Islanders," and there were proposals on the table for "multi-racial" as a catchall designation replacing the present racial variations. U.S. Senator Daniel Akaka and the Office of Hawaiian Affairs sought a new

Census classification changed

ethnicity classification of "Native Hawaiian." In October 1997, the Office of Management and Budget approved "Native Hawaiian or other Pacific Islander" as one of the five race categories for the 2000 census. The data will be used for federal civil rights compliance, statistical reporting and grant administration. Still unresolved by the October decision is the definition of Hawaiian. Presumably it will be left to individuals to decide which ethnic root they wish to recognize.

Cast aside U.S. citizenship?

In human terms the definition of Hawaiian already is a critical problem for those who espouse a Hawaiian nation. What do they propose for their ancestral Chinese, Filipino, Japanese or Caucasian family members? Would they expect them to give up the American citizenship they or an ancestor worked so hard to achieve?

The second and perhaps most important issue that needs clarification involves the 1893 Revolution and Hawai'i's land. The land issue arises from the Revolution that overturned the Monarchy. In order to understand the land problem, the Revolution itself needs to be better understood.

"Theft" of lands an erroneous cry

The emotional and economic basis for each of the various sovereignty efforts is the carefully crafted, controversial and misleading double-edged claim that land (a) was taken from the Hawaiian people by the United States in the 1893 Revolution and (b) it was done without their approval—and therefore the United States should make some kind of reparation. The process toward reparations has started with the misunderstood congressional apology resolution passed in 1993.

The land argument is based on the controversial claim that the U.S. government was a party to the Revolution, took the lands from the Monarchy, and therefore should pay its former Native Hawaiian subjects for the "theft."

The charge of American participation comes about because U.S. Minister to Hawai'i John L. Stevens brought U.S. troops ashore in 1893 to protect American lives and property. In itself, this was not unusual. It had been done by his predecessors a number of times in earlier Hawai'i history. When the Revolution looked as if it were going to succeed, he recognized the rebels as the new government of Hawai'i. The Republican president at the time, Benjamin Harrison, approved, confirmed recognition of the new government and submitted to the U.S. Senate a treaty of Annexation.

Harrison Administration favored Annexation

Two months later, Democrat Grover Cleveland took over in Washington. Cleveland withdrew the treaty but did not withdraw recognition of the new government. However, he said Stevens had recognized it too early, before it had complete control, and that the Revolution would not have succeeded without the U.S. troops standing by. Therefore, he said, the U.S. government should reject the rebels and restore the Queen to power.

Cleveland withdrew treaty; a political act

Whether the United States was accountable for success of the Revolution is a gray area, at best. My studies convince me it was not; that as testified to by those who brought it off, the Revolution would have succeeded if there had been no U.S. troops onshore. There are others who disagree completely. But all historians recognize that at Annexation five years later, the situation had changed; the United States was an arms-length negotiator when the treaty was put together that made Hawai'i a Territory.

Author believes U.S. troops weren't needed

At the time of the Revolution, following the time-honored international practice of revolt as a last-ditch means for people to change their governments, control of the Islands was seized from the Queen by a volunteer army of Hawai'i residents. They created a Republic whose leadership was not Hawaiian.

The new leadership took over administration of the government lands. These lands had been set aside by King Kamehameha III in 1848 for the support of all Hawai'i residents and have been used by successor governments only for that purpose from then until now. The lands never were owned by individuals. The Republic negotiated an Annexation treaty with the United States in 1898, transferring to it control of the lands. The United States thereafter acted only as a trustee before returning the lands to Hawai'i at Statehood in 1959.

Lands were transferred by Republic

Thus, however one characterizes the exchanges themselves, the undisputed sequence of events makes clear that the United States did not get the lands from Native Hawaiians or from the Monarchy. The transfer of lands was made by the independent, five-year-old Republic that had been fully recognized by the international community.[1] The Republic Senate, moreover, which by 1898 included several Native Hawaiians, voted unanimously for Annexation, approving the transfer of lands to be held in trust for Hawai'i residents. The House of the Republic, with a majority of Native Hawaiians, did not have to act on the proposed treaty, but undoubtedly would have voted the same way. Speaker of the House John L. Kaulukou was a highly respected, full-blooded Hawaiian who spoke out strongly for Annexation. As a later chapter discusses, the alliance with America in 1898, contrary to sovereignty views, was approved by residents of all races—a majority of each, incidentally, in the case of all except for Native Hawaiians. The five thousand-member Annexation

Annexation Club had many Hawaiian members

Club—out of the thirteen thousand registered voters when it was formed in 1892 and '93—included one thousand and two Native Hawaiians.

As mentioned above, the Revolution, which took place two months before the end of the Harrison presidency, was not challenged by that administration. Along with every other nation with interests in the Pacific, the United States recognized the new Provisional Government. Subsequently, under the Cleveland administration, it recognized the Republic of Hawai'i.

U.S. recognition

A change in U.S. administration does not in itself automatically undo diplomatic relationships, and while President Cleveland denounced the Hawaiian Revolution and tried personally and unsuccessfully to reinstate the Monarchy, he did not try to undo the diplomatic relationship with the Hawaiian Provisional Government.[2] He withdrew the treaty of Annexation proposed by President Harrison, but even while trying to subvert the revolutionary government, he superficially observed the diplomatic niceties of dealing with it as a recognized foreign nation. Cleveland did apologize to Queen Lili'uokalani for what he called U.S. involvement and withdrew U.S. Minister John Stevens, who he charged had overstepped his bounds.

Cleveland tried to reinstate the Monarchy

Cleveland also sent a new minister to Hawai'i, A.S. Willis, to order leaders of the Provisional Government, a majority of whom had American ties, to return the Kingdom to the Queen. They refused, and Cleveland backed off. Politically, he could not bring war against the independent nation of Hawai'i. He was on risky political ground even to interfere in its internal affairs.

Willis mission to restore Queen ended in failure

It is possible he could have found some way to sanction the U.S. citizens involved, but it would have been politically difficult for him to try to punish American citizens for helping to create a republic by overthrowing a monarchy. As William A. Russ, Jr. notes in *The Hawaiian Revolution,* the Russian minister, Prince Cantacuzene, put it succinctly to U.S. Secretary of State Walter Q. Gresham in 1893: ". . . is it not a little singular that your Government, a Republic, should establish a Monarchy?"

Willis saw trouble with Lili'uokalani

Further, even before the Revolutionists rejected Cleveland's demand that they give back the Monarchy, it had become clear to the president's minister that there were problems with that tactic.

Russ notes further in *The Hawaiian Revolution:*

[Brackets] in quoted material indicate words added by author for clarity

"Already Willis was evidencing some skepticism regarding the results of his mission, for he informed Gresham, in a regular despatch, that if the Queen were reinstated 'there will be a concerted movement [by the Queen] . . . for the overthrow of that constitution [of 1887] which would mean the overthrow of constitutional and limited government and [reinstatement of] the absolute dominion of the Queen.'"

Willis doubted abilities of ex-Queen's advisers

Willis knew this would not sit well with the community, nor would it have lasted. History had shown it was an unacceptable condition to the Annexation-minded businessmen, attorneys and other residents. The Queen's efforts to make such a change in January 1893 had led to the very Revolution he had been sent to overturn. Moreover, he questioned the political ability and personal honesty of most of her advisers, naming "such as J.E. Bush, R.W. Wilcox, Joseph Nawahi, and John Richardson."

Willis' actions made clear at that point, mid-1893, that the new government was not a U.S.-backed endeavor. In fact, in what the Republic later charged was a breach of international neutrality laws, the Cleveland administration in November 1894 did not stop a shipment of arms from the West Coast to the Queen's forces who were plotting a counter-revolution in 1895. The Hawaiian Republic had notified U.S. officials that the shipment was being loaded in San Francisco and was about to be smuggled into the Islands, and demanded the United States impound the ship under neutrality laws.[3] When the shipment went through despite that, it set off an international brouhaha. The counter-revolution did not succeed, but the protests to the United States over the arms smuggling went on.

Cleveland Administration charged with breaching neutrality

No further efforts were made by Cleveland to overturn the Revolution or nullify the original recognition by the United States of the new government. He turned the whole problem over to Congress with an impassioned speech repeating his charges of U.S. participation. His charges were rebutted by the majority of the members of the U.S. Senate Committee on Foreign Relations in a subsequent hearing which produced the Morgan Report.

Two sides to question of American involvement

Obviously there are two sides, then, to the question of U.S. involvement in the Revolution, and politics appears to have played a major part in the so-called "findings of fact." If you supported Annexation, you generally did not find Stevens' sympathy with the Revolutionist viewpoint to be an indictment of his actions. If you were opposed to Annexation, you could build a case for his possible support—or at least too-quick recognition—of the Revolutionists' new government.

Facts behind the larger issue that grows out

of the Revolution itself, the status of government land, have been needlessly confused. They are very clear. Most sovereignists speak of the lands as "stolen." They say the lands were wrested from the Hawaiian people without their consent and without remuneration. The facts are simple. They show the land was not stolen, no matter which side of the overthrow argument you prefer. This book will develop the argument more fully, but the following nine paragraphs outline the facts that show the lands in question were not "stolen."

"Ceded lands" benefit all residents

We are talking about the public, government lands of Hawai'i, the so-called "ceded lands." These lands were set aside by Kamehameha III in the 19th century for the benefit of all residents of the Kingdom. Today the income from these lands still is used for the benefit of all residents of the state, though one-fifth of the income is being earmarked for the use only of persons with 50 percent Native Hawaiian blood. At the time of the 1893 Revolution, the ceded lands included lands set aside as government lands by Kamehameha III in 1848, combined with lands he had retained as crown lands. He and his successors considered the crown lands their personal property, but court and legislative actions, in 1865, made the crown lands an inalienable part of the government lands. Today the combination is known as "ceded lands" because they were ceded to the United States by the Republic at Annexation, as detailed below. These are lands that Lili'uokalani controlled when she was Queen, but did not own personally. No individual has owned any part of them personally since Kamehameha III made his magnificent gift for, he said, "the benefit of the Hawaiian Government."

Monarch didn't own these lands

When the Provisional Government took over on January 17, 1893, the control and administration of those public lands became a responsibility of the new government. None of the lands went into private hands at that time. (Homestead acts of the various governments put a small fraction into private hands at later dates.)

Government workers stayed on

No government workers were replaced by the new government except for the Queen, her four Cabinet officers and Charles B. Wilson, her marshal. The proclamation that set up the new government asked all other officers and employees of the old government to continue to serve.

The government workers in the land department were the same individuals who had been appointed or hired under the Queen's rule. The income from those government lands still flowed for the benefit of the same residents who had enjoyed benefits of that income under the Queen, including the Queen herself.

Lands passed from government to government

The Republic of Hawai'i was formed in 1894 and the lands became an administrative and control responsibility of that new government. Nothing else changed; the lands were still public lands and the income still went to the benefit of the same people it always had.

Annexation occurred in 1898 and control of the lands shifted from the Republic to the U.S. government. Terms of the Annexation agreement required the United States to hold these ceded lands separate from federal lands as a whole, in a sort of trust for the people of Hawai'i. Administration of the lands, however, remained with the new Territorial government and the income remained in Hawai'i for the benefit of all of its residents.

Income from lands stayed in Hawai'i

Statehood came along in 1959. Control of the lands came back from the federal government to go under the control and administration of the new state government, intact except for lands that had been removed for national parks, the military, other federal government uses and homesteading. A relatively small percentage of the whole, these retained federal lands were significant and valuable lands. But although still under control of the federal government, they were and are of considerable benefit to the people of Hawai'i, too.

False claim of stolen land is divisive

So today we have under our control and for our benefit pretty much all of the lands that were under the control of Queen Lili'uokalani. She tried in court to get title to some of them for herself but both the Hawai'i Supreme Court, earlier, and the U.S. Court of Claims, on May 16, 1910, ruled that they were government lands and not lands owned by any individual, royal or otherwise.

So what was "stolen"? Obviously nothing. No lands were taken from the Hawaiian people or anyone else in the Revolution. **They were government lands then and they still are.** It is a divisive disservice and clearly wrong for sovereignty leaders and others to continue claiming falsely that these lands were stolen from the Hawaiian people.

Lands were not "stolen"

In the process of trying to set the record straight, this book will undertake a quick review of Hawai'i's history after Western contact. It will show among other things that the Hawaiian leadership of the Kingdom wanted Annexation to the United States as early as 1848 but that U.S. policy then, as well as in 1893, did not include taking over these Islands. It will also document, as indicated above, that the lands the sovereignists call theirs were never stolen from the Hawaiian people, that the Revolution was not a missionary movement and that its leaders were not land-lusting sugar plantation owners, nor were they trying to kill the language or eliminate

Hawaiian culture. False claims like these are often made by those attempting to rewrite the history of these Islands. They would like to make their followers look and feel like victims. They think it makes a better case for sovereignty.

We need to look at the character and culture of the Hawaiian people and how ordinary people were treated by early rulers in order to understand why the Revolution clearly benefited Hawaiians who were not members of the royal family. Things are much better for today's Native Hawaiians than if they were still subjects of a Monarchy.

Caution against victimization

Objective consideration of all this may lead many to question whether sovereignty in any of the forms now being promoted is something that would be good for Hawai'i. Frankly, in most of its proposed forms sovereignty would not be good except possibly for those few who might emerge as sovereigns if there were a new nation. Sovereignty would do little to meet the needs of today's Hawaiians and it could divide this community as nothing has done before. It could be a tragedy.

Sovereignty might only benefit leaders

In one sense, some sovereignty activists seem to be trying to move Native Hawaiians against the tide of human events. They seem to be seeking to put Hawaiians back on the land, to re-establish them as agriculturists at a time when the rest of the advanced nations of the world are looking to new horizons.

As Alvin Toffler put it in his 1981 book, *The Third Wave,* the world has seen two major waves of change and is currently being swept over by a third. He describes the first as the agricultural revolution, which started perhaps ten thousand years ago. The world was changed forever by the second wave, the industrial revolution, beginning in the 18th Century, and today it is undergoing a third, most overwhelming wave of all, what Toffler calls the brain wave. To ignore these powerful events and seek to put Hawaiians, in effect, back into the Third World doesn't make much sense.

Look to what's best for all

We need to consider instead other courses of action that could be productive and fulfilling today and in the future for all of the people of Hawai'i, whatever their ancestry.

The next chapter will attempt to put in perspective how Hawai'i related to the rest of the world at the time of the 1893 Revolution. It will show that association of Hawai'i with some stronger, foreign, nation was virtually inevitable.

Chapter Two

$\mathcal{C}$olonialism and Missionaries:
Facts of Life in the 19th Century

The international context in which the government of Hawai'i changed from Monarchy to democracy made that change virtually unavoidable and, in 1893, it seemed overdue. It was an inevitable step along with the decline of the native population in the evolution of today's Hawai'i. The demise of the Hawaiian Kingdom was simply part of the process, the Revolution, but a step along the way.

Global context of late 19th Century

When Captain James Cook opened Hawai'i to the Western world in 1778, he also set in motion factors that were life-threatening to its status as an independent kingdom: exposure to diseases that devastated the native population and exposure to the ambitions and greed of colonial powers.

Discovery brought disease, colonial greed

Most of the arguments for sovereignty pay scant attention to what was going on in the rest of the world during the 19th Century and what this meant for Hawai'i. Colonialism, unacceptable to us today, was a way of life then, and actions taken in its name were a normal part of international relations. Hawai'i could expect to be viewed with covetous eyes by every colonial power, and it was.

Colonialism had been way of life

17

In fact, although attempts to seize it were made variously by French, British and Russian representatives, Hawai'i remained one of only five Pacific-area kingdoms still independent toward the end of the 19th Century, the others being Japan, China, Tonga and Thailand. Hawai'i's strategic location and limited powers, however, made its eventual acquisition by some foreign power a certainty. Partly for this reason Kamehameha I had discussed cession to Britain with Captain George Vancouver as early as 1793, and his son, Liholiho, Kamehameha II, had placed the Islands under the protectorate of Britain's King George IV in 1824. Kalākaua threw a Far East twist into this equation some sixty years later with his attempt to arrange for his niece, Princess Ka'iulani, to marry the nephew of the Emperor of Japan. Queen Lili'uokalani's diary entry of January 29, 1894, outlines this proposed Asian tie for her anticipated successor if she were reinstated. Earlier kings had sought closer ties to America (in the case of Kamehameha III) or Britain again (in the case of his successor, Kamehameha IV).

Kamehameha I explored protection

Other Pacific island groups had, or were about to become, colonial outposts throughout the 19th and into the early part of the 20th centuries. In fact, a Naval Chart filed with the Morgan Report shows all of the Pacific islands except Hawai'i and the Carolines clearly under control of some colonial power, and the Carolines probably were under control of Japan or Germany, which claimed the adjoining Marshall and Solomon Islands.

Pacific Islands under foreign control

France was making a sweep through the Pacific during the period and laying claim to much of Polynesia, particularly Tahiti. France's flag was first raised there in 1768. In 1843 France established Tahiti as a protectorate, and in 1880 annexed it. It also claimed the Marquesas, the Loyalty and Tuamotu Islands as well as the rest of the Society Islands besides Tahiti.

Samoa was divided between Germany (Western Samoa) and the United States in 1900. The Dutch took possession of the western sector of New Guinea in 1828; in 1884, a British protectorate was established in Southeast New Guinea and a German protectorate in the northeast. By 1905, Australia was handling administration of the British area and in 1914 occupied the former German territory. The Gilbert Islands (Kiribati) fell into British hands in 1877.

Spain had control of the Mariana Islands from the 16th Century, but sold them to Germany in 1899. The Japanese had been covetous of those islands and assumed control of them by 1914. Japan and China fought for centuries over Okinawa, and the Japanese took it over in the 1870s.

As Lorrin A. Thurston stated in his widely distributed 1894 *Handbook on the Annexation of Hawai'i:*

> "Within the past eighty-five years, Hawai'i has been taken possession of (Ed.— though not for long):
>
> "Once by Russia.
>
> "Once by England.
>
> "Twice by France.
>
> "And by reason of hostile demonstrations by foreign governments, creating the fear of foreign conquest, an absolute cession of the sovereignty of the country to the United States was executed and delivered in 1851, and a treaty of annexation negotiated in 1854.
>
> "Since 1874, on four separate occasions, internal disturbances have required the land-

The state of other Pacific countries

Hawai'i was a prized jewel

ing of foreign troops from war ships, for the protection of the interests of the several nations there represented."

A permanent takeover of some kind was a constant threat, and what happened to Hawai'i in 1893 could be viewed simply as an event that was inevitable. Its sizable land area, splendid harbors and strategic position as a refueling station in the mid-Pacific made it the most valuable outpost in that vast ocean.

Takeover a constant threat

Hawaiian monarchs, using the advice and skills of trusted foreigners, had adroitly played world powers off one another in the first century of Western contact and thus no takeover lasted more than a few months. When the French threatened a second time in the late 1840s, Kamehameha III signed a treaty of "friendship, commerce and navigation" with the United States in 1849. In 1851, he ordered his ministers to negotiate Annexation with America despite objections from the French and the British, but the United States wasn't eager then, nor was it in 1893, to accept these Pacific islands as part of its continental-based nation. The treaty took three years to negotiate, and Kamehameha III died before it could be signed.

Kamehameha III looked for Annexation

As Honolulu historian-community leader Robert R. Midkiff pointed out in a Yale thesis in 1942, however, the negotiations underscored America's position as protector of Hawai'i in the mid-19th Century, a role of great benefit to the Island Kingdom but one that was subject to shifting political winds in Washington and elsewhere. America, he pointed out, could not be counted on forever as a protector of the small Kingdom or its people.

U.S. Secretary of State Daniel Webster, in a

dispatch to his commissioner in Hawai'i, Luther Severance, on July 14, 1851, noted:

> "You inform us that many American citizens have gone to settle in the islands; if so, they have ceased to be American citizens. The government of the United States must, of course, feel an interest in them not extended to foreigners, but by the laws of nations they have no right to demand the protection of this government . . ."[4]

Americans in Hawai'i lost citizenship

On December 9, 1868, President Andrew Johnson wrote to the U.S. Senate:

> "It is known and felt by the Hawaiian Government and people that their Government and institutions are feeble and precarious; that the United States, being so near a neighbor, would be unwilling to see the islands pass under foreign control. Their prosperity is continually disturbed by expectations and alarms of unfriendly political proceedings, as well from the United States as from other foreign powers. A reciprocity treaty, while it could not help but materially diminish . . . revenues for the United States, would be a guarantee of the goodwill and forbearance of all nations until the people of the islands shall of themselves, at no distant day, voluntarily apply for admission . . . ."[5]

U.S. expected Hawai'i to want admission

On February 25, 1871, American Minister to Hawai'i Henry Pierce wrote to U.S. Secretary of State Hamilton Fish:

> "A majority of aborigines, Creoles and naturalized foreigners of this country, as I am credibly informed, are favorable, even anxious for the consummation of measure named (Ed.–Annexation)."[6]

The Kingdom at that point was declining rapidly in economic and political power, largely due to the catastrophic falloff in native population. From an estimated three hundred thousand or more Native Hawaiians in 1778, the native population had fallen to fewer than fifty thousand in 1878 and about forty thousand by the time of the Revolution in 1893.

Kingdom in decline

Development by foreign investors was holding the economy together, but these business interests were seriously threatened by autocratic and spendthrift actions of King Kalākaua and, subsequently, Queen Liliʻuokalani.

By the 1890s, leaders of the community knew a weakened Hawaiʻi was fair game for some colonial power, and rather than see their investments and their lives fall under control of England, France, Germany or Japan—the four most likely candidates other than the United States—they opted for a permanent tie with America through Annexation. There were more Americans in Hawaiian business and community leadership roles than any other kinds of foreigners, and those who had come to Hawaiʻi from European countries saw America as a compromise they could live with. There were some, though, who wanted to continue the status quo, each hoping his own mother country could be motivated to acquire Hawaiʻi.

Weakened Hawaiʻi prey to takeover

Christian missions, too, were a way of life in the 19th Century. Missionaries went out from America in every direction, as they did from other countries around the globe. These missionaries were a benign counterpart to colonialism in the development of lands abroad. The American missionaries today are criticized for the rigid standards of their Calvinist faith that inevitably led to the suppression of certain aspects of native cultures they deemed incompatible with their views of Christianity. The missionaries were much admired in the United States at the time, however. For example, a pamphlet in circulation in the 1870s refers to Asa Thurston, one of the pioneer missionaries to Hawai'i, as a "Hero of Fitchburg," his home town in Massachusetts.

Missions were way of life

The story of how Yale-educated missionaries happened to come to Hawai'i at the urging of young Henry Obookiah (as his name was spelled at Yale) is well known and has been chronicled in numerous books, of which *Grapes of Canaan* by Albertine Loomis is one of the most complete and accurate. Suffice it to say here that those missionaries responded wholeheartedly to Obookiah's plea to bring Christianity to his people. They came to do good and indeed accomplished many things of lasting benefit to the Hawaiian people. The old canard that they "came to do good and did very well indeed" is a serious distortion of their efforts. They worked under difficult and demanding conditions and often suffered as much physically as they were uplifted spiritually.

Henry Obookiah urged mission to Hawai'i

When the missionaries arrived in Hawai'i in 1820 they found a population already suffering from the effects of forty years of visitors to paradise. After the initial exposure to Western civilization in 1778 the Hawaiian people had made the transition to Western ways very quickly and without the extended combative problems of first contact that often occur between two distinctly different cultures.

Though capable of being fierce warriors, Hawaiians in 1778 basically were a hospitable people and they welcomed the foreigners from afar. There were a few problems. The continuing inter-island wars that brought the Kingdom under the control of

Missionaries found adverse effects of Western contact

Kamehameha I by 1810 caused Hawaiian chiefs to enlist as many as thirty foreigners as advisers of the rival armies. In addition, several fatal outbreaks of hostility with foreigners occurred in the first ten years of Western contact—largely the fault of rough and ready seafaring men. Most of these early foreigners were tough and thoughtless seamen, some would say the scum of the earth—or the sea. When they slaughtered Hawaiians over some transgression, other Hawaiians slaughtered the next visitors. But in the long run, the viruses the visitors brought in the first forty years of contact—ranging from measles to smallpox to venereal diseases—were the worst danger. They decimated the population.[7]

Foreigners enlisted by Hawaiian chiefs; diseases were worst enemy

The dwindling nation had other problems as it faced survival in a Western world. Hawaiians had no written language and in fact had no religion when the missionaries arrived in April 1820. King Kamehameha I had died shortly before the missionaries began their six-month trip to Hawai'i, and his successor, Liholiho, under the direction of the dowager Queen and later regent Ka'ahumanu, had capitalized on the dwindling importance of the idols and *kapu* (taboos) that had been worshiped or observed since prehistoric times and abolished them. The ancient religion included the practices of infanticide and human sacrifice, with daily life guided by strict observance of many restrictive taboos. In some cases, the strict taboos serendipitously served as protective ordinances, particularly in the field of public health, but many were typical of a male-dominated society where warfare was common. Until Liholiho's precipitate action in 1819 of sitting down to eat with the women of his court, women were forbidden to eat with men or to eat certain foods and had few of the rights enjoyed by Western women even at that time

Kapu broken

in history.

The young missionary arrivals, coming at the end of the first forty years of Western contact and the end of the ancient religion, were given a mission of stunning scope, considering the limited tools they had. An extract from the instructions given them in 1819 by the American Board of Commissioners for Foreign Missions reads as follows:

Women had few rights

> "Your views are not to be limited to a low, narrow scale; but you are to open your hearts wide and set your marks high. You are to aim at nothing short of covering these islands with fruitful fields, and pleasant dwellings and schools and churches, and of raising up the whole people to an elevated state of Christian civilization. You are to obtain an adequate knowledge of the language of the people; to make them acquainted with letters; to give them the Bible, with skill to read it; to introduce and get into extended operation and influence among them, the arts and institutions and usage of civilized life and society; and you are to abstain from all interference with local and political interests of the people and to inculcate the duties of justice, moderation, forbearance, truth and universal kindness. Do all in your power to make men of every class good, wise and happy."[8]

The missionary mandate

They set about their task with incredible drive and the energy of dedicated men and women in their twenties. The pioneer missionaries had learned rudiments of the language from Obookiah and became fairly fluent later in conversations with the Hawaiian youths aboard the Brig *Thaddeus* on the six-month voyage from Boston. Within weeks of their arrival they began teaching a written version.

Liholiho, King Kamehameha II, reluctant at first even to allow them ashore, eventually allowed a one-year trial visitation. Well before the time was up, about two hundred of his people had become eager students and by April 1824, all of his subjects were ordered to learn to read and write.

Missionaries quickly learned language

The natives were good students, and when Richard H. Dana of Boston visited Hawai'i in the late 1850s he wrote a letter to the New York *Tribune* that was published on June 5, 1860, and which reads in part:

> "It is no small thing to say of the Missionaries of the American Board, that in less than forty years they have taught this whole people to read and to write, to cipher and to sew. They have given them an alphabet, grammar, and dictionary; preserved their language from extinction; given it a literature, and translated into it the Bible and works of devotion, science and entertainment. They have established schools, reared up native teachers, and so pressed their work that now the proportion of inhabitants who can read and write is greater than in New England; . . . and the more elevated of them [are] taking part in conducting the affairs of the constitutional monarchy under which they live, holding seats on the judicial bench and in the legislative chambers, and filling posts in the local magistracies."

Hawaiians were ready students

Some sovereignty activists find it politically expedient to say that the missionaries "stole" or sought to kill the Hawaiian language and tried to destroy the culture of the Hawaiians. But far from stealing or killing the language, the missionaries saved it! Without its conversion to a written form it would have died as the population dwindled and the remaining natives dealt with new arrivals in the language of the foreigner or the patois of pidgin. Oral languages of isolated Native American tribes, Eskimos and distant African tribes have been lost under similar circumstances.

Missionaries preserved Hawaiian language

The missionaries were Calvinists, strict interpreters of the Scriptures but also imbued with the idea that Christianity required the doing of good works as well as accepting Christ. It is true that in their belief, if you weren't a Christian, you were a heathen. This seems a bit harsh today and has been seized upon by critics as an excuse to paint those early missionaries as cold and discriminatory. The missionaries didn't want their children associating with heathens, for example, and tried to keep them apart from young natives who they feared might corrupt them in the eyes of the Lord. They and their children interacted openly, however, with Hawaiians who became Christian converts.

Ban against contact with non-Christians

This strictness was an integral part of the missionaries' religion at the time and has no more relevance to their character as human beings than the practice of infanticide and sacrifices by early Hawaiians implies that Hawaiians were savages. The American missionaries to these Islands were good people, respectful of the natives as free people, and a boon to Hawaiians and their culture. In 1898, for example, a missionary descendant introduced, and the Legislature of the Republic passed, a bill authorizing the government to acquire and preserve the sites of ancient *heiau* and *pu'uhonua* (temples and places of refuge). The good attitude and respect afforded Hawaiians by the American missionaries contrast strikingly with the mistreatment of native peoples that occurred elsewhere in the Pacific—

Missionary descendant worked to preserve heiau

French Polynesia and New Zealand, for example.

Perhaps the worst distortion, which appeared in 1995 in various letters from sovereignty activists printed in *The Honolulu Advertiser,* is the attempt to label the missionaries as slave owners or sympathetic to the slave trade. Almost every missionary family came from a New England home on the "underground railroad" that helped slaves flee from the South to safe havens in the North.

Missionaries worked against slavery

In fact, missionary descendants played important roles in the Civil War on behalf of Union forces. One, Punahou School graduate Samuel Chapman Armstrong, became in his early twenties a Union general of African-American forces and stayed on in the South after the war to found Virginia's Hampton Institute for black students. He served as its president until his death in 1893.[9]

The missionaries' particular brand of Calvinism and their belief in the Preamble of the American Constitution saw worth in every human being and the treatment of them as equals—once they became Christians. This is the most significant reason that Hawaiian Polynesians never suffered the mistreatment imposed by missionary movements in other parts of the Pacific, which combined with colonial influences to classify native populations as second-class citizens. This problem still exists in parts of Polynesia under French control and in New Zealand under British influence. Hawaiians, while they battled to the death in their own internal wars, never faced foreign troops sent out from a colonizing country to wipe them out and seize their lands, as did their distant cousins, the Maori, in New Zealand, for example. Native Hawaiians and all who call Hawai'i home are fortunate that American missionaries were the first ones to get a foothold here.

No mistreatment by missionaries in Hawai'i

The American missionaries arrived in what were called "companies." The companies included men of the cloth, but they also included printers, storekeepers, builders and teachers, who brought all of the skills considered necessary at the time to build a Western community. Support from the mainland began to dwindle in 1845 and was almost gone by the early 1850s. The American Board of Missions severed its relationship in 1863 except for continued financial support of the teaching of native pastors and the maintenance of a few partial pensions. The remaining American ministers either went on to missions elsewhere or continued their work in Hawai'i with the support of local congregations. The lay members of the mission companies entered the world of commerce or continued their professions in Hawai'i or abroad.

Missionaries respectful of Hawaiians

The missionary concern for the welfare of the common people extended to concern for their governance as well. Their pact with the church, however, required them to resign as churchmen when they yielded to the pressure of the King to serve his political cause. All told, four missionaries as well as four descendants of missionaries served as counselors to Kamehameha II, III, IV and V, and Lunalilo.[10] Though influential, these eight obviously did not constitute a very large percentage of the one hundred one foreigners who took Cabinet posts between 1838 and 1893. The missionaries who resigned from the mission to become Cabinet members were Dr. G.P. Judd, Richard Armstrong, (father of the Civil War general), William Richards and E.O. Hall. The four descendants were W.N. Armstrong (brother of the Civil War general), W.R. Castle and A.F. Judd, sons, and L.A. Thurston, a grandson.

Background of mission "companies"

While their missionary background no doubt

continued to live within them, those first four listed advisers technically no longer were missionaries, nor, of course, were the four listed descendants.

Kamehameha II, in his early twenties when the missionaries arrived in 1820, died of the measles in London in 1824. His orders, however, that everyone be educated in reading and writing meant that in addition to the rest of his subjects, all of the younger members of the royal family went to school almost immediately. In 1840 Kamehameha III directed formation of The Chiefs' Children's School, run by the missionary Amos Starr Cooke and his wife, Juliette, to give the young royals and children of the highest chiefs a more comprehensive education. Its enrollment of 15 students included every Hawaiian who was to assume a leadership role in Island history for the next fifty years, ranging from King Kamehameha IV to Queen Lili'uokalani. Also among them were Hawai'i's two greatest Hawaiian benefactors, Princess Pauahi, whose legacy is the Bishop Estate, and the Englishman John Young's granddaughter, Emma Rooke, who was to marry Kamehameha IV and with him found Queen's Hospital as well as St. Andrew's Priory School.

Chief's Children's School

Hawaiian benefactors

Other great benefactors attending the royal school, who no doubt learned there of the joys of giving and the responsibilities of wealth, included Lili'uokalani, whose trust helps needy Hawaiian children, and King Lunalilo, whose trust runs a home for aged Hawaiians.

Blaming "the missionaries" for the ills of Hawai'i has been going on for one hundred seventy-seven years. First it was the whalers who resented missionary efforts to cut down on promiscuous sexual practices and party times in general. Whalers and local businessmen also resented the active missionary role in temperance movements. Alcoholism was a serious problem with Hawaiian royalty as well as much of the rest of the population, but sailors landing in these Islands after months at sea were in no mood to have their rowdy enjoyments curtailed.

The missionaries may not have been much fun for those bent on wild parties, but there's no doubt that without their stern presence the condition of Native Hawaiians would have sunk lower and more quickly than it did. About two-thirds of the population, or a net loss of nearly two hundred thousand people, had been wiped out in the forty years after Western contact and before the missionaries arrived, and the population fell another eighty thousand or more in the seventy-three years from then until the Revolution.[11] Missionary doctors undoubtedly were responsible in large measure for that slowdown in the death rate, but doctors of the 19th Century did not possess the skills that today help us to defeat more successfully the kinds of scourges that ravaged the Native Hawaiian population.

The kings and their chiefs used the counsel of missionaries, missionary descendants and other foreign members of the community in most of their government and economic undertakings. But the missionaries should not be branded as seeking power. The fact they constituted only 4 percent of the foreigners filling Cabinet posts in the 19th Century shows it simply isn't true. What this use of foreign advice by the kings really demonstrates is that Hawaiians were a strong people, capable of getting what they wanted, using the tools and methods of Western civilization where they were useful.

However, "the Mission Boys" became a term of derision in the 1870s and continued on through the period of the Revolution as if to imply that the missionaries were behind the Revolution itself.

An examination of the number of missionary descendants involved in the Revolution and the subsequent Provisional Government shows that the assertion of "missionary plot" by sovereignty activists and others is greatly exaggerated.

Annexation Club had few missionary descendants

The Pacific Commercial Advertiser in 1897, as Russ points out in *The Hawaiian Revolution*, reviewed the two thousand names then on the rolls of the Annexation Club and found that only thirty-four or about 1.5 percent were missionary descendants.

Nor did any of the planning for or execution of the Revolution involve their church or religious associations.

Mainland offices of the United Church of Christ, the organizational descendant of supporters of the original churches of Hawai'i, did a huge disservice to the early missionaries when they formulated an apology in 1993 for the erroneous claim that the church played a role in the 1893 overthrow. Their effort still is a matter of controversy in many Hawai'i congregations with members who know

Church apology inappropriate

their churches were not a party to carrying out the Revolution.

In 1996, the mainland churches went another step beyond their local members with the decision to turn over millions of dollars from church endowments, as well as certain church lands, to various Hawaiian associations.

The church apology falls into the same category as the U.S. congressional apology of October 27, 1993. Both appear to be unfortunate attempts to make political hay. Both apologies were conceived in haste and adopted without public input from citizens of Hawai'i. No public hearings were held to consider errors in the "whereas" clauses of the congressional apology or to weigh long-range consequences of either apology, a subject dealt with separately in a later chapter.

Apologies conceived without public input

If it weren't missionary zeal that caused the Revolution in 1893, what did, beyond the inevitable evolution of colonialism? The next chapter examines causes that led to the Revolution, and the subsequent chapter takes a look at intriguing evidence that the Queen herself was a major immediate cause.

Whatever the causes, Hawai'i was eliminated in 1893 from the shrinking list of monarchies and added to the expanding list of democratic nations.

Chapter Three

Seeds of Revolution

As we have seen, the pressure of colonialism from both Western and Eastern nations coupled with the downward trend in its population was moving Hawai'i inevitably on a path away from independence.

Kamehameha III saw that independent future was unlikely

Kamehameha III, Hawai'i's longest-reigning king and arguably the monarch who best served Hawai'i's people, saw this coming. Early on, he sought to combine Hawai'i's future with America's through Annexation or Statehood. He was the first Hawaiian king to proclaim a constitutional government for the Islands and perhaps most importantly, he authorized the Great *Mahele* to get land ownership from his sole control into the hands of the common people. He was a master at using the advice and counsel of his foreign advisers in ways that benefited his people, and the Great *Mahele* may be the best example of that. By distributing two-thirds of his former lands to the government, the chiefs and the commoners, as we will see in a later chapter, he revolutionized the way land was held in these Islands. The *Mahele* provided the base for economic growth and governance that prevails even today.

King revolutionized way land was held

His successor, Kamehameha IV, in the mid-19th Century allied himself more with British influences and veered away from moves to bring about Annexation to the United States. Kamehameha V moved the constitutional government concept slightly backward toward a stronger Monarchy by promulgating on his own initiative—illegally under terms of the Constitution he had sworn to uphold—a new Constitution. His action set a fateful example for Queen Liliʻuokalani forty years later. He got away with it; she didn't.

Kamehameha IV more aligned with British

Kamehameha V was the last of the Kamehameha line to rule—he died without naming a successor, though members of the bloodline were alive and would have been fitting leaders had they chosen to accept the responsibility. With his passing, Hawaiian government entered a new phase characterized by elected monarchs who sought expanded powers. The new monarchs had fewer ties with the great genealogies of Hawaiian history and associated with foreign advisers of a far different sort from the missionary advisers of early years.

New monarchs less tied to great genealogies

The missionary teachings had laid thoughts and ideas before the early Kamehameha kings that led to expanded roles for the people. The constitutional Monarchy brought elected legislators who shared the role of creating laws, formerly a province entirely of the king. Greater autonomy for chiefs and regional governors spread political power. The dispersion of land ownership through the Great *Mahele* started building an economy based on stability and on caring for one's own land. Early practice had required a tenant to work one day in every week (Tuesday) for the king and one day (Friday) for his *konohiki* (landlord). This later was reduced to thirty-six days in the year for the king and an equal number for the landlord, and at the *Mahele*, the requirement was dropped completely.

Unfortunately, Native Hawaiian population figures continued to plunge. The common people, inexperienced in ownership of their own land and suffering the destruction by disease of their families, abandoned agricultural development of their plots of land and often sold them, falling prey in some cases to foreigners, more astute neighbors, chiefs and *konohiki*. William L. Lee, chief justice of the Kingdom in 1848, had written countless letters to the missionaries over the limited period of time the *Mahele* was available, seeking—and getting—their help in reaching Native Hawaiians who under terms of the *Mahele* could claim their *kuleana* (the piece of land, usually small in area, that they had been working). Thousands of natives did so—about twenty-nine thousand acres worth all told—but the ideal of widespread land ownership did not succeed on the scale Lee had hoped.

Lee worked diligently to get land for Hawaiian commoners

His letters and replies from the missionaries give eloquent testimony to the efforts he and the missionaries both made to get land ownership into the hands of the people. A number of these letters are detailed in Chapter Nine.

When the Kamehameha dynasty died out with Kamehameha V, the Legislature began a new system of monarchical selection, an election by vote of the combined houses.

The first of the elected kings, Lunalilo, could do little in his fourteen months as ruler. The second elected king, Kalākaua, was plagued by unscrupulous advisers who played to his ego and desires for power, pomp and ceremony—the seeds of destruction and discontent that were to lead to revolution. His election was hotly disputed, a large faction of Hawaiians

Kalākaua plagued by unscrupulous advisers

preferring Queen Emma over the doubtful lineage and abilities of Kalākaua. He and his appointed sister-successor, Queen Lili'uokalani, seemed motivated more by desires for individual power and privilege than desires to improve the welfare of their people, though both did much to build pride and self-esteem for the race among many Hawaiians. Both were monarchical in appearance, musical and talented in many ways. But neither provided the leadership that was required to keep Hawai'i politically stable, economically strong and capable of existing as an independent nation.

Power and privilege seemed paramount

Lorrin A. Thurston, instrumental in bringing down the Monarchy in 1893, in his early years believed in the concept of an independent Hawaiian monarchy and thus initially was a supporter of Kalākaua. Thurston was a member of one of Kalākaua's many cabinets during the early part of his reign and acted as his prime minister before 1887 but turned against him in later years.

In his *Memoirs of the Hawaiian Revolution,* Thurston is often snide and rancorous about King Kalākaua. He describes a distinct decrease in the quality of leadership from the Kamehameha line of monarchies to those of Kalākaua and Lili'uokalani.

Quality of leadership declined

This is his summary of the King:

"Kalākaua displayed diverse qualities; a personal charm and a kingly demeanor; an unbalanced mentality and a total inability to grasp important subjects intelligently; a fundamental financial dishonesty; personal extravagance, which merged into the control of community finances to such an extent that community financial collapse loomed; an immoral disposition, or it might be termed 'unmoral;' a bent to indulge in political intrigue, a reckless disregard of political honor, which made impossible the continuance of honest government; personal cowardice."

Queen Emma, who was Kalākaua's opponent in the legislative election of a monarch after Lunalilo's death and whose lines of descent were called impeccable, saw Kalākaua as an "arrogant pretender, using paid genealogists to give substance to his flawed pedigree," in the words of Gavan Daws in his widely acclaimed history of Hawai'i, *Shoal of Time.*

Ralph S. Kuykendall, in his definitive, three-volume history of Hawai'i, *The Hawaiian Kingdom,* reported that Emma had written to a cousin about Kalākaua's good points: "With Taffy's faults, we must give him credit for a great ambition—he has worked & exerted himself both lawfully & to be sure unlawfully . . . to obtain his desire but there is the fact he has exerted himself . . . to secure his coveted object—the Throne."

U.S. Minister Henry Pierce called Kalākaua "ambitious, flighty & unstable. Very energetic; but lacks prudence and good sense."[12]

Daws said Kalākaua "continued to encourage his official genealogists in their reconstruction of family lines of the old ruling chiefs."

Thurston in his *Memoirs* pointed to the 1886 election as particularly noteworthy of Kalākaua's improper behavior. The King was determined to get his slate of candidates elected to the Legislature and bought those votes with cheap "sandpaper gin"—virtually raw alcohol that felt as if it were taking the lining off your throat.

William De Witt Alexander, early historian and a contemporary of Kalākaua's, told former U.S. Representative James H. Blount, sent by President Cleveland in 1893 to investigate the Revolution, that

"The election of 1886 was the most corrupt one ever held in this Kingdom." He said the King supplied cheap gin to flood the districts and "he paid for it by franking other liquor through the customhouse free of duty, . . . thereby defrauding the Government of revenue amounting to $4,749.35."

More than $60,000 worth of liquor was supplied by Kalākaua for this election, according to Thurston's *Memoirs*. This came to light, Thurston said, when the books of the dealer were seized by the Reformists after the 1887 Constitution was enacted.

1886 election "most corrupt" in history

Under the law at the time, no duty was levied on goods imported for use by the King or the royal family, and Kalākaua signed the necessary papers so the gin was tax-free. According to historians of the period, Kalākaua had used the same maneuver in the 1884 election to get duty-free gin.

He had a list of royalist candidates prepared, along with a careful schedule showing the number of cases of gin to be sent to each. This liquor was used by the candidates to cajole voters for support.

Shady liquor franking

While the tax break lightened the financial load, the King still needed a large sum of money to pay for the gin itself. To cover that, Thurston said, Kalākaua stamped "duty free" on additional amounts of gin for the liquor importer so that the importer could evade duty in an amount equal to the price of Kalākaua's election gin.

Besides supplying gin, Kalākaua played a personal role in the elections of 1886. Thurston reports the King sat himself in an armchair at the polls in Kona and urged Native Hawaiians to vote against G.W. Pilipo, whom he disliked, and then watched to see for whom the voter cast his ballot. Thurston pointed out that for the Native Hawaiian commoner, raised in traditional subservience to the monarch, this was intense pressure. Other historians such as Alexander and Kuykendall also report this poll-watching behavior of the King.

Sanford B. Dole, a Supreme Court justice under the Monarchy and later president of the Provisional Government, tended to be restrained about Kalākaua in his *Memoirs of the Hawaiian Revolution.* Nonetheless, he said of the King:

"He showed a tendency to gather subservient advisers about him and to delve into politics in efforts to control the elections and legislation."

Dole further said, "With the growing tendency of the King to base his selection of cabinet members on their subservience, rather than on their ability, much looseness crept into the administration of public affairs. Funds were transferred from one legislative appropriation to another; roads, landings, and wharves were neglected; appropriations were made for fantastic enterprises and for the personal aggrandizement of the royal family; little was done to promote the material prosperity of the kingdom . . ."

Hawai'i was very prosperous at the beginning of Kalākaua's rule in 1874, and at first he helped assure that prosperity with successful negotiation of the Reciprocity Act of 1876, which provided Hawai'i with duty-free trade arrangements, eventually in return for the use of Pearl Harbor. But Kalākaua was a spendthrift by nature and the tiny Kingdom was in trouble. There are repeated reports in the literature of allegations that Kalākaua was willing to sell Hawai'i to the highest bidder among foreign nations. Indeed, in her diaries, his sister, Lili'uokalani, reported that the King raised the notion to her: "Supposing I should sell the country, what then?" she claimed Kalākaua asked her.

Thurston in his *Memoirs* discussed the budgets for two years—1872, prior to Kalākaua's ascension, and 1886, the year before the Reform Constitution was forced on the extravagant monarch.[13]

In 1872, the cost for maintaining the King, the royal family and the military was $144,350. In 1886, it had risen to more than three times that amount, $462,436. Within that number, military costs had doubled, but support for the royals more than tripled.

Costs skyrocketed under Kalākaua

In addition, the budget included:
- $40,000 for bands, flags and salutes.
- $15,000 for celebrating the King's birthday.
- $22,867 for coronation costs.

The final tally for the two-week coronation, an event held nine years after Kalākaua took the throne, actually was closer to $50,000. In addition, during his world tour (for which $22,500 in travel expenses was appropriated), he had bought two crowns at $10,000 each for himself and his Queen. Apparently taken with the pomp of European courts, he copied some of that style for his coronation. The coronation pavilion, built for the occasion, still stands on 'Iolani Palace grounds, an intriguing memento for Hawai'i's visitors.

Kalākaua attracted by pomp of Europe

Alexander told Blount during his interview that the event "was boycotted by Queen Emma, Princess Ruth, Pauahi Bishop and by a large part of the foreign community, as an expensive and useless pageant."

Charles R. Bishop, an American who married Princess Bernice Pauahi and became very close to the royal family, earlier had lost confidence in King Kalākaua. Harold Winfield Kent, in his biography, *Charles Reed Bishop, Man of Hawai'i*, relates that Bishop and his wife both wanted Kalākaua to succeed, as did most of the leadership in Honolulu, and for the most part, kept criticism of the sovereign under wraps. Bishop remained in close contact with Kalākaua, and was at his deathbed in California.

Nonetheless, Bishop was an astute man, and despite his affection, he could see that Kalākaua and later Lili'uokalani were not living up to promise. Kent points out that the Bishops felt so strongly about Kalākaua's "extravagances and reckless public actions" that they did not attend his elaborate coronation, nor any of the festivities surrounding it.

The Bishops found Kalākaua excessive

While he supported the Monarchy, Bishop could see its shortcomings. In June 1887, he wrote, "I do not think it possible for the King to clear himself of the damaging charges made against him so plainly. And that he is guilty of much more not exposed or made public I have no doubt."

After the 1887 public uprising against King Kalākaua's excesses, the new Reform Constitution curtailed the Monarchy. Bishop wrote, "Good men here [in San Francisco] seem surprised when I tell them that I prefer a monarchical government in Hawai'i with proper restraint upon the sovereign to a republic."

In her book, *Hawai'i's Story by Hawai'i's Queen,* Lili'uokalani defends her brother's excess:
"It was necessary to confirm the new family . . . by a celebration of unusual impressiveness. There was a serious purpose of national importance; the first line of the 'Kamehamehas' having become extinct. . . . It was wise and patriotic to spend money to awaken in the people a national pride."

Lili'uokalani applauded Kalākaua coronation

Prior to the Reform Constitution, Kalākaua had a penchant for dismissing cabinets and appointing new ones, sometimes in the middle of the night. He appointed thirty-seven ministers. According to Daws, that was "more than all the kings before him had made among them."

One such appointment was Celso Caesar Moreno, a recent arrival with questionable ethics and a way of flattery that ingratiated him with the King. Kalākaua named him minister of foreign affairs, but the diplomatic corps, representing the various nations with offices in Hawai'i, refused to deal with him, Daws and others note, and he was removed in a matter of days.

Talk around Honolulu at the time was agitated and ranged from "the abdication of the King, the crowning of Queen Emma, annexation to the United States, [to] the lynching of Moreno . . . ," reported U.S. Minister General J.M. Comly to his home office.

Daws reports that the nation "had never been so prosperous, yet the national debt kept growing." The Kingdom and Kalākaua himself remained in financial stress due to poor management by the King and his premier, Walter Murray Gibson. Both the King and Gibson were heavily in debt to Claus A.

Spreckels, an American sugar baron who apparently viewed this as a means of wielding power in the Islands. People at the time said he held the Island government in his hands. What finally tipped the balance away from Spreckels, probably, was that he was openly being referred to as "King Claus" or "His Majesty, King Spreckels," and Kalākaua did not like it. Spreckels never lost his power completely, however, and after the Revolution he tried to get Lili'uokalani restored to the throne.

A $2 million loan from the British was the King's idea of a means to get out from under Spreckels' control. The loan was an unrealistic idea: Kuykendall reports the government was able to realize only $725,000 of the proposed $2 million. Daws reports it appears the loan was for $1 million with over $250,000 going out in fees before the government netted its remainder. Lili'uokalani's diaries indicate Kalākaua tried to get her to sign off on crown lands as a means of providing collateral for this loan.

Spreckels told Hawai'i's longtime minister to the United States and Europe, H.A.P. Carter, that he was sorry he'd gotten control of Kalākaua and the Legislature. According to U.S. Secretary of State Thomas Bayard, Carter reported that Spreckels "found that when he sought to stay the current of corruption which he himself had set in motion, . . . it proved too strong for him."

Spreckels sorry about backing Kalākaua

Charles C. Tansill, Ph.D. of Fordham University, writing in 1940 on the life of Secretary Bayard, said that Kalākaua had been elected partly through the efforts of Americans because they feared Queen Emma would align the Islands too closely with Britain. Tansill wrote, "It was difficult, however, for the American Government to continue to look with favor upon the Kalākaua administration which was shamelessly corrupt." Led by Gibson, he said, the regime was filled with "vice and venality."

Americans favored Kalākaua over Emma

Carter also reported, according to Bayard, that Kalākaua "had the idea he would receive more personal consideration at the hands of the British Government than at the hands of the United States; that they would probably give him a title—make him a duke or something of that kind, and secure him a better income, but he thought if the United States would keep up his personal dignity and secure as good treatment for him, that then he would be perfectly willing to act in accordance with their wishes."

While Kalākaua was willing to sell the Kingdom as a way out of his troubles, he was working on other ideas as well. One was to collect all of the independent kingdoms of the Pacific under one umbrella, which he would hold. Another was for an Asiatic confederation, of which Hawai'i would be part, and toward that end he sought to marry his niece, Princess Ka'iulani, to the son of the Emperor of Japan.

Kalākaua wanted Ka'iulani to marry Japanese

The event that appears to have been the straw that led to forcing of the Reform Constitution on his regime, however, involved the opium license.

Opium sales had been illegal for some time in the Islands. In the early 1880s, Kalākaua himself had vetoed two bills that would have allowed sale of the addictive narcotic. Then, for whatever reason, he signed into law a new licensing. According to various reports, a Chinese rice mill operator named Tong Kee paid Kalākaua a total of $71,000 for the license. The payments were made to the King in three installments, according to Daws in *Shoal of Time*. These were made at night, in gold, in a basket carried by Tong and accompanied by a baked pig as a gift. But Tong, known as Aki, didn't get the license. The Cabinet had sold it to another man, Chun Lung, for $80,000.

Twice-sold opium license

Aki asked for his money back. The King said it was all gone, and, said Thurston in his *Memoirs*, "Aki blurted out the whole story to the public, and lay down and died." Aki's estate finally was reimbursed by the government. Kalākaua, who admitted taking the money from Aki, again according to Daws, couldn't pay it back because he was a quarter million dollars in debt.

This incident, exemplifying the corruptness

of the Kingdom under Kalākaua, was followed by a horrendous example of the impractical grandiose schemes he launched, which made his government an embarrassing laughingstock to local residents.

The incident that made him a laughingstock involved his sending first a delegation and then a gunboat to Samoa in 1886 to form the beginnings of his Pacific empire. A former guano ship, the *Kaimiloa*, was to have been a man-of-war, the cornerstone of his royal navy. Mid-course, its purpose was changed to a naval training vessel, although the Hawaiian delegation in Samoa was expecting a fighting ship to back them up in their attempts to unify Polynesia.

The whole affair would have been an amusing failure if it hadn't been so costly. The *Kaimiloa* voyage reportedly was a besotted expedition, led by a drunken captain. The delegation already in Samoa had achieved a dubious reputation of drunkenness and crudeness. John E. Bush, the Native Hawaiian head of the group, was the subject of an official protest from the Samoan government and the mission was recalled.

When Kalākaua died in 1891, his sister, Lili'uokalani, succeeded him, and the community for a short time thought things were going to get better.

But Lili'uokalani was not a good ruler. She was a caring, generous person to those around her, but as a monarch, she came up very short, as had her brother before her.

Russ, in *The Hawaiian Revolution*, reported that Lili'uokalani's reputation had been purposefully tainted by John Stevens, the U.S. minister in Honolulu. Many of the rumors swirled about her private life. Yet rumors about personal conduct aside, there were grievous concerns among her subjects about Lili'uokalani and her ability to administer the country.

Business leaders who had anticipated a better government from her than from her brother were quickly shaken in that belief. Hawai'i's government bonds were declining on the London market with the increased instability of the government under Lili'uokalani, and according to some reports of the day, the nation was going bankrupt.

Hawai'i reportedly going bankrupt

Reports show, too, those agitating against the Monarchy, or against this particular monarch, also included Native Hawaiian leaders both in the Legislature and within the community. Lack of confidence in her was growing, particularly because of her continued support for Charles B. Wilson, who was serving as marshal of the Kingdom.

At a meeting of *Hui Kālai'aina* (a Native Hawaiian political club) in December 1891, Hawaiian activist Robert W. Wilcox expressed community discontent. Rumors were rife about a personal relationship between Lili'uokalani and Wilson. At that December meeting of *Hui Kālai'aina,* Wilcox said Wilson was "carrying on high jinks" while running Lili'uokalani's administration. Wilson was accused of allowing opium rings to operate right under his nose.

Hawaiian group concerned about marshal of Kingdom

The government, Wilcox said, was rotten and loose from top to bottom and it was a disgrace to Hawaiians to allow this to continue.

During the campaign of 1891, Wilcox said "We must all be loyal Hawaiians, and tell the Queen that her present Government is an injustice and a disgrace to the nation. We must not flatter her."

His Liberal Party did not carry the day in that election, but it continued to attack the Queen's government in 1892 and one of its most articulate spokesmen, John E. Bush, went so far as to predict its demise. Bush was the editor of *Ka Leo o Ka Lāhui,* a widely read Hawaiian language newspaper. In a three-part series in February issues, Bush reviewed the history of the Monarchy, pointed out it couldn't last forever, and, in the final article, said "no candid student of current Hawaiian history can fail to see that the course of events has been, and now is running steadily in one direction, and that toward democratic institutions." In later articles, he predicted and applauded the idea of Annexation to the United States.

Hawaiian opposition to Queen

There was concern throughout the community that the party, largely Native Hawaiians but including Caucasians and part-Hawaiians, would overthrow the Queen, establish a republic and seek Annexation to the United States. The rumors became so widespread that Marshal Wilson arrested Wilcox and seventeen others, charging them with treason. The case was later dropped but it was apparent there was considerable dissension within the Hawaiian community.

Hawaiian language paper saw democracy coming

Marshal Wilson and the Queen's continued support of him were also key ingredients in the climate that led to the 1893 Revolution. Hawaiian leaders in the Legislature as well as in the community at large had strong, negative feelings about Wilson, and the Queen's seemingly blind support of him shook many Hawaiians' faith in her.

A resolution was introduced in the 1892 Legislature that would have ousted Wilson. The proposed resolution, introduced by Rep. S.K. Pua, a long-time supporter of the Queen, read in part ". . . and whereas the said Marshal [Wilson] is commonly reported to exercise a pernicious, illegitimate and

Queen's support of Wilson upset many

49

occult influence at the court of Her Majesty the Queen, which tends to bring Her Majesty's government into contempt and disrespect . . ."

Pua's reference to the Queen and the occult is noteworthy. Some of the rumors about the Queen before and just after the overthrow involved her alleged reliance on *kahuna*, Hawaiian spiritualists. In her diary she pointedly notes she refused the offer of services of a *kahuna*, but in that case her comments indicate she apparently was suspicious of the reason for the offer and not necessarily against advice from such a source. Kuykendall, however, in *The Hawaiian Kingdom*, in notes transcribed by his colleague Charles H. Hunter, says ". . . she refused the services of *kahuna*, even one who claimed the power to free her from evil influence by prayer. The Bible, she said, was her only guide."

The Queen's German fortuneteller

Lili'uokalani was strongly influenced also by a German teacher and fortuneteller, Miss Wolf, or Fraulein, as the Queen refers to her in the diaries.

Lili'uokalani recounts listening as Fraulein read the cards late one night after a ball at the palace. Fraulein told about a man who would come at a precise hour with "a bundle of papers that would bring money from across the waters," and indeed at the precise hour, the man came. He came regarding establishment of a lottery in Hawai'i. This Queen, so distrustful of many more-level heads, listened carefully to the Fraulein, and never once in her diaries does she ask herself if perhaps there might be some hanky-panky behind the readings of the cards.

Reading the cards predicted lottery visitor

Her diaries show she was suspicious in many instances and cautious at other times about people surrounding her. She made frequent loans of money, for example, to her close associate Sam Parker, in spite of privately questioning in her diary his motivations. He was the flamboyant grandson of the founder of today's Parker Ranch on the Big Island, a Cabinet minister and adviser to Kalākaua, and later minister of foreign affairs in Lili'uokalani's last Cabinet. She also questioned the motives of Paul Neumann, her personal attorney, adviser and Cabinet minister, to whom she had given her power of attorney. Neumann later wrote the masterful letter of surrender in 1893 in which she professed to be surrendering to the United States instead of the Provisional Government.

Queen questioned motive of key supporters

In so many ways, her diaries show her to be an astute and cautious politician. For the counsel of the Fraulein, however, she seemed totally gullible.

Lili'uokalani supported the lottery bill because she believed it would bring needed revenues into her government. But she also believed it would bring her personal money. She was informed by this occult figure that the lottery operators would provide her $10,000 to $15,000 a year in pocket money.

She saw cash cow in lottery

Lili'uokalani, who wrote with distaste of bribery allegedly taking place in the Legislature, who held a high moral stance against it, did not see this "pocket money" as a bribe. She did not question Fraulein's motivations and believed the medium's sources were otherworldly.

Queen never questioned motivation of Fraulein

The Fraulein meddled in affairs of state beyond the lottery, but probably related to it. Miss Wolf makes specific recommendations as to whom Lili'uokalani should appoint as Cabinet ministers and in her diary, Lili'uokalani lists their initials. The queen wrote that the medium told her "they will make a good Cabinet, but you are going to appoint and the house will reject you, send down again and they refuse, but I must be firm after that and everything will be all right. When C.S. gets here, he will spend $25,000 among the members."

C.S. is undoubtedly Claus Spreckels, the leading sugar baron in the Islands, who was away from Hawai'i at the time. The entry indicates that C.S. would use the $25,000 to buy the support of legislators, and subsequent events prove he did.

Another day, the Fraulein read her cards and told the Queen that "Mr. S. Parker and Mr. Neumann knew about lottery papers and would be the means of bringing the measure before the house." Again, the medium predicts that the lottery man would come at 10 a.m." and tell me things important." Mr. T.E.E. [Thomas Evans?] did arrive at 10 and told the Queen "of Sam [Parker] seeming favorable to the lottery" and that Peterson, later to be her attorney general and along with Parker a member of her final Cabinet, was also a "friend." Peterson, in the Legislature at the time, was the only *haole* (foreigner, usually meaning white) member to vote for the lottery, which passed by one vote. *The Advertiser* said at the time "he forfeited his reputation in the eyes of all men."

More cards directed Queen on lottery

Peterson not respected

Fraulein also told Lili'uokalani that she would remarry. "How can that be, and to whom?" the Queen asks in her diary. A later entry notes that a new dress arrived on the *Mariposa* and the Queen wonders if it will be her wedding dress.

Miss Wolf spun an elaborate story about Lili'uokalani's deceased husband, John Dominis, and his possible royal lineage. The Queen wrote to sources abroad, based on what the Fraulein told her, to try to get proof of these things.

A second marriage for Queen?

On the one hand, here is a Queen, prey to the mumbo-jumbo pronouncements of a card-reading medium; on the other, Lili'uokalani was a ruthless political tactician, not above bribery and deceit.

The longtime *Advertiser* columnist Samy Amalu (he insisted on using only one "m" in Samy), who often proclaimed his descent from Hawaiian royalty, nevertheless said, as he did in a column that ran September 4, 1975: "How many living Hawaiians of today would go back to yesterday—would exchange being an American citizen for being the subject of a Hawaiian monarch? There may be some. But not I for sure."

Samy Amalu on Monarchy

He also had scant praise for Queen Lili'uokalani:

"There were two barren women in the history of Hawai'i who through their own personalities, their own innate natures, brought drastic changes to their people. Each of them . . . wielded power in their own right.

"The first of these was Queen Ka'ahumanu, the widow of the great Kamehameha. The second was Queen Lili'uokalani . . . . They were both arrogant.

"They were both haughty. They were both imperious. They were both alike. The difference between them lay only in what they accomplished for their people.

"Ka'ahumanu saved her people and gave them a chance to survive in a new world. Lili'uokalani lost her people and lost for them everything that they had—their throne, their crown, their scepter, their orb, their kingdom, and their independence.

Amalu compared Lili'uokalani to Ka'ahumanu

"And that is the basic difference between the blood of the Kamehamehas who founded the Hawaiian Kingdom and the blood of the Kalākauas who lost that same kingdom . . ."

Charles R. Bishop, through his marriage to Princess Bernice Pauahi, had become Lili'uokalani's adopted brother-in-law. He was dedicated to the

53

Hawaiian Monarchy, as indicated earlier in this chapter, but he, too, in the end, saw Annexation as the best course.

Excerpts from his correspondence reported in *Charles Reed Bishop, Man of Hawai'i,* cast considerable light on the Queen.

Bishop, with his close relationship, knew the Queen well and discounted stories of her liaison with Marshal Wilson—"no known facts," he said. But while he apparently didn't believe she was having an affair with the marshal, he, too, found her to be an inadequate monarch, one who was "treacherous and deceitful."

Bishop concerned Queen was deceitful

Bishop had once been guardian to Lili'uokalani, who had been adopted by his wife's parents. Lili'uokalani thus was the *hānai* (adopted) younger sister of Bernice Pauahi, and after Bernice's marriage, the future queen lived with the Bishops. After strongly supporting Lili'uokalani, treating her with affection and great deference, giving her wise and kind counsel during her reign, he, too, came to the conclusion change was needed.

"The frequent changes of Ministry and other disturbing acts and reports, with the impression that the business of the country is not prospering, have injured the credit of the Government abroad . . . ," he wrote.

Bishop concluded change needed

This was about a month before the Revolution and overthrow. A month after the Revolution, he wrote, ". . . Much as I dread it, annexation to this country (the United States) seems to be the wisest action suggested so far for all concerned."

Bishop saw Claus Spreckels as a principal opponent of Annexation and of the Provisional Government. Bishop wrote that Spreckels "will, no doubt, do all he can to defeat the efforts of the Provisional Government." Bishop feared the Provisional Government was wobbly. If Annexation were not possible, he favored Ka'iulani as monarch, "not getting the ex-Queen back."

Bishop's thoughts after the Revolution

Bishop, who had "a life-long hope of a sturdy, independent, Hawaiian nation," had come sadly to the conclusion: "It looks to me that the best interests of natives and haoles will be promoted by annexation . . ."

Bishop was bothered that the leaders of the new Republic were making too much out of Lili'uokalani's private habits before the Revolution, with "too little made of the political acts of the Queen which led to the Revolution."

"Had the Queen been a law-abiding and honest ruler—though her private character might not have been pure—the case would have been a different matter," he wrote.

Bishop believed public, not private, acts were Queen's downfall

The Queen was not above altering facts to fit her story. There are many examples. After the unsuccessful counter-revolution in 1895, when Lili'uokalani was under arrest, Paul Neumann, Sam Parker and Charles Wilson went to Judge A.S. Hartwell's law office and asked him to draw up Lili'uokalani's abdication paper, Hartwell reported in a letter to Thurston. Working in confidence with only his clerk informed, Hartwell said he redrafted the paper three separate times as her advisers brought changes she wanted made. Then she signed her abdication declaration, he said, in his presence with Neumann, Parker, W.G. Irwin, H.A. Widemann and Curtis Iaukea as additional witnesses, the latter two being additional Hawaiian advisers and supporters.

Queen's discrepancies of fact

Yet in her book, *Hawai'i's Story by Hawai'i's Queen*, she said she was deceived and that Hartwell was acting as attorney for the other side. Hartwell made it clear he kept the confidence of the group until the former monarch had signed the papers, and therefore had never even discussed the subject with anyone in the Provisional Government. Hartwell, however, did not blame Lili'uokalani. He said the misinformation was from Julius Palmer, who helped her write the book.[14]

Stories between diary and book differ

Another example of a discrepancy of facts concerns James Dowsett. In a diary entry during Kalākaua's reign, Lili'uokalani says that Dowsett came to see her and "told me that they [the Wilcox group plotting the overthrow of Kalākaua in 1889] wanted me to be Queen." She said she would, but "only if it became necessary for the King to abdicate if he was doing wrong."

Later, in her book, Lili'uokalani describes Dowsett as "a mere boy eighteen years of age," and makes much of the rebels sending such a young fellow, as if to belittle his report of the incident. She said she told him that such a proposal was not to be considered. "My answer would be 'No,' and this was final."

Dowsett was no boy

Thurston, in his *Memoirs,* points out Dowsett was no boy; a part-Hawaiian, he was involved in politics of the day, and in fact was elected to the Legislature the year after his meeting with Lili'uokalani. His birth records, according to Thurston, show he was 30 years old the year he approached Lili'uokalani about taking the throne from her brother.

Thurston wrote that Lili'uokalani "was in an almost continuous maelstrom of negotiation and scheming to bring about Kalākaua's abdication and her own elevation to the throne." Thurston, who was a member of Kalākaua's Cabinet for three years, said her actions were well known to him, but that he later also checked various sources for corroboration.

In another section of her diary (January 16, 1888) Lili'uokalani recounts telling two of her supporters it was time to go to the King and propose his abdication, if only for a year. Kalākaua, according to Lili'uokalani, said he'd think about it.

Lili'uokalani supported abdication of her brother

Yet in her book, she claims she refused all discussion of such matters, including with W.R. Castle, who she says approached her about it. Castle's story is quite different. He said he went to ask her if the rumors that she thought Kalākaua should abdicate were true. "She gave me a positive statement that she thought her brother should abdicate, and that, if he did, she would accept the position as sovereign."

Thurston, while minister of the interior for Kalākaua, got a signed statement from Charles Wilson that he, Wilson, and a group of others went to the King and demanded he abdicate in favor of his sister, and that if he didn't, they'd oust him by force. Kalākaua refused to abdicate, but the argument went on so long, according to Wilson, that the Wilson supporters outside got cold feet and disappeared, so the ringleaders gave up and went home, too. This was shortly before the well-documented 1889 Wilcox insurrection, designed to achieve the same end. Incidentally, that insurrection was the second time in Kalākaua's regime that U.S. troops had been landed to preserve order, the first being the riot of 1874 when Kalākaua was elected by the Legislature over the popular Queen Emma. The 1889 insurrection was put down in favor of Kalākaua by the same men who ousted Lili'uokalani four years later. Each of those earlier times they were successful without the active, physical help of U.S. troops, who merely stood by, as they subsequently did in the 1893 Revolution.

Wilson and others demanded Kalākaua abdication

U.S. troops landed to help preserve order for Kalākaua

Lili'uokalani's statements to Blount and her own diary are discrepant regarding the lottery bill, too. She clouded the truth to Blount, perhaps because she sensed his sentiments would be against a lottery. She knew by the time of his arrival that, while he was in the Islands to investigate the Revolution, his main purpose was to consider her reinstatement as Queen, and she didn't want to make a bad impression. Her diary entries make clear her avid support for the lottery, but she told Blount that the lottery and opium bills had been railroaded through the House by Representative William White, and that her new ministers "advised me to sign the opium and lottery bills . . . I had no option but to sign." As Kuykendall points out, this is not true. Veto was the personal prerogative of the monarch and was not dependent on advice from the ministry.

Discrepancy on lottery

As we see from her diaries and other reports of the time, she handpicked the members of her new Cabinet because they would support the lottery bill. Some have maintained that she swapped her support for the lottery bill in exchange for legislators' support to oust the former Cabinet and to get native support for a new Constitution. From her diaries, one can conclude that while she may have used the lottery bill as political leverage, she also supported the bill on its own merits.

Cabinet hand-picked for lottery support

Whatever the argument, community perception was that they were her bills. This added to the concerns over her efforts to roll back the constitutional Monarchy that had served Hawai'i well for 50 years. She had become a liability so far as the business community and its friends were concerned. They were joined in their concerns by people from all walks of life, including members of her own Legislature and, for a while, her own Cabinet. The seeds had taken root: There was no holding back the inevitability of revolution.

$\mathcal{T}$he Queen's Own Men Wanted Her Out

Queen Liliʻuokalani was very nearly deposed by her closest supporters three days before the January 17, 1893, climax of the Revolution that overthrew the Monarchy.

Hand-picked Cabinet balked at proposed Constitution

Members of her Cabinet approached the community for help in accomplishing this on Saturday, January 14, minutes after her abortive effort to promulgate a new Constitution. Sworn testimony before U.S. Senator John T. Morgan's Committee on Foreign Relations by several witnesses and the writings of several other sources affirm the four Cabinet members agreed to oust her if she persisted in her revolutionary attempt to circumvent Hawaiian law and illegally change the 1887 Reform Constitution. Her agreement with them the next day to back off the constitutional issue for the time being saved her from facing an immediate revolt within her own ranks.[15]

Cabinet considered ousting Queen

The four were Samuel Parker, minister of foreign affairs; John F. Colburn, minister of the interior; W.H. Cornwell, minister of finance, and A.P. Peterson, attorney general, all Royalists. The 1887 Constitution gave the Cabinet extraordinary powers, which they interpreted as empowering them, as a Cabinet, to oust her. Their basis was that when she proposed to change the Constitution unilaterally, she was violating her oath "to maintain the Constitution . . . whole and inviolate . . . ," thus vacating the throne. But admittedly this was an interpretation and they wanted assurance of support from the community at large in case the Queen fought back. Under the existing Constitution, the Cabinet was in some ways the most powerful element of government. The Queen was going to change that in her new Constitution. At the moment, though, no actions of the Queen were valid without their approval, or in some cases, just the approval of one of them, and they shared the executive power with the monarch. By law, Cabinet members were appointed by the Monarch, but they could be removed only by the Legislature. She was going to revoke the sharing of executive power and provide for removal of the members "at the pleasure of the Queen."

Cabinet shared executive power

These were the Cabinet members she had appointed on January 13, the day before the Legislature ended. Colburn and Parker, both popular Hawaiians, were appointed to satisfy the Hawaiian community. Peterson and Cornwell were supposed to be men the American community would approve of, but they were not perceived by that community as good choices. The Queen had appointed them on the basis they would approve the opium and lottery bills. They did that, and she thought they also would approve the new Constitution. To her apparent surprise, on January 14 they advised her as a group that they would not support it. A lengthy and emotional argument broke forth in the palace as the Queen tried to get at least one of them to back her up, but they refused despite threats she and two of her other

Cabinet appointed to approve opium, lottery bills

supporters reportedly made. Testimony shows the Cabinet members feared for their lives after making this break with their Queen. They kept the approach to the community that same day a secret from her; she did not find out until eleven months later that they had discussed what she viewed as a treasonous act with the Annexation group, and then only because a report of their action appeared in a letter written by Thurston and published in Washington.

Lili'uokalani later found out about Cabinet plan

After learning belatedly of their action, she notes in her diary for Monday, December 4, 1893 (indicating that even though she no longer was a ruling Queen, she was still functioning in a queenly manner: meeting, planning new cabinets, etc.):

"Told Mr. Richardson (Ed.—Native Hawaiian John Richardson, her close adviser) he had better tell Mr. Parker to resign when I told him to. He, as one of the Cabinet had committed a great crime of treason—in fact they all had—turned against me and followed Mr. Thurston the Agitator's instructions and allowed themselves to be guided by him until the overthrow of my throne . . . and it was Colburn who asked Thurston that they must support the Cabinet against the Queen (what a confession) or they would resign. (Thurston's letter published in Washington last month and received here December 4th)."

Queen called behavior treason

Quoted material in (parentheses) are words of source, not this author unless preceded by Ed.-

In retrospect, it can be argued that the Cabinet members were not performing a treasonous act. It was their job to hold the Queen in check and when she proposed to violate the Constitution, they had a duty to stop her. The same argument applies to the Committee of Safety's actions. Having found the Queen in revolution, their counter-revolution was not really a treasonous act. As subjects they were reacting against a treasonous act on the part of their Queen.

Cabinet sought help from community

Testimony of the events of that January day indicates the Cabinet members sought backing from the community. Some of the Queen's diary remarks indicate perhaps the Cabinet sought to put the blame elsewhere once she learned of their contemplated desertion.

Lengthy testimony on this subject was given before the Morgan Committee by John A. McCandless, a member of the Committee of Safety in the 1893 Revolution and also a participant in the reform efforts of 1887 that reined in Kalākaua.[16] He had been a resident of Honolulu since 1881, in the business of sinking artesian wells in the 'Ewa plain.

McCandless testimony on Cabinet actions

He testified that on January 14 after the Queen had deferred her promulgation of the new Constitution and was arguing with her Cabinet members over their unwillingness to support it, a messenger from the Cabinet came to the office of W.O. Smith, soon to become an attorney member of the Committee of Safety and later attorney general of the Republic. McCandless said members of the community were gathered there to consider what to do about the Queen's plans for a new Constitution. He said the Cabinet members wanted to know what support they could get in the event they continued to resist the Queen.

Cabinet asked for citizen support

McCandless said "someone took a piece of office paper, brown paper such as lawyers use, the size of a sheet of legal cap, and then wrote a heading in lead pencil stating that 'We hereby agree to stand by the ministers against the encroachments of the Queen'—something to that effect. It was only a line or two, and the people as they came in signed that."

He testified that about a hundred persons signed it and that he did not see any visitor to the office decline to sign it. He said signers included Paul

Neumann, the Queen's personal attorney, and a number of other people in opposing political parties. He said the petition remained on the desk at Smith's office all day Sunday and into Monday, continuing to gather signatures before it disappeared. (L.A. Thurston, writing about the incident later in his *Memoirs*, recollected it disappeared on Saturday and believed it was taken by Neumann.)

McCandless testimony about Cabinet

McCandless said that about 2 p.m. Saturday, two of the Cabinet members themselves came to the office. He identified them as John F. Colburn, the Queen's minister of the interior, and A.P. Peterson, her attorney general. He said by then there were about 700 to 800 people in the vicinity.

He said Colburn was prevailed upon to "make a speech, tell us the story."

In his testimony, McCandless said Colburn then said ". . . he had information that morning that the Queen intended to promulgate the new constitution. He said that he immediately carried the news to Judge Hartwell and Mr. Thurston. They (Ed.—the Cabinet members versus Hartwell and Thurston) had been political enemies, of course, and they had advised the ministers to resist—that is, to refuse to countersign the new Constitution, and to do all they could with her to keep her from signing the new Constitution. After the legislature had been prorogued (Ed.—adjourned) they proceeded to the palace, right across the street, and there she made the speech (which of course is a matter of history) to the effect that she proposed to give the people a new Constitution. She asked the ministers to countersign it, and they refused to do so. Mr. Colburn told the story of her becoming very angry, and Mr. Peterson made the remark that the Constitution was faulty in some respects, whereupon he said she replied: 'You

Proposed Constitution shook Cabinet

Queen angry with Cabinet

have had it in your possession for a month and you returned it without any comment, and I took it that it was all right.'

"He (Ed.—Colburn) stated that they had escaped from there (Ed.—the palace, each going out a different direction) and thought that their lives were in danger; that she had sent for them again, and that at this time she had concluded not to promulgate the new Constitution . . . for the time being.

Colburn felt Queen would do it again

"'Now,' said he (Ed.—Colburn), 'gentlemen, we want to know what support we can get as against the Queen, because she is apt to do this at any time.' He said that the only reason she had desisted was that she was unable to get them to sign the constitution. She got it into her head that it would not be legal unless countersigned by the cabinet, and if she could get the cabinet to sign she felt that she had a legal constitution . . . she did not believe that it would be valid without the signatures of the ministers."

In retrospect, there's a nice bit of irony here. On the one hand, the existing Constitution provided that only the Legislature—and it took two sessions— could recommend changes in the document, which then would have to be approved by a two-thirds vote in the second legislative session before the amendment became a part of the Constitution. On the other hand, the Queen was proposing to bypass that involved process and proceed on her own. Yet she clung to the idea of her actions being invalid without the signature or signatures of the strong Cabinet required by the existing Constitution. Her new Constitution, even though it contained the same language on this point, in effect would have removed the requirement for approval by the Cabinet by providing that the Cabinet could be replaced at her pleasure.

Strange logic on proposed Constitution

McCandless testified that "immediately it

66

was proposed that we must have a Committee of Safety appointed," and it was done. He said the Cabinet ministers and Neumann were still there when the Committee was appointed. He said it was about 4:30 or 5 p.m. at the time and the Committee met on into the night.

Committee of Safety appointed

In his *Memoirs,* Thurston writes of waking Colburn up at 6 a.m. the next morning, Sunday. He and Colburn woke Peterson up shortly thereafter to pursue the matter of citizen support requested the day before by the Cabinet. Thurston said he told them "the citizens were prepared to support the cabinet against Lili'uokalani, declaring her in revolution against the government, the throne vacant, the monarchy abrogated, and favoring annexation to the United States. If the ministers would lead, the committee would back them; otherwise the committee would act alone." He said they—the Cabinet members—weren't ready to answer then, but would consider. Thurston reported this to the Committee at its 10 a.m. Sunday meeting at the home of W.R. Castle.

Citizens ready to back Cabinet efforts to stop Queen

President Cleveland's investigator, Blount, also reports this meeting, but his handling of it in his official report gives a different twist to the tale. An affidavit signed by all four Cabinet members appears in the Blount Report confirming this meeting, but it is the only reference by Blount to the Cabinet's discussions with the Committee of Safety. Nothing in the Blount Report acknowledges the Cabinet had approached Thurston and his group on their own the day before. Blount in his report to U.S. Secretary of State Walter Q. Gresham therefore said the whole effort to get the Cabinet to revolt was Thurston's idea. If Blount knew of the earlier meeting, he was guilty of a grave distortion by failing to mention it. If he didn't know of it, his refusal to interview

Blount ignored Cabinet's role

Thurston and Dole or take statements from them and other of the Revolutionists is at fault.

McCandless in his testimony said the Committee at that Sunday morning meeting decided to call a mass meeting for 1:30 Monday afternoon, the 16th.

On Monday morning about 9 o'clock, he said, he first saw the proclamation by the Queen calling her own mass meeting for the same time. It was *Mass meetings* shown to members of the Committee of Safety by all *set* four of the Queen's ministers.

McCandless testified the Committee met soon after in Thurston's office and reviewed a formal request from the Cabinet that had been received on Sunday, seeking a conference with the Committee of Safety.

"William Wilder, F.W. McChesney, and myself [were] constituted a [sub]committee" for that purpose, McCandless said.

"We were instructed to go and hear what they had to say, and say nothing. We went up to the Government building (Ed.—the Ali'iolani building, today the state courthouse) and the foreign office. *Cabinet* They were all there. We were ushered in, and they *changed mind* were on the other side of the room. We were opposite to them. Finally there was a pause—one of the ministers said, 'What is it, gentlemen?' And we said 'We have come up here to see you on account of the appointment you asked of Mr. Thurston.'"

He said they replied, "'We have decided that there is nothing to say, just now; the Queen has just signed a paper that she will not commit an act of this kind again, and agreed to abide by the Constitution.'"

At this point in his testimony came the bombshell that surprisingly has been largely underplayed or ignored by historians. It was not included in the report to President Cleveland by his special investigator, Blount, where it might have given the administration pause in its rush to reinstate Lili'uokalani. McCandless put it this way:

". . . there was at that time, as we afterward ascertained—did not know it then—a proclamation drawn up by the ministers, and it was even signed— I think drawn up and in their possession ready to be proclaimed at any time—**declaring the Queen deposed and reorganizing the Government** (Ed.—emphasis added). This letter from the cabinet to Thurston, asking for the conference, was in regard to the ministers taking charge of the Government and deposing the Queen entirely, and their entering into the movement with us, we supporting them."

McCandless testimony is telling

It is strange that this turn of events is not given more weight in accounts of the Revolution. It would appear to be key to determining its root causes and certainly a good indication of what the Queen's supporters really felt about her as a ruler. Blount, then, and sovereignty advocates now, are fond of saying the Queen was beloved and supported by all Native Hawaiians. This action by her closest supporters shows there were Native Hawaiians who were very concerned about her ability to govern— indeed, who even sought to depose her.

McCandless' report is backed up by testimony before the Morgan Committee from a number of other members of the Committee of Safety, who also were not interviewed by Blount.

McCandless testified that the proclamation sought by the Cabinet was drawn up with the approval of the Cabinet on Saturday afternoon by Judge Hartwell and Thurston, and probably W.O. Smith and Peterson, the Queen's attorney general. McCandless testified the proclamation declared that

Proclamation to vacate thrown drawn up

the Queen had violated the Constitution, declared the throne vacant, and that at the Monday morning meeting with the Cabinet, "they showed us the original copy."

In response to questions from the Morgan Committee, McCandless testified he believed the reason the proclamation was never issued was that the ministers decided between Saturday and Monday that their safest course remained with the Queen. He said existing political rivalries also were always hanging over the negotiations and "if there was any way in which they could get out of it (the agreement with the Committee of Safety) they would do it." He said the Queen's signing of a declaration that she would not proceed right away with the new Constitution apparently satisfied them.

Political rivalries

McCandless went on to detail events that took place in the period leading up to and during the actual Revolution the next day.

He read into the record the key resolution adopted at the mass meeting on Monday, January 16. History has made light of the Queen's violation of the Constitution as a basic cause of the Revolution, many analysts preferring the simplistic reasoning that the Revolution was just an excuse for business and sugar interests to gain control. This key resolution makes clear that high in the minds of those faced with the problems that day were reasons far removed from mere financial and personal gains. They wanted freedom, continuation of the right to vote and a strong and stable government, all of which they believed would be lost to them under her proposed new Constitution. It would have given her the right to appoint the nobles (the upper house members) instead of allowing for their election, and would have disenfranchised the foreign community.

Desire for freedom & stable government prompted Revolution

McCandless read the mass-meeting resolution from *Two Weeks of Hawaiian History*, published by *The Hawaiian Gazette* in Honolulu shortly after January 28, 1893:

Resolution from mass meeting

"1. Whereas Her Majesty, Lili'uokalani, acting in conjunction with certain other persons, has illegally and unconstitutionally, and against the advice and consent of the lawful executive officers of the Government, attempted to abrogate the existing constitution and proclaim a new one in subversion of the rights of the people;

"2. And whereas such attempt has been accompanied by threats of violence and bloodshed and a display of armed force; and such attempt and acts and threats are revolutionary and treasonable in character;

"3. And whereas Her Majesty's cabinet have informed her that such contemplated action was unlawful, and would lead to bloodshed and riot, and have implored and demanded of her to desist from and renounce such proposed action;

"4. And whereas such advice has been in vain, and Her Majesty has in a public speech announced that she was desirous and ready to promulgate such constitution, the same being now ready for such purpose, and that the only reason why it was not now promulgated was because she had met with unexpected obstacles, and that a fitting opportunity in the future must be awaited for the consummation of such object, which would be within a few days;

Queen ready to promulgate new Constitution

"5. And whereas at a public meeting of citizens, held in Honolulu on the 14th day of January, instant, a committee of thirteen, to be known as the 'Committee of Public Safety,' was appointed to consider the situation, and to devise ways and means for the maintenance of the public peace and safety, and the preservation of life and property;

"6. And whereas such committee has recommended the calling of this mass meeting of citizens to protest against and condemn such action, and has this day presented a report to such meeting, denouncing the action of the Queen and her supporters as being unlawful, unwarranted, in derogation of the rights of the people, endangering the peace of the community, and tending to excite riot, and cause the loss of life and destruction of property;

Queen's actions denounced

"Now, therefore, we, the citizens of Honolulu, of all nationalities, and regardless of political party affiliations, do hereby condemn and denounce the action of the Queen and her supporters;

"And we do hereby ratify the appointment and endorse the action taken and report made by the said Committee of Safety; and we do hereby further empower such Committee to further consider the situation and further devise such ways and means as may be necessary to secure the permanent maintenance of law and order, and the protection of life, liberty, and property in Hawai'i."

McChesney testimony

F.W. McChesney, another member of the Committee of Safety and one of the three men who met with the Queen's Cabinet, did not appear in person at the Morgan hearings. He submitted a sworn affidavit, which includes these statements regarding the efforts by her Cabinet to gain support of the Committee of Safety and others:

"I signed a roll with other citizens in the office of W.O. Smith on the afternoon of Saturday, January 14, 1893, pledging myself as a special police officer in support of the cabinet against the proposed aggression of the Queen . . . . It was reported by Mr. Thurston [at a meeting the next day] that the

Queen's cabinet had gone back on us, so we decided to proceed without them."[17]

The third member of the Committee that visited the Cabinet was William C. Wilder. He also submitted a sworn affidavit, which included these comments:

Committee went forward without Cabinet

"The conduct of the Queen became such toward the end of the [legislative] session as to lead me to believe that she was determined to regain the powers taken away by the constitution of 1887; things went on from bad to worse until the 14th of January, 1893, when the Legislature was prorogued. When it was reported on that morning that the opium and lottery bills were signed and the Cornwell-Parker-Peterson cabinet came in, the tension of public feeling became most intense; every one felt that there was trouble in the air, but it was not on account of the ousting of the Wilcox reform Cabinet. If matters had ended there, there would have been no uprising.

Wilder described buildup of tension

"The reform members of the Legislature did not attend the prorogation, more as a protest against the unlawful acts of the Queen than anything else. When, however, after the prorogation, the Queen attempted to abrogate the constitution and proclaim a new one, which would have restored the ancient despotic rights of the throne, and would have trampled under foot all further semblance of liberty in Hawai'i, the respectable, conservative, and property interests of the country, without any prior meeting or plans, simply arose in protest and to defend their rights. From what I saw, **I would have no hesitation saying that the Queen's act in attempting to abrogate the constitution and promulgate a new one brought about the revolution**[18] (Ed.—emphasis added)."

Constitution would have trampled liberty

Regarding his subcommittee's meeting Monday with the Cabinet, Wilder had this to say: "Some negotiations had been going on between members of the Queen's cabinet and Mr. Thurston, on behalf of the Committee of Safety, of which I knew nothing except the fact of such conference; but at that meeting [earlier Monday morning with the Committee of Safety at Thurston's office], I was appointed one of a [sub]committee to wait on the cabinet to receive their communication in answer to the matter discussed by them with Thurston. We went to the government building and met the cabinet; they stated that they declined any further negotiations."

Cabinet declined further negotiation

The testimony of these three men some thirty years before Thurston wrote his *Memoirs* differs slightly in details with some of his recollections, but overall is strikingly similar.

In his *Memoirs of the Hawaiian Revolution*, Thurston recalled he was in his office that Saturday morning, January 14, "sorting papers preparatory to resuming law work." (For much of the previous year Thurston had been working on Annexation plans for the secret Annexation Club, including a trip to Washington to feel out the Harrison administration on the subject, actions the Queen would have considered treasonous.)

He said Colburn came in looking much excited and since the Queen had appointed him her minister of the interior only the day before, "I was surprised to see him. He immediately burst out: 'Lorrin, we've been having a hell of a time up at the Palace, and I have come to tell you about it.'" Colburn said he had come to get Thurston's advice, while Peterson had gone to the office of W.O. Smith to seek Smith's. Colburn, of Hawaiian ancestry, and Thurston, though of opposite political persuasions, had grown

Colburn sought Thurston's advice

up together in the Islands and were good friends.

Colburn recounted the Queen's angry efforts to get the Cabinet members to approve the new Constitution and their refusal to do so. Thurston suggested they consult with Judge Hartwell, who in turn suggested further review with Smith. "Our united advice to Colburn was to stand pat in his refusal to approve the Queen's action, and we agreed to undertake to raise support for him among the men downtown," Thurston wrote.

Colburn was promised support of community

His *Memoirs* continue: "After lunch, Mr. Smith and I went to the office of Attorney-General Peterson, in Ali'iōlani Hale; there we met Colburn, Peterson, and Cornwell, several other men also being present. Messrs. Peterson and Cornwell corroborated the statement made to us by Mr. Colburn. They all agreed that Lili'uokalani was furiously insistent on their joining her in promulgating the new Constitution . . . .

Queen "furiously insistent" on new Constitution

"Mr. Smith and I, as well as the other men present, advised the cabinet to counter upon the Queen, declare her in revolution against the government and the constitution, declare the throne vacant by reason of her treasonable attitude, and call upon the people to sustain them.

"During the conversation, Samuel Parker, minister of foreign affairs and head of the cabinet, entered the room. He did not have much to say, but he was practically of the same mind as the other ministers . . . . [All four] were in a blue funk as to their course.

Cabinet in a "blue funk"

"I offered to draft for the cabinet a declaration along the lines that we had advised. They did not agree to make the declaration, but assented to my suggestion of drafting it; and I drafted it then and there (Ed.—in Peterson's office). At that stage, a messenger came from the Queen, demanding the immediate return of the cabinet."

Thurston said Colburn, Peterson and Cornwell stated they did not intend to go, but that Parker said: "'I'm not afraid. I'll go to the palace and see what the Queen wants us to do.'" He left the meeting.

Thurston's *Memoirs* continue, covering one of the most important points in the argument over United States participation in the Revolution and further confirming the Cabinet's intention to depose their Queen: "I then suggested that the cabinet officially request John L. Stevens, United States minister, to land forces from the *U.S.S. Boston* in order to prevent violence on the part of Lili'uokalani, which Peterson and Colburn both said they feared. **Three members of the cabinet having agreed to my doing so** (Ed.—emphasis added), I drafted, and Peterson had typewritten, a request to Mr. Stevens, that he cause men to be landed from the *Boston* to preserve the peace; **and the request was signed by the three ministers** (Ed.—emphasis added) . . . .

Cabinet members agreed to ask Stevens for help

"Taking the paper, I started down town with William O. Smith. As we reached the door of the office, however, Peterson called me back and said: 'I think you had better give me that request; I'll deliver it to Minister Stevens myself.' Though I urged him to let me deliver it, he insisted that I surrender it to him, and I reluctantly complied. I have never seen it since, and Peterson did not deliver it to Minister Stevens."

Peterson took paper, never delivered it

Later that day, after the events described below, a special committee of the newly formed Committee of Safety called on Minister Stevens for the first time. It was comprised of Thurston, W.C. Wilder, an American member of the Committee (Blount, as he did in identifying other members of the Committee of Safety who were Hawaiian subjects, did not mention his American connection, listing him only as a "naturalized citizen of the Hawaiian Islands, owing no allegiance to any other country") and H.F. Glade, German consul—who resigned from the Committee the next day in view of the potential conflict with his diplomatic status. They called on Stevens to inform him of the situation and "ask him if he was going to support the Queen against her cabinet and the citizens." A letter from Thurston to U.S. Secretary of State John W. Foster shortly after the Revolution says:

Stevens approached by Committee

> "Mr. Stevens replied to us that on three occasions he had been applied to by those representing the Queen for support against those opposed to her, and that he had always given her assurance of such support as lay within his power; but that in this case he considered the position taken by the Cabinet and people a just and legal one, and the attempt made by the Queen a revolutionary one; and that if asked by her for his support he would not give it; and on the contrary he should recognize the cabinet as the supporters of law and as possessing the authority of Government so long as they were supported by any respectable number of responsible citizens, and if they called on him he would give them the same assistance that had always been afforded to the Hawaiian Government by the United States Representatives."[19]

Thurston account to U.S. secretary of state

Stevens apparently was juggling three balls in the air at once, with requests during that two-day period for support of the Cabinet itself, support later from the Cabinet for the Queen and support for the Revolutionists. Except for the Blount Report's adverse finding, other accounts of the period and Stevens' own testimony indicate he played all the requests right down the middle and said he would back none of them. He said he would protect American lives and property.

Thurston's account in his *Memoirs* of the Saturday events continues:

Proclamation signed, later disappeared

"Mr. Smith and I returned to his office, where several dozen men were excitedly discussing the situation. We informed them of what was occurring at the Government Building. A declaration was immediately drafted to this effect: since Lili'uokalani had announced her intention of subverting the constitution and arbitrarily promulgating a new one, the undersigned declared her to be in attempted revolution against the constitution and government and pledged their support to the cabinet in resisting her. Signatures were affixed, and messengers were sent out to bring in other men to sign . . . ."

Thurston said the signing was under the direct supervision of Paul Neumann, the Queen's attorney, among others, and that in several hours nearly a hundred leading members of the community had signed it. It later disappeared and "the general belief of those present was that Neumann had sequestered it . . . ."

Neumann supervised signing

Similar testimony and affidavits from Castle and others further confirm how close the Cabinet members came to deposing their own Queen. Principals from both the Reform and Royalist parties agreed that her attempts to promulgate a new Constitution were indeed revolutionary and did not have the support of many of her own advisers. They therefore called the successful Revolution of 1893 in actuality a "counter-revolution."

Blount called the Revolution a "conspiracy"

between Stevens and the Committee of Safety, a point often made by sovereignty activists. A conspiracy is defined by Webster as a "secret agreement to do an unlawful act." The evidence demonstrates the buildup of the Hawaiian Revolution was anything but secret. Thurston's *Memoirs*, testimony before the Morgan Committee and statements from the Royalists make this clear. One point in particular, supported by all three of the above sources, occurred on Monday morning, January 16, as the Committee gathered in Thurston's law offices upstairs over the old Bishop Bank, Kaʻahumanu and Merchant streets, a half-block from the police station on Merchant at the foot of Bethel.

Revolution no conspiracy

Thurston describes it:

"While the committee was in session, a knock sounded at the door. Charles B. Wilson, marshal of the Kingdom and chief of police, was there; he poked his head into the room and noted the persons present. Withdrawing, he said to me: 'Thurston, I would like to speak with you a minute.' I accompanied him into the hall; he resumed: 'I know what you fellows are up to, and I want you to quit and go home.'"

Revolution plans were not secret

Thurston said he told him it was too late; the die was cast. Thurston later said that after the Revolution was over, he talked again with Wilson, who told him, "'When I came to your office that Monday morning, the cabinet were all over at the police station. I told them that the entire Committee of Safety were in your office, and I asked their permission to swear out a warrant and arrest the whole lot of you, but the damned cowards would not give me permission.'" We can assume today that in addition to any concerns the Cabinet members may have had about arresting many of the town's leading citizens, they

Wilson wanted to arrest Committee

must also have worried about their own involvement being discovered by the Queen.

Obviously the Queen, her Cabinet, the chief of police and probably most of the other key government officials knew a revolution was brewing. It was no secret maneuver and it didn't occur in a single day. It was openly planned and carried out over a four-day period. The Committee of Safety kept the Queen's key people informed at all stages. And those

Royalists knew Revolution brewing

key people made clear their own displeasure with the direction their Queen was heading. There was no conspiracy about it. Her decision to seek a more absolute Monarchy through a new Constitution was her undoing.

One of her key Cabinet members told Blount there were other reasons as well. He was Minister of Foreign Affairs Samuel Parker, by his own description a seven-eighths Hawaiian. He said, "My honest opinion is this: I think it (the Revolution) never would have taken place if the Reform ministry had not been put out." This was the four-member Cabinet that the Queen replaced a few days before the Revolution with Parker and Colburn—two Hawai-

Parker said ministry change was cause of Revolution

ians—and Cornwell and Peterson, two Americans. Parker explained to Blount that had the former Cabinet not been discharged at the Queen's behest, there would have been no opium bill, no lottery and assuredly no attempts at a new Constitution, actions that stirred the community to the point of revolution. But he told Blount in his opinion the Revolution would have occurred even if the Queen had not tried to promulgate a new Constitution:

"A majority of the capitalists of the town had no confidence in our ministry. I think it would have come about anyway," he replied to a question from Blount.

Although loyal to the Queen until after the counter-revolution in 1895 when he opted for Annexation, Parker had strong words with her about the propriety of her actions.

Parker saw Revolution as inevitable

In recounting, for example, at Blount's request the "circumstances attending the conference between the cabinet and the Queen [wherein the cabinet refused to sign] the new constitution," Parker said he and the Cabinet told the Queen:

"Your Majesty, we have not read the constitution, but before we read it, you must know it is a revolutionary act. It can not be done . . . . We advise you to give it up—not to think any more about it." He said at this point "she got pretty well excited, and some of my colleagues said: 'If you insist upon it, we will resign.'"

He later told Blount that while he believed the majority of the people were for the Queen, he did not think her reinstatement would survive as a government without the protection of an outside power.

Cabinet told Queen her Constitution was act of revolt

"There is a feeling that unless we are under some country like the United States it would be the same old revolutionary trouble coming up all the time . . . . So that I say I do not think it will ever be a stable government unless we are under a protectorate. If we are under a protectorate I say let it be the United States . . . . I would not accept the same position I had before the revolution unless there was a protectorate . . . . It is no use looking to England, Japan, France, or Germany. All our benefits are derived from the United States," he told Blount.

Reading similar accounts of other interviews in the Blount Report, one has to wonder why Blount apparently made no effort to get a balanced picture of what was going on in Hawai'i at the time. Dole said it was because he did all his "fact-finding" from with-

Parker told Blount protectorate needed

in his hotel room; that he did not go outside and see what the community felt like. Here were her own ministers pointing out the Queen's faults and their disagreement with them and Blount did not follow those reports up with any substantive interviews with members of the revolutionary group or other leaders outside of the Royalist party. Flying in the face of contemporary accounts in his own report of dissension and lack of confidence among her closest supporters, he proceeded as if his mind were already made up to recommend reinstatement of the Queen.

Blount didn't follow leads

Chapter Five
$\mathscr{R}$*evolution*

little more than one
hundred years ago a
four-day, virtually
bloodless Revolution changed Hawai'i forever. Gone
was the Monarchy that had controlled these Islands
for eighty years of the 19th Century. The Kingdom
had dwindled from a self-sufficient nation in 1810 of
some two hundred thousand Native Hawaiians and a
handful of immigrants to a struggling collection in
1893 of forty thousand Hawaiians and about as
many immigrants.[20] Most of the immigrants were
Asians brought in to provide the work force to maintain an economy based on sugar. A few thousand
were Caucasians from America and Europe, many
from Portugal.

*Kingdom's
population
decimated*

    The Revolutionists wanted a stable govern-
ment and Annexation to the United States, but the
U.S. administration, to put it simply, didn't want
Annexation, at least not then.

    (For the sake of simplicity, this book is calling
the 1893 action that led to formation of a provisional government a "revolution." There is good reason it
could well be called a "counter-revolution," the
Queen having committed a revolutionary act by

*Revolution really
a counter-revolt*

attempting to promulgate a new Constitution in violation of the terms of the existing Constitution she had sworn to uphold. This point is developed more fully in Chapter Four and will be developed again later in this chapter—Ed.)

Today, some descendants of the forty thousand Hawaiians then residing in the Kingdom, mostly from families mixed with the blood of immigrants from many other nations, are attempting to undo the results of the 1893 Revolution and re-establish some form of Hawaiian sovereignty. Their sovereignty movement depends on portraying the Revolution as a conspiracy between a group of Caucasian Revolutionists and the United States. They claim that conspiracy brought the Islands under control of the United States. Both aspects are important: First, they must prove there was a conspiracy, which is not supported by any factual evidence, and second, that the result was U.S. control. Since President Cleveland demonstrated that the U.S. control part wasn't there, as did the Provisional Government of Hawai'i, the latter claim rests on thin ice, too.

Sovereignty movement depends on implicating U.S.

This interpretation of conspiracy and seizure is key to potential claims against the U.S. government for reparations and title to Hawai'i's government lands. Central to these claims is the interpretation of the role played by 162 U.S. marines and bluejackets on January 17, 1893. And a part of interpreting that role objectively is understanding what U.S. foreign policy was at the time, and who had the responsibility for determining it.

Revisionists draw inaccurate pictures

Those who are trying to rewrite history and those who have become their unwitting assistants in the process persist in calling what happened simply an "overthrow." For sure, Queen Lili'uokalani was overthrown, but describing the event in that narrow a term ignores the far-reaching realities of what was taking place at that time in Hawai'i's history and why these changes occurred.

Government practices not acceptable

The Revolution did not occur in a vacuum. It did not happen overnight, though once it was triggered it moved with incredible speed. It probably was inevitable in the tide of America's "manifest destiny" that was shaping things internationally. Its timing was the result of years of questionable governmental practices on the part of late-19th-Century monarchs of Hawai'i, some of which are detailed later in this chapter and in other chapters. These practices would be unacceptable today to almost everyone living in these Islands, and they were unacceptable then to many of the subjects and residents of the Kingdom. The Monarchy wasn't going to change by itself; as in any revolution, the people living under the Monarchy were the only ones who could bring about change.

Since no polls were taken in those days, no one can prove whether a majority of residents— Hawaiians, Caucasians and others, subjects or otherwise—favored the Revolution or not. Most comments by Royalist leaders of the day claim that at least 80 percent of Native Hawaiians would have opposed it in a secret ballot, and perhaps a quarter of the remainder of the population. But the record of what transpired makes very clear that no majority rose to undo that Revolution once it had succeeded and that people of all nationalities supported its end result, Annexation.

No majority rose to undo Revolution

The Annexation Club, from which sprung the Revolutionary troops, had started in early 1892 as a closely held, small, secret group. By July 1893, however, its rolls included more than a thousand Hawaiians, according to J.W. Jones, its secretary. At

Hawaiians joined Annexation move

Blount's request, Jones submitted a report in July 1893 certifying that of the 5,500 members on the rolls at that time, 1,022, or 18 percent, were Native Hawaiians—11 percent of the native population as a whole. There were 1,218 persons he described as Americans, constituting 22 percent of the club but 90 percent of the Americans in residence. There were 251 Englishmen, "being 26 percent of those on the islands and 4 percent of club rolls." He said there were 2,261 Portuguese, "being 73 percent of Portuguese on [these] islands and 41 percent of club rolls." Half the Norwegians in Hawai'i, 69, representing 1 percent of club rolls, were members. Three hundred fifty-one Germans, 53 percent of those in the Islands, representing 6 percent of club rolls, were members, along with 328 persons "unclassified."

Annexation Club members from all races

The change the Revolutionists sought in government has to be described as a revolt. It was undertaken by residents of the Island nation, seething under the conduct of affairs by their government. Those who led the revolt were changing a form of government by a method with long historical and legal precedent. They were not just getting rid of one leader to put in a replacement leader and continue an existing pattern of government. They were throwing out a system they felt was not working for the residents of Hawai'i as a whole. The Revolutionists knew this kind of movement from monarchy toward democracy had been used on many other occasions, in particular by the people of the United States in 1776, when they threw off the yoke of King George III, and by the French in 1789, when a populist uprising threw off that Monarchy.

Revolution has long history as way to change governments

The Revolutionists believed the people of Hawai'i would support them, as popular opinion in America and France had supported those earlier revolutions. Indeed, since no successful counter-revolution occurred in Hawai'i, it is not unreasonable to describe the movement as having wide acceptance.

Why was there no mass uprising in Hawai'i against the Revolution? In part, because in the opinions of Native and Caucasian leaders expressed in 1898, the Revolution of 1893 and the subsequent Annexation of Hawai'i by the United States were the best things that could have happened to the people of these Islands at that point in history. This viewpoint was held by those in leadership positions, but whether it was held by a majority of the general populace or not will never be known because no votes were taken. The absence of a successful counter-revolution appears to confirm it was, but the Revolutionists admittedly did not want to take the chance of an open vote on the matter.

Colonialism, as we saw in Chapter One, was rampant in the 19th Century, and the Hawaiian Monarchy was but one of five Pacific-area kingdoms still extant. Colonial powers were casting covetous eyes at Hawai'i's strategic position. By mid-century, the French and the British each had seized control of the Islands and the Russians had tried to get a foothold on Kaua'i. Each had backed off under pressure. German and Japanese interests also could have moved into the game.

Pressures were building enormously in the 1890s and there is good cause to believe Hawai'i could not have remained independent beyond 1900. Japanese efforts were particularly strong because of the population dominance that had come about with the influx of Japanese laborers arriving to work on the sugar plantations. Their government was demanding voting rights for the immigrants. These men had not yet become subjects of Hawai'i or

American citizens and still were closely tied to their native country. Giving them the right to vote could immediately, in effect, have put control of the Legislature in Japanese hands.

That Hawai'i remained independent as long as it did is astonishing. The innate ability of Hawaiian kings and the use they made of their *haole* advisers to play external powers against one another had kept foreign governments at bay. If the domestic government had found a way to be representative of all its subjects and residents and become stable enough to develop the confidence of investors, thus providing the economic growth needed to keep the Kingdom strong, the Revolution might never have occurred. But this still would have left Hawai'i open to the colonial pressures of other powers.

Foreign governments had been kept at bay

Kamehameha III in the late 1830s had wisely seen the benefits of replacing his absolute Monarchy with a constitutional Monarchy, which he did in 1840. The move served his people well, though from time to time his successor monarchs made changes in such things as voting rights that today we would consider steps backward. In 1864, for example, Kamehameha V abrogated the Constitution of 1852 and replaced it with a new Constitution that returned certain powers to the Monarchy and introduced a property ownership requirement for voting.[21]

Kalākaua led Kingdom toward bankruptcy

By the late 1880s, King Kalākaua, with extravagant notions of his own and Hawai'i's stature in the world, was leading the Kingdom to bankruptcy. Community leaders of all nationalities felt restraints had to be put in the Constitution to rein him in.[22]

A Reform Constitution was adopted in 1887. Opponents called it the "Bayonet Constitution" because it was forced on the King. But the forcing

The Bishops

Princess Bernice Pauahi Bishop, a direct descendant of Kamehameha I, refused the throne. Probably Hawai'i's ultimate benefactress.

Charles Reed Bishop arrived by accident in Hawai'i. Important businessman and philanthropist who married Princess Pauahi, he created the Bishop Museum and predecessor of First Hawaiian Bank.

Photo: © The Hawaiian Historical Society

Photo: © The Hawaiian Historical Society

Photo: © W.T. Brigham Collection, The Bishop Museum

The Bishop Home in downtown Honolulu, at what is now the corner of King and Bishop Street.

The Thurstons

Photo: © The Hawaiian Mission Children's Society

Asa and Lucy Thurston, photographed in Honolulu in the 1860s. They arrived in Hawai'i in 1820 among the first missionaries, and are the great-great-grandparents of the author.

Photo: © The Hawaiian Mission Children's Society

Photo: © The Hawaiian Mission Children's Society

Their son, Asa G. Thurston, above, father of Lorrin A. Thurston, died when the boy was one. His widow, Sarah Andrews Thurston, right, taught school to support their three children.

Lorrin A. Thurston, lawyer, firebrand patriot, Revolutionist, public servant, journalist, adventurer, pictured shortly before Revolution.

The Royals

Kamehameha I, most powerful chief in Hawaiian history, united Hawai'i after bloody wars throughout the Islands.

Photo: © The Hawaiian Historical Society

Kamehameha II, brave king who challenged superstition by breaking *kapu* and eating with women.

Photo: © The Hawaiian Historical Society

Kamehameha III, longest-term Hawaiian ruler, promulgated first written laws, moved nation toward constitutional form of government. Ordered the Great *Mahele*.

Kamehameha IV, grandson of King Kamehameha I, favored Britain over the U.S., founded Queen's Hospital, brought in Episcopal Church.

The Royals (continued)

Photo: © The Hawaiian Historical Society

Kamehameha V, pushed new Constitution through Legislature, died without naming successor, prompting first popular election of Hawaiian king.

Lunalilo, first popularly elected king, created Lunalilo Trust with more land than the Bishop Estate, but it was sold in the 19th century to build Lunalilo Home for aged Hawaiians.

Photo: © The Hawaiian Historical Society

Queen Emma

Photo: © The Hawaiian Historical Society

Queen Emma Rooke, popular choice for Monarch, lost to Kalākaua in 1874 election by Legislature; widow of Kamehameha IV, founded Queen's Hospital and St. Andrew's Priory.

King David Kalākaua

David Kalākaua, merrie monarch, who ruined Hawaiʻi economy, leading to a Reform Constitution; bloody but unsuccessful overthrow attempt of 1889 put down by same men who later led Revolution against his sister, Liliʻuokalani.

was done by a coalition of people of all races meeting in the largest public gathering up to that time in Hawaiian history. Speakers attacked the King on many counts of abusing his powers and favoring unsavory friends, and the crowd adopted a resolution demanding reform. Many thought his most unsavory friend and adviser was Walter Murray Gibson, who had been given lands and other special favors by the King. At that moment, Gibson was prime minister, minister of foreign affairs and president of the Board of Health. He was ordered out of the Kingdom and left on the next ship.

Kalākaua excess brought new Constitution

Kalākaua was succeeded after his death in January 1891 by his named successor, his sister, Lili'uokalani, and it soon became clear that her interest lay in returning the government to the powerful, self-centered Monarchy it had been earlier in the 19th Century. She was not interested in broadening participation in government by her subjects and other local residents.

Lili'uokalani didn't support representative government

Early in 1892, with the Annexation Club already talking privately about a move to replace her and seek Annexation to the United States, one of its organizers and more outspoken members, Lorrin A. Thurston, had gone to Washington to check out the possibilities. Annexation had been advocated by a long series of U.S. presidents, secretaries of state and ministers to Hawai'i.

He found the Harrison administration sympathetic to the idea, providing it came as a request from the Hawaiian government. He returned to Honolulu more than ever convinced that the best future for his homeland lay in Annexation to the United States. As it turned out, the U.S. interest in possible Annexation would be temporary; the Cleveland administration a few months later reverted to an ear-

Thurston found Harrison open to Annexation idea

lier non-expansionist policy for the United States.

Annexation would give Hawai'i needed protection from conquest by other foreign powers and a much stronger position in the world sugar market. At that time sugar was the kingpin in Hawai'i's economy. Sugar interests, however, were not behind the Revolution or Annexation. Most sugar growers, particularly English and German owners, were concerned that an alliance with America would adversely affect their abilities to bring in foreign laborers. Ironically, once Annexation occurred, the benefits to the sugar industry became evident. By 1906, The *Advertiser*, in an anniversary edition on July 2, called Annexation "the greatest single factor in the development of the sugar business . . . since the reciprocity treaty."

Sugar interests not behind Revolution

Before Annexation, however, Claus Spreckels, richest and biggest of the sugar barons, was a staunch supporter of the Monarchy, which he was able with considerable success to manipulate. After the Revolution, the Queen wrote in her diaries for May 1893 that one of her advisers, Sam Parker, told her Spreckels "would be the means of putting me back on the throne."

Sugar barons opposed Annexation too

Paul Isenberg, a German national who had made major investments in Hawaiian sugar but lived mainly in his homeland, and a number of British sugar men, such as Theo H. Davies and W.H. Rickard, also were opposed to both the Revolution and Annexation. Davies, whose successor firm still operates in Hawai'i though no longer in sugar, strongly supported the Monarchy, but after the Revolution agreed Lili'uokalani should not be reinstated as queen. An ardent foe of Annexation to the United States, he journeyed to Washington from London with the 17-year-old Princess Ka'iulani, the Queen's niece and designated successor, and jumped into the 1893 Annexation struggle. He suggested Ka'iulani, who was studying in London at the time, be substituted for Lili'uokalani in a regency government under Dole for three years, after which, he suggested, she should be made queen. The suggestion went nowhere.

Davies proposed Ka'iulani as monarch

As mentioned earlier, the U.S. administration had told Thurston it could not act on Annexation without a request from the government of Hawai'i. While predecessor monarchs had favored Annexation from time to time, Queen Lili'uokalani was not so inclined. There didn't seem to be much hope in 1892 for a Hawaiian government that favored Annexation.

The Annexation group continued informally in its planning on how to proceed toward its goal. The feeling of most of the men who made up the loosely formed club was that the Queen probably should be removed eventually from office, but with a stable Cabinet—the Jones-Wilcox group—in power and the Queen quiescent, there seemed to be no immediate urgency. U.S. Minister Stevens and the *U.S.S. Boston* left for a ten-day trip to Hilo on January 4, 1893, convinced all was well.

Kingdom appeared stable with Jones-Wilcox Cabinet

The Queen's quiescence did not last long, however, and in a little over a week, her opponents were talking revolution, convinced she could not be allowed to continue.

The final straw for Lili'uokalani's opponents came on January 14, 1893. Ignoring the counsel and advice of Cabinet ministers she personally had selected, she served notice of plans to promulgate a new Constitution. It would have done away with the safeguards and balance of power between the monarch and the Legislature that had guided the

New Constitution plan was straw that brought revolt

Kingdom for six years. Her proposal was a clear violation of constitutional provisions for amending the existing document.

The 1864 Constitution had been promulgated by similarly illegal means, but Kamehameha V got away with it. The 1887 Constitution also was done in a manner contrary to constitutional procedure, but it was done with the backing of a mass meeting of his subjects—all voters. Kalākaua had no choice *Queen's plan* but to adopt it and swear to uphold it. In the minds *considered* of many legislators, businessmen, homeowners and *illegal act* professional people and even her own hand-picked Cabinet members, Lili'uokalani's proposal to do it again in 1893 was not acceptable. They considered it an illegal, revolutionary move.

Feelings ran high that something had to be done before she could act. The town was boiling with rumors.

The buildup toward Revolution had begun ten days earlier when she tried unsuccessfully through her supporters in the Legislature to replace her widely approved Jones-Wilcox Cabinet with new members more likely to go along with her plans, *Politicking to* including her proposals for opium licenses, a lottery *remove Cabinet* and the new Constitution. She couldn't even get all the Hawaiians in the Legislature on her side. She lost the first effort to remove her highly regarded Cabinet by a vote of 22 to 19, and in view of claims today that Hawaiians universally were behind her, it is worth noting that the 22 nays included 11 Hawaiians and part-Hawaiians and 11 *haoles* while the 19 ayes included 15 Hawaiians and part-Hawaiians and 4 *haoles*.[23]

In the next few hectic days, the Queen's supporters rammed through the opium and lottery bills, and she twisted enough arms (there were open reports of bribery) to dump the respected Cabinet, which had opposed those bills, by a vote of 25 to 16 on January 12. Five Hawaiians still voted against her effort. Her good friend, brother-in-law and adviser, Archibald S. Cleghorn, whom she had appointed governor of Oʻahu, also opposed her on this point. Married to her sister, Miriam Likelike, Cleghorn was the father of Kaʻiulani, the young princess whom the Queen considered her successor. He wrote his daughter, who was in school in London: "The Legislature passed the wretched Lottery Bill yesterday—and I am afraid your Aunt has taken bad advice, still she may not sign it. I told her months ago not to have anything to do with it."

Opium & lottery bills rammed through

The next day, however, with her new Cabinet in place, the Queen signed both bills and her action was announced by the Cabinet the following morning, Saturday, January 14, at the Legislature's final session. Hours later, when she was finalizing plans for announcing her new Constitution, a hitch developed: Her new Cabinet decided it could not approve it. The four Cabinet members held a flurry of meetings and conferences with various community leaders and ministers of all of the foreign governments represented in the Islands, and found them all opposed to the Queen's proposal.[24]

Cabinet balked at new Constitution

That Constitution, among other things, would have enabled the Queen to appoint or remove her Cabinet without approval of the Legislature. It would have given her the power to appoint the upper house of Nobles instead of their continuing to be elected. She proposed barring anyone but native-born or naturalized subjects—only males, as was still the case in the United States—from voting, disenfranchising about one-quarter of the electorate, including most of the business community.[25] Since

Queen sought to expand her powers

this group paid most of the taxes, they were less than enchanted. Her new Constitution would have given her more power than Kalākaua had before the Reform Constitution reined him in.

When her Cabinet strongly opposed her, she did not promulgate the new Constitution that Saturday morning. She told the crowd she had invited to assemble that she would do so within a few days. Her intentions also were set forth in the Hawaiian language newspapers of the day, making a strong point that the delay was temporary.

Queen indicated delay was temporary

As word of her proposed action spread, alarmed leaders of the community also gathered that Saturday morning. Business came to a halt. Honolulu merchant John Emmeluth, exemplifying the problems faced by Honolulu businessmen, complained that Lili'uokalani's actions were paralyzing business, that he had to shut his doors three times and let his men off work in order to attend meetings dealing with the problems she was creating.[26]

What started that morning as a gathering of concerned residents quickly became a mass public meeting. After a number of fiery speeches, members of the gathering, many of them also members of the Annexation Club, appointed a committee of thirteen to figure out how to deal with the Queen. The Committee called itself the Committee of Safety, and its assignment was to formulate plans for immediate action.[27] We'll learn more about its members in the next chapter. They included three—Castle, Smith and Thurston—born in Hawai'i of American parents and, because of their birth, subjects of the Kingdom; four American citizens born on the mainland but at the time residents of Hawai'i; two additional American citizens who had become naturalized subjects of Hawai'i, and four Europeans, two of whom also were

Committee of Safety formed

naturalized subjects of Hawai'i. In summary, the Committee was comprised of seven subjects of Hawai'i, four citizens of America and two Europeans. All were residents of Hawai'i. Three also were missionary descendants and a fourth, Henry Waterhouse, had married a missionary descendant.

Hawaiian subjects were majority on Committee

Blount, in his report, characterized only six as subjects of Hawai'i. The difference comes because he referred to McCandless as a U.S. citizen who had not been naturalized. McCandless, however, told the Morgan Committee a few months later that he was a "citizen of both countries" and voted in Hawai'i.

As a curious aside, Blount referred to the three who were born in Hawai'i of American parents as "a Hawaiian of foreign parentage" in the case of Castle; "a native of foreign origin" in the case of Smith; and "a native-born subject of the Hawaiian Islands, of foreign origin," in the case of Thurston. He made no mention of their American ties. One wonders why, and how this was interpreted by the administration in Washington, which for the most part had never heard of these individuals nor their ancestry.

Blount ignored American ties of key members

No crystal-clear, universally accepted, complete record of the Revolution that followed exists, though the chronology of actual events is well documented. Interpreting what is known is difficult, clouded as it is with political intrigue. The following account may be as accurate as it is possible to get:

After hearing an impassioned plea that Saturday from members of the Queen's Cabinet for support if they were to move against her—see Chapter Four—the Committee of Safety met into the night and decided no other course remained but to depose the Queen and install a provisional government. They would back the Cabinet if it chose to move, or

How Revolution evolved

go it alone if it didn't. They favored early Annexation to the United States, which was opposed by the Queen and her legislative supporters. It was a clear-cut choice: stay with the Queen and endure her proposed return to a more absolute Monarchy, or break with the crown and head for an unknown destiny that could lead to Annexation.

U.S. was
unofficial
protector

The United States had been the unofficial protector of Hawai'i since the 1840s and it was clearly the foreign nation most likely to become involved at this point in case of a breakdown of government power in the Kingdom. Both sides called more than several times on U.S. Minister John L. Stevens to seek his support. He was absent from Honolulu from January 4 until noon on January 14, having gone to Hilo on the cruiser *Boston*, which later was to land U.S. troops to keep the peace. A subcommittee of the Committee of Safety called on him that Saturday night to inform him of the Committee's formation and its agreement to back the Queen's Cabinet members. They wanted to get his support, or at least to find out his position, both as to their moves and the possible Cabinet moves. The post-Revolution Blount Report, relied on by President Cleveland in his political, one-sided denunciation of the overthrow, quoted W.O. Smith, secretary of the Committee of Safety, on the results of that meeting. Smith reported that Minister Stevens would only say to the Revolutionists that "U.S. troops on board the *Boston* would be ready to land [at] any moment to prevent the destruction of American life and property...[and that] if a new government were established, and was actually in possession of the Government Building, the executive departments and archives, and in possession of the city . . . ," it would have to be recognized by his ministry.

Stevens would
not back revolt

Lorrin A. Thurston put it this way in his *Memoirs:*

". . . William O. Smith and I called on the American minister, Mr. Stevens, and informed him of the facts. He assured us that he would protect American lives and property, but emphasized that he could not recognize any revolutionary government until it was actually established, and repeated that **the United States forces, if landed, would not take sides with either party** (Ed.—emphasis added), but would protect Americans."

On Saturday afternoon, members of the Queen's Cabinet, in the midst of seeking support from the community to depose the Queen themselves, were present when the Committee of Safety was formed to carry out the Revolution. There certainly was no secret conspiracy going on between the U.S. minister and the Revolutionists. Everyone was keeping everyone else, friend or foe, fully informed— the antithesis of conspiracy. As noted, Minister Stevens had left for Hilo on January 4, firmly believing that the Queen would remain quiescent and the Jones-Wilcox Cabinet would continue in control until the 1894 legislative session. His absence makes clear that he could not have been conspiring with the Revolutionists as their decision to move ahead was made.

On Sunday morning, January 15, the Queen's four Cabinet members were told by the Committee of Safety it intended to move against the Queen whether the Cabinet was with it or not.[28] The Cabinet, meanwhile, believed it had gotten a promise from the Queen to abandon her thoughts of a new Constitution. It therefore declined to proceed further with the Committee of Safety. But its members immediately informed the Queen of the impending takeover. She took no action against the small group of thirteen. Since their proposal was clearly treasonous from her point of view and she had an army of several hundred armed men, her failure to act remains one of the mysteries surrounding the Revolution. It could lead to the conclusion that the Queen and her advisers had mixed feelings about what to do as well as what would be the reaction of her other supporters if she chose to act against an uprising. Memories of the similarly widely representative mass meeting that had forced the Reform Constitution on Kalākaua less than six years earlier may have been on her mind. The threat was coming largely from the same men, who as community volunteers, had put the Reform Constitution into effect in 1887, and later had put down the bloody 1889 revolt by a Hawaiian group under the auspices of Liliʻuokalani against her brother, Kalākaua. That attempted coup had been planned in a house owned by Liliʻuokalani, but while she admittedly was in favor of his ouster, she denied any part in the attempted move against him.

Queen was told of revolt, but did not act

Cabinet knew even more than Queen

Most important, it is vital to bear in mind that this discussion between the Queen and her key people was taking place well before any U.S. troops had been brought ashore or been asked to come ashore, so there were none around to be construed as a deterrent to her taking action. Do not overlook also that her own Cabinet members, only hours earlier, had been contemplating removing her themselves. They may have been hesitant to recommend action on her part in fear of their own action being exposed. As discussed in the preceding chapter, the Cabinet had a duty to the Kingdom under its Constitution

No U.S. troops on shore yet

and if they believed, as they indicated to the community, that she was breaking the law under Hawai'i's constitutional Monarchy, it was not a treasonous act on their part to try to depose her. But the Cabinet knew she would view the matter otherwise and no doubt thought it best to keep it secret. She did not find out about their plan to remove her until nearly eleven months later, and then labeled it treasonous.

Cabinet unsettled on what to do

Members of the Queen's Cabinet met with Minister Stevens later that Sunday to find out what his position would be in the event of a community-wide insurrection against the Queen and were told he would not take sides with the Queen or anyone else.[29] Earlier, Saturday night, he had been visited by a delegation from the Committee of Safety seeking his view on a revolt led by the Cabinet members. He knew the powerful position held by the Cabinet under the Hawaiian Constitution and told the Committee of Safety he would view the Cabinet as the government if it deposed the Queen—recognize it as such and back it up if it so requested. The Committee of Safety and a large number of members of the community already had indicated their support of such a move by the Cabinet, so there would have been no disagreement between those forces had this course been followed. In that case, it would have been the Cabinet and U.S. troops maintaining peace and order with the support of the community. The Queen might or might not have received the support of the government troops and police force.

Stevens would back Cabinet if it dumped Queen

Stevens maintained throughout subsequent investigations by Washington that he was concerned only with protecting American lives and interests in case of a pitched battle between the Monarchy and a revolutionary group. He testified he had made it clear to each side that he would directly back neither

Stevens maintained he wanted to protect Americans

side.[30] But since he was an avowed supporter of the idea of annexing Hawai'i to the United States, his personal sympathies undoubtedly lay with the Revolutionists and were known to them and to the Monarchy. Queen Lili'uokalani assumed he would have supported the Revolutionists had a battle broken out. The Committee of Safety was not unhappy with this assumption on her part, but its members testified later in the hearings before Senator Morgan's Committee on Foreign Relations that it was not their fault she made the assumption nor their role to tell her she was wrong.

Assumptions are not always facts

Captain G.C. Wiltse, commanding officer of the *Boston*, had included this language in his three-paragraph order to the troops, setting forth their mission as he landed them on January 16:

Wiltse's order

". . . for the purpose of protecting our legation, consulate, and the lives and property of American citizens, and **to assist in preserving public order** (Ed.—emphasis added)."

He had gone beyond what Stevens asked for, which was simply that Wiltse land troops:

". . . for the protection of the United States legation and the United States consulate, and to secure the safety of American life and property."

Steven's request

The extra language could have come from the personal warning that U.S. Consul General H.W. Severance sent to Captain Wiltse, independent of Stevens and two hours earlier, saying "the troops might be needed to preserve order and protect American property." Severance was worried about what might happen at the two mass meetings that had been called for that day. Kuykendall's colleague, Professor Charles H. Hunter, who took over the manuscript of Volume III of *The Hawaiian Kingdom* at this critical juncture, notes that Severance sent his message about 1 p.m., an hour and a half before the angry mass meetings were to start. Severance told Wiltse that if other means of communication were cut, he would lower his flag to half staff to indicate help was needed. The consulate was on Merchant Street, clearly visible from the harbor, while Stevens' office, the legation, was at Nuʻuanu and School streets.

In retrospect, and weighing the testimony of Stevens and the ship's officers, the U.S. forces in all probability would not have taken action against the Queen's forces if she had moved against the Committee of Safety on Sunday or Monday. This would have been before the Revolutionists had taken the government building and been recognized by Stevens as in control of the city. The officers of the *Boston* were experienced naval commanders, well-schooled in Navy regulations, international law and past practices in disputes in foreign countries where there were American interests. They would not have jumped into action against an entrenched and recognized government in favor of rebels who had not yet made their move. This international policy was well known to the Queen's Cabinet as well.

U.S. officers would not have acted against recognized government

Lieutenant Commander W.T. Swinburne, executive officer of the *Boston* and the senior officer on shore, had made that clear to the revolutionary forces on the morning of January 17, when they were on their way to seize the government. He testified before the Morgan Committee that he told them, "If the Queen calls upon me to preserve order, I am going to do it."[31]

Swinburne stood ready for Queen's call

It is reasonable to assume the Revolution succeeded simply because the Queen did not seize the moment nor heed the advice of her military leaders, who wanted to move against the impending Revolution while it was still in its formative stages, Sunday and Monday. At that point, the only Revolutionists planning action were the members of the Committee of Safety, thirteen in all. The Queen's military commander, Marshal Wilson, knew he could arrest them easily. He advocated doing so, but the Queen and her Cabinet said no.

No matter how one interprets the actions of Minister Stevens, it must be conceded he had no quick way of getting counsel or advice from his superiors in Washington and had to act on his own in any situation offering a threat to American lives and security. He had done so, as had his predecessors, on a number of occasions. Cable communication from Hawai'i to the United States did not become operative until 1903. The fastest way to communicate between Honolulu and Washington in the 1890s was to send a message by ship to San Francisco and direct that it be sent by telegram from there to Washington. This took eight to ten days, depending in part on whether a proposed telegram was able to catch a ship from Honolulu right away. Because the ultimate link was a telegram, the message had to be short and somewhat sparse, with details often missing. The answer would come by telegram to San Francisco and then by the first available ship to Honolulu, so it was a sixteen- to twenty-day process all told to send a message and get a reply.

No quick way to get advice from Washington

At the time, the United States was not actively interested in expansion. Statements by President Cleveland and Secretary of State Gresham, the two people in the next administration involved in setting foreign policy, make it clear they were not likely to commit the United States to a policy of acquiring Hawai'i. The preceding Harrison administration had told Thurston it would act on a proposal for Annex-

U.S. not expansionist

ation only if requested to do so by the government of Hawai'i, clearly indicating the United States at that time, too, had no policy calling for unilateral acquisition of the Island Kingdom. Characterizing the actions of Minister Stevens, therefore, as a determination of U.S. policy is a stretch. He had no authority to determine policy. The most that can be said, and President Cleveland said it, is that Stevens acted without specific authority when he moved U.S. troops ashore—although testimony at the Morgan hearings revealed that it was Captain Wiltse who ordered the troops ashore, not Stevens. But even here, similar action had been taken by his U.S. predecessors in earlier outbreaks in Hawai'i, such as the riots surrounding Kalākaua's election in 1874 and the abortive effort to unseat Kalākaua in 1889.

U.S. wasn't actively seeking Hawai'i

Details of those two earlier landings show that preparations for this kind of action did not always await a formal request from the Island government, as was later claimed by Blount to be a requirement that Stevens had failed to observe. In 1874, for example, U.S. Minister Pierce became concerned about potential rioting as the Legislature assembled to carry out the contentious election of Kalākaua over Queen Emma. He alerted the troops in the harbor and set up a shore-to-ship signal, "thinking it to be a prudent measure to be prepared against any violation of the public peace." When Lunalilo's minister of foreign affairs, Charles Reed Bishop, King-elect Kalākaua and Governor John O. Dominis became alarmed and asked Pierce to help, the troops were ashore in minutes. In 1889 U.S. Minister G.W. Merrill brought a squad of marines ashore on his own to guard the American legation, then received permission of the government to bring a larger force in as the fighting escalated, which was done.

Troops had landed before

Troops aided King-elect Kalākaua in 1874

It obviously was well within their general authority for U.S. ministers and military commanders abroad to take actions on their own to protect American lives and property and maintain order.

The Revolutionists met several times on Sunday and Monday, putting together the documentation they would need to establish a provisional government. They drafted Sanford B. Dole, a respected associate justice of the Hawai'i Supreme Court, to be president after L.A. Thurston declined on the basis he considered himself too controversial a figure to bring about a community-wide feeling of peace and order.

Dole chosen as president

On Monday, the Committee decided it was not far enough along with its planning to bring about the Revolution.

Says Thurston in his *Memoirs:*

"Our plans were inchoate—we had no plan of action to meet the Queen's government, should it move first; we lacked particulars of the military at our command; at the moment (on Monday), we lacked organized troops. We did not know just what the government intended, or what Minister Stevens had in mind, whether he proposed to land armed forces from the *Boston*, or what the [Hawaiian] government would do if men were brought ashore, though we feared that the government might resist. Time for thought and planning was overwhelmingly essential.

Committee's plans not solid; delay sought

"Therefore, the committee decided, the first thing to do, before being compelled to act, was to gain time. The critical state of affairs might induce Mr. Stevens to land forces to protect American lives and property; a landing might precipitate action by the

Queen's government, before the committee had evolved a plan. W.O. Smith and I were appointed to wait upon Minister Stevens immediately and urge him to delay the landing of American troops, if he had it in view. We went to the residence of the minister, near the corner of School and Nuʻuanu Streets, and were informed by his daughter that he had left a short time before to go aboard the *Boston*, which was lying in the harbor. He returned within a few minutes, and we told him of our mission.

Thurston & Smith urged Stevens to wait

"Mr. Stevens' reply was: 'I do not know what your plans are, gentlemen, and I cannot afford to take chances to find out what the plans of the government may be. The conditions are so serious, and the possibilities of trouble so great, that it is my duty to protect the lives and property of American citizens with every available means within my power; and I am going to land American troops immediately for that purpose. I have already given orders to that effect, and it will not be long before the troops are ashore. That's all I have to say.' Such was the first information given to the committee, or to Mr. Smith or me individually, that troops were to be landed. There was no suggestion by Mr. Stevens as to what he intended to do with the troops, or what the committee should do. The members of the Queen's cabinet stated afterward that they called on Mr. Stevens that evening to ask his support for the Queen's government against the revolutionists, and that his reply was evasive and ambiguous. His reply to them was no more evasive and ambiguous than his reply to Mr. Smith and me a few hours earlier. The Committee of Safety had

Stevens restated his duty to protect Americans

Stevens did not tell them his plan for the troops

exactly the same information from Mr. Stevens that the cabinet had—no more, no less."

Thurston continues on the subject to say that later that day, "I met Mr. W.H. Rickard, then the manager of Honokaa Plantation, who had been a member of the Legislature, and was a supporter of the Queen. He shook his fist in my face and exclaimed: 'Damn you, Thurston, you did this!' 'Did what?' I wished to know. 'Had these troops landed,' replied he. 'You credit me with considerable influence, to be able to direct the United States troops,' I answered. 'I had no more to do with their coming ashore than you did, and I have no more idea of what they are going to do than you have.' I mention the incident simply to indicate the exaggerated idea of the royalists as to our control over the American forces. That misapprehension undoubtedly had much to do with their subsequent supine submission to the Committee of Safety." (Ed.—Rickard was another powerful sugar figure opposed to the Revolution and Annexation.)

Royalists had exaggerated notion

Thurston concludes: "That is the correct story of the landing of the American troops from the cruiser *Boston* . . . . Nothing else was ever done; there was no other understanding or agreement between the Committee of Safety, or any member, and the United States Minister Stevens, or with the officers of the *Boston* . . ."

No understanding with Stevens

Other reports, including that of Lucien Young, an officer aboard the *Boston*, indicate that when Stevens went aboard on Monday to talk about landing troops, Captain Wiltse told him the decision had already been made. Wiltse and Young apparently made the actual decision, not Stevens. Testimony at the Morgan hearings by Lieutenant Charles Laird said Stevens did not return to the *Boston* from the time he got back to Honolulu at noon Saturday until Monday afternoon, leaving Captain Wiltse and his officers to consider and prepare to act on rumors the ship's officers picked up in town.[32] Stevens obviously was not plotting strategy with his military forces.

Ship's officers, not Stevens appear to have landed troops

The next day, Tuesday, January 17, the Revolutionists occupied the government building, installed Dole in office and proclaimed the new government. It had been a quick and bloodless coup. Initially just Dole, Henry Cooper and most of the rest of the Committee of Safety were on the scene at the King Street door of the government building (now our courthouse) when the proclamation of a new government was read. (Several key members of the Committee, including Thurston and Castle, were in bed with the flu.) The word went out quickly into the community, and volunteer riflemen, as they had on previous occasions, grabbed their arms and hurried to the scene. The volunteers were largely members of the Annexation Club, either at the moment or shortly after the Revolution, and probably did not include Native Hawaiians, who did not join the club until after the Queen was removed. The Revolutionists seized the other buildings Stevens had said they would need to control before he would extend recognition to their new government. They received that recognition about 4:30 to 5:30 p.m., but they had not yet gained control of the police force or the army barracks, where most of the Queen's troops were located, buildings that had not been mentioned by Stevens. Obviously, however, surrender of those forces was necessary to preserve the peace. This was achieved about 7 p.m. after the Queen surrendered and directed her armed forces to give up. Within the

Revolutionists take control

hour, the Revolutionists took over the city police department and the army. The following morning they took over the palace.

Critics later made much of Stevens' "precipitate" action in recognizing the new government an hour or so before it had taken over the police and the army. He had recognized it sometime between 4:30 and 5:30 p.m. from his sickbed. He apparently was afflicted by the same virus that felled a number of the Revolutionists and government workers.

Did Stevens act too soon?

Historian Russ, for one, concludes that while there is no direct evidence, Stevens was precipitate in recognizing the government before the Queen's troops had surrendered. Stevens, however, had not acted without sending an emissary to Dole's office to determine whether the Revolutionists actually held the seat of government, which they did. (Blount in his report belittled the importance of this building, Ali'iōlani Hale, claiming it was not a building prepared for defense against attackers. It was, however, the seat of government, housing the Cabinet, the attorney general, the minister of foreign affairs, the Department of Land and other departments except for the Queen's army and the city police.)

Revolutionists had seat of government

In Stevens' defense, too, he knew the men he was dealing with. The Revolutionists were mostly the same men with the same leadership who had prevailed in the outbreaks of 1887 and 1889 without the aid of U.S. troops, who in both cases, as in the 1893 Revolution, had been landed to protect American lives and property. In neither of the earlier outbreaks had these men depended on surrender of the royal forces to achieve their objective. It was not unreasonable for Stevens to assume a similar ability to dominate existed in 1893.

Stevens knew Revolutionists' ability

There's no doubt the presence of U.S. troops,

however, helped lead the Queen's advisers to urge surrender on her part. But it wasn't just the troops and the recognition by Stevens that led to that decision. Her principal adviser, her longtime legal counsel Paul Neumann, saw a parallel with the return of Hawai'i by the British government after the Islands had been seized in 1843 by an overzealous British task force. Neumann also had been present—some say he supervised it—when a petition of support was being signed on January 14 by townspeople on behalf of the Cabinet's proposal to oust the Queen on their own, and he remained for the mass meeting afterward when the Committee of Safety was formed. He knew, therefore, that the Revolution was a widespread local, community reaction. But he reasoned at the time of surrender on January 17 that if the United States were seen as responsible for the current takeover, Washington might be persuaded to take action similar to that taken by the British. He agreed with other of the Queen's advisers present at a meeting to consider her surrender that alternatively an attempt to resist the Revolution could have led to a doubtful and probably bloody outcome.

Neumann's role

E.C. Macfarlane, one of the Queen's closest advisers, is the principal source for naming who was there when the surrender was accomplished. He told Blount that S.M. Damon, whom the Queen respected, was there from the Provisional Government "to inform Her Majesty that she had been deposed, her ministers dismissed, and likewise the marshal, Mr. Wilson." He said that when he, Macfarlane, arrived he found the four Cabinet ministers; Judge H.A. Widemann, the Queen's confidant; J.O. Carter, another close adviser of the Queen; Neumann, and "the two princes" (probably Kūhiō Kalaniana'ole and David Kawananakoa).

Macfarlane's account of surrender

Neumann is believed to have been the principal author of the document in which the Queen surrendered "to the superior power of the United States" and claimed to be leaving the possibility of her reinstatement up to the United States. A master stroke in content and timing, that document has been a major cause of confusion over the Queen's surrender and the U.S. role, if any, in it, and has given opponents of the Revolution a basis for arguing that the United States had played an active role in it.

Neumann believed to be author of surrender protest

A consideration of the Revolutionists'. viewpoint, however, leads to a different interpretation. Damon had been sent by Dole to meet with the Queen and seek her surrender. Damon, along with everyone else involved in the meeting with the Queen on the 17th, sought a bloodless resolution. When her surrender was delivered to Dole at the end of that tumultuous day, he was careful only to acknowledge its receipt, not even addressing the question of agreement with its wording. In no way, Dole said later, did her letter constitute a negotiated agreement nor was Damon authorized in the first place to negotiate for the Provisional Government.

No agreement about U.S. arbitration

He likened delivery of the Queen's protest to the arrival of a letter in the mails, with the messenger wanting a signature as evidence of delivery.

Dole makes no comment in his *Memoirs* about its wording, nor does it receive any comment from Thurston in his. But in his December 23, 1893, letter to U.S. Minister Willis, some of which is produced below, Dole develops a clear case against there being any agreement to submit the Revolution to arbitration by the United States. His defense, however, was too late to stop the political fallout—both then and now—of Blount's unilateral investigation and Cleveland's summary denouncement of the Revolution. Both were announced in Washington without the prior knowledge of the Provisional Government. In fact, both announcements took place months before the Provisional Government was informed of what Blount was doing or what the president had concluded. Had Blount been willing to interview Dole or other leaders of the Revolution, or even more important, had he, perhaps more properly, chosen to consider their reasons for revolt in order to develop a balanced report, the results would have been much different.

Blount's unilateral investigation

    The ambiguous wording of the Queen's protest in the surrender document probably was critical to getting the Queen to agree to give up without a fight. Neither side wanted a battle, and a quick and bloodless surrender of the Queen's armed forces was what Damon was after. Semantic niceties no doubt took a backseat to getting the job done. The Revolutionists probably weren't bothered at the time by the language because they hadn't been asked to agree with it as a condition of her surrender, and they anticipated the United States would quickly accept Annexation. The question then would have become moot. They knew that the Monarchy was surrendering to them and not to the United States, and they knew her protest didn't make them a party to a request that the United States arbitrate the action. Gresham and Cleveland, however, seized on the document as an excuse for the United States to enter the situation in the role of arbitrator rather than meddler, ignoring the facts that the United States under President Harrison had recognized the new Provisional Government, that the Provisional Government was obviously running the Island nation, and no agreement existed that its role was subject to arbitration by the United States. Nor did the United

Revolutionists knew she surrendered to them

States let the Provisional Government know it was contemplating an attempt to arbitrate the Revolution until U.S. Minister Willis made his demand upon Dole at 1:30 p.m. on December 19, 1893.

As Dole later pointed out in his extraordinary letter on December 23 to Minister Willis, if such an agreement existed between the Provisional Government and the Queen, the Queen had not mentioned it to President Harrison. She had written him a letter dated January 18, 1893, which accompanied the Provisional Government's envoys on their mission to Washington two days after the Revolution.

Queen made no mention of arbitration to Harrison

Dole states in the letter to Willis:

"If any understanding had existed at that time [of her surrender] between her and the Government to submit the question of her restoration to the United States, some reference to such an understanding would naturally have appeared in this letter (Ed.—the January 18 letter written to President Harrison), as every reason would have existed for calling the attention of the President to that fact, especially as she then knew that her attorney would be seriously delayed in reaching Washington.

Team went to Washington for recognition, Annexation

"But there is not a word from which such an understanding can be predicated. The [Provisional] Government sent its commissioners to Washington for the sole object of procuring the confirmation of the recognition by Minister Stevens of the new Government and to enter into negotiations for political union with the United States.

"The protest of the ex-Queen, made on January 17, is equally with the [January 18] letter devoid of evidence of any mutual understanding for a submission to the United

States of her claim to the throne. [It] was received exactly as it would have been received if it had come through the mail. The endorsement of its receipt upon the paper was made at the request of the individual who brought it as evidence of its safe delivery. As to the ex-Queen's notice of her appeal to the United States, it was a matter of indifference to us. Such an appeal could not have been prevented, as the mail service was in operation as usual. That such a notice, and our receipt of it without comment, should be made a foundation of a claim that we had submitted our right to exist as a government to the United States had never occurred to us until suggested by your Government (Ed.—by Willis on December 19 when he presented the U.S. demand that the Provisional Government return the Queen to her throne).

"If [it is] your contention that President Cleveland believes that this Government and the ex-Queen have submitted their respective claims to the sovereignty of this country to the adjudication of the United States . . . , then, may I ask, when and where has the President held his court of arbitration?

"This Government has had no notice of the sitting of such a tribunal and no opportunity of presenting evidence of its claims. If Mr. Blount's investigation were a part of the proceedings of such a court, this Government did not know it and was never informed of it; indeed, as I have [told you earlier] we never knew until the publication of Secretary Gresham's letter to President Cleveland a few weeks ago, that the American Executive had a policy of interference under contemplation. Even if we had known that Mr. Blount was

Dole takes issue with U.S. significance in Revolution

Queen's statement received without comment

authoritatively acting as a commissioner to take evidence upon the question of restoration of the ex-Queen, the methods adopted by him in making his investigations were, I submit, unsuitable to such an examination or any examination upon which human interests were to be adjudicated."

At this point, Dole, as a longtime associate justice of the Hawai'i Supreme Court, proceeded to pick holes in Blount's procedures, his secret examinations of witnesses, his leading questions, and the lack of opportunities for cross-examination and explanations.

Blount methods unsuitable to fair review

"It is hardly necessary for me to suggest that under such a mode of examination some witnesses would be almost helpless in the hands of an astute lawyer, and might be drawn into saying things which would be only half-truths, and standing alone would be misleading or even false in effect . . . . Surely the destinies of a friendly Government, admitting by way of argument that the right of arbitration exists, may not be disposed of upon an ex parte and secret investigation made without the knowledge of such Government or an opportunity by it to be heard or even to know who the witnesses were.

Dole outlined flaws in Blount Report

"In view, therefore, of all the facts in relation to the question of the President's authority to interfere . . . I am able to assure your excellency that by no action of this Government, on the 17th day of January last, or since that time, has the authority devolved upon the President of the United States to interfere in the internal affairs of this country through any conscious act or expression of this Government with such an intention."

Dole then suggested the matter was a problem for the United States and the Queen. He wrote:

"You state in your communication, 'After a patient examination of Mr. Blount's Reports the President is satisfied that the movement against the Queen if not instigated was encouraged and supported by the representative of this Government [Stevens] at Honolulu; that he promised in advance to aid her enemies in an effort to overthrow the Hawaiian Government and set up by force a new government in its place; that he kept his promise by causing a detachment of troops to be landed from the *Boston* on the 16th of January 1893, and by recognizing the Provisional Government the next day when it was too feeble to defend itself and the Constitutional Government was able to successfully maintain its authority against any threatening force other than that of the United States already landed.'

Dole said Cleveland had no right to interfere

"Without entering into a discussion of the facts I beg to state in reply that I am unable to judge of the correctness of Mr. Blount's Report from which the President's conclusions were drawn, as I have had no opportunity of examining such report. (Ed.— Neither Blount nor Gresham made a copy available to the Provisional Government until long after Cleveland's decision to send Willis out to reinstate the Queen!) But I desire to specifically and emphatically deny the correctness of each and every one of the allegations contained in the above-quoted statement; yet, as the President has arrived at a positive opinion in his own mind in the matter, I will refer to it from his standpoint.

Dole can't judge Blount's Report without seeing it

"My position, briefly, is this: If the

American forces illegally assisted the revolutionists in the establishment of the Provisional Government, that Provisional Government is not responsible for their wrong-doing. It was purely a private matter for discipline between the United States Government and its own officers. There is, I submit, no precedent in international law for the theory that such action of the American troops has conferred upon the United States authority over the internal affairs of this Government.

Dispute is between U.S. Government and its officers

Should it be true, as you have suggested, that the American Government made itself responsible to the Queen, who, it is alleged lost her throne through such action, that is not a matter for me to discuss, except to submit that if such be the case, it is a matter for the American Government and her to settle between them. This Government, a recognized sovereign power, equal in authority with the United States Government and enjoying diplomatic relations with it, can not be destroyed by it for the sake of discharging its obligations to the ex-Queen.

Provisional Government protested U.S. actions

"Upon these grounds, Mr. Minister, in behalf of my Government I respectfully protest against the usurpation of its authority as suggested by the language of your communication."

Dole then reviewed events of the previous two decades leading up to the Queen's attempt to promulgate a new Constitution, saying at one point:

"For long years a large and influential part of this community, including many foreigners and Native Hawaiians, have observed with deep regret the retrogressive tendencies of the Hawaiian Monarchy, and have honorably striven against them, and have sought through legislative work, the newspapers, and by personal appeal and individual influence to support and emphasize the representative features of the Monarchy and to create a public sentiment favorable thereto, and thereby to avert the catastrophe that seemed inevitable if such tendencies were not restrained.

Dole described retrogression of Monarchy

"These efforts have been met by the last two sovereigns in a spirit of aggressive hostility . . ."

Reviewing the major problems of the reign of Kalākaua and its financial instability, Dole moved on to the reign of Queen Liliʻuokalani:

"The ex-Queen's rule was even more reckless and retrogressive than her brother's. . . . She, to all appearance, unhesitatingly took the oath of office to govern according to the constitution, and evidently regarding it merely as a formal ceremony began, according to her own testimony to Mr. Blount, to lay her plans to destroy the constitution and replace it with one of her own creation. With a like disregard of its sanctions, she made the most determined efforts to control all of the appointments to office, both executive and judicial. The session of the legislature of 1892 was the longest . . . in our history, and was characterized by a most obstinate struggle for personal control of the Government and the legislature on the part of the Queen. . . .

Liliʻuokalani more reckless than brother

"Although the situation at the close of the session [January 14] was deeply discouraging to the community, it was accepted without any intention of meeting it by other than legal means.

"[But] the attempted coup d'état of the Queen followed, and her ministers, threatened with violence, fled to the citizens for assistance and protection; then it was that the uprising against the Queen took place, and gathering force from day to day, resulted in the proclamation of the Provisional Government and the abrogation of the Monarchy on the third day thereafter (January 17).

Ministers fled for help from community

"No man can correctly say that the Queen owed her downfall to the interference of American forces. The revolution was carried through by the representatives, now reinforced, of the same public sentiment which forced the Monarchy to its knees in 1887 [putting into place the Reform Constitution], which suppressed the insurrection of 1889 [when Lili'uokalani tried to oust her brother], and which for twenty years has been battling for representative government in this country. If the American forces had been absent the revolution would have taken place, for the sufficient causes for it had nothing to do with their presence."

Public sentiment battled for representative government

Dole then ended his lengthy letter by rejecting the blunt request by Willis that the Queen be reinstated:

"I, therefore, in all friendship of the Government of the United States, which you represent, and desiring to cherish the good will of the American people, submit the answer of my Government to your proposition, and ask that you will transmit the same to the President of the United States for his consideration.

"Though the Provisional Government is far from being 'a great power' and could not

118

long resist the forces of the United States in a hostile attack, we deem our position to be impregnable under all legal precedents, under the principles of diplomatic intercourse, and in the forum of conscience. We have done your Government no wrong; no charge of discourtesy is or can be brought against us. Our only issue with your people has been that, because we revered its institutions of civil liberty, we have desired to have them extended to our own distracted country, and because we honor its flag and deeming that its beneficent and authoritative presence would be for the best interests of all of our people, we have stood ready to add our country, a new star, to its glory, and to consummate a union which we believed would be as much for the benefit of your country as ours. If this is an offense, we plead guilty to it.

"I am instructed to inform you, Mr. Minister, that the Provisional Government of the Hawaiian Islands respectfully and unhesitatingly declines to entertain the proposition of the President of the United States that it should surrender its authority to the ex-Queen."

"We have done your Government no wrong"

Dole refused to reinstate ex-Queen

The letter was delivered on the evening of December 23. Willis, admittedly stunned, forwarded the letter at 4 o'clock the next morning by a waiting U.S. Revenue Cutter, the *Corwin,* to Secretary Gresham. He was so concerned that word not leak out of the Provisional Government's firm position in defiance of the president that he ordered the *Corwin* not to enter San Francisco Bay until after dark, and not to allow anyone ashore for several days so that his envoy would be able to forward it secretly by courier to Washington, where it arrived on January 9. There

Willis stunned by Dole letter

was no further action from the administration to reinstate the Queen. On January 12, 1894, Gresham instructed Willis that "you will until further notice consider that your special instructions have been fully complied with."

There followed additional long and interesting correspondence between Willis and Dole as the two governments tried to put their various spins on the exchange. Willis in particular asked for a long list of specifics as a result of Dole's December 23 letter. Dole complied with excruciating detail. As President Cleveland later said, it was a "most extraordinary correspondence."

"Most extraordinary correspondence"

The president's subsequent behavior—or perhaps more to the point, his lack of further action—can well be interpreted as a change of mind on his part. The emotional charges against the Revolutionists embodied in his message to Congress after the Queen turned down his demand for amnesty were not the kind of thing one would expect to be a president's final words on the matter. Yet he had nothing more to say publicly about the Hawaiian Revolution for the rest of his term. He had given that message to Congress before he read the "extraordinary correspondence" between Dole and Willis. In other words, he gave the message before hearing the Provisional Government side of the story, depending only on Blount's one-sided report for his information. The cool logic of Dole's presentation of the case may well have persuaded him that he was fighting a losing battle, that the Revolution was warranted after all. In the light of his and Gresham's earlier emphasis on the moral principles involved in the Hawai'i matter, the lack of any follow-up is striking in its absence.

Cleveland apparently changed his mind

Meanwhile, to return to the narrative of the

Revolution, later in the evening of the Queen's surrender, the Revolutionists began notifying the other seventeen foreign legations of their formation of a Provisional Government and received recognition from all within 48 hours. Interestingly, they were helped at this point by Prince David Kawananakoa, who, along with all other members of the Queen's government except the Queen herself, her Cabinet and her marshal, was asked by the Provisional Government to remain on duty to serve the new government and keep things going.[33] Kawananakoa, a potential successor to the crown if the Monarchy had continued, soon left the government, however, and maintained an opposing, Royalist, position throughout the following five years.

Legations recognized Provisional Government

Incidentally, one of the first administrative actions of the new government was repeal of the odious opium and lottery bills.

Both sides, meanwhile, rushed emissaries to Washington, the one to present a case for Annexation, the other to make a case for return of the Islands to the Queen. The Revolutionists got there first—they had quickly made arrangements to charter a ship owned by Committee member William C. Wilder. They left on January 19 and arrived in Washington on February 3, more than a month before the Harrison administration was due to leave office. They succeeded in getting a proposed treaty of Annexation negotiated and introduced by the sympathetic Harrison, but President Cleveland took office before the Senate could act on it.

Opium & lottery laws repealed

Cleveland withdrew the proposed treaty and, as mentioned earlier, sent James H. Blount, the former chairman of the U.S. House Committee on Foreign Relations, to Hawai'i, under secret instructions to study the Revolution and its causes. Subsequent events can lead to the conclusion that Blount came predisposed to restoration of the Queen. His voluminous report does not delve into the causes of the Revolution, focusing mostly on the role Stevens—and hence by Blount's erroneous extension, the United States—had played in it.

Blount predisposed to restoration of Queen

The U.S. troops had been carefully kept out of sight during the actual time the Revolutionists were occupying the government building and doing their other acts of conquest, in an effort to make clear they and the United States were not parties to the Revolution. They had dipped their colors to the Queen as they passed the palace to demonstrate their neutral and respectful position. Lieutenant Laird testified before the Morgan Committee that reading of the proclamation took place out of sight of the U.S. troops. Nor, he testified in language directly opposed to Blount's assertion, were his troops in position between the Queen's forces and the Provisional Government forces. The specific U.S. position, incidentally, was selected by the military force and not by Stevens after several other possible sites had fallen through. But these cautions on Stevens' part did not prevent the situation from becoming interpreted otherwise. In his investigation on behalf of President Cleveland, Blount blamed the whole affair on Stevens. He charged that the United States thus was illegally involved, in violation of international law that holds that a diplomat, recognized by a foreign government, should not get involved in an effort to overthrow that government.

U.S. troops kept out of sight

Stevens, watching a cause that he strongly believed in unfold before his eyes, admittedly was walking a fine line between his duties as a diplomat and his personal notions as to what was best for his country. The same problem, but in the opposite sense, was to face his successor, Albert S. Willis. President Cleveland sent Willis out to Hawai'i as U.S. minister to the Provisional Government, a friendly government that the United States had recognized. But he carried secret orders to do all he could to subvert it, to force that government to return the Monarchy to the Queen. His orders, which of course he did not reveal to the government in Hawai'i, were a clear violation of international law, coming from the seat of the offending government itself and not merely from the actions of an agent in the field.

Willis, outwardly friendly, came to subvert Government

Blount had conducted his study in secret, with no sworn statements and no public hearings. He did not interview key members of the Committee of Safety, though he did talk with two members on a limited basis and accepted a written statement from another. He also did not interview officers involved in the landing of U.S. troops, nor leaders of the new government. Altogether he interviewed or took statements from sixty Royalists, including everyone who could be considered a leader of that party, and only twenty Annexationists, none of whom was a key figure in that movement or the Revolution.

Blount didn't interview key people

A few months later, an investigation by the nine-member Senate Committee on Foreign Relations reached an opposite conclusion to Blount's, exonerating Stevens on a five-to-four basis. The committee heard out under oath anyone who wanted to testify at public hearings in Washington. The hearing was conducted by its chairman, John T. Morgan, an Annexation-minded Democratic senator from Alabama. The committee had announced its hearing in Honolulu newspapers and accepted sworn statements from those who could not make the trip to Washington. The committee report is clear in its conclusions and in general was approved in its entirety by all of its nine members.

The four Democrat members, however, disagreed with their Democrat chairman and that part of his committee report that dealt with Stevens' role. They agreed instead with the Blount finding that Stevens had erred and should be censured. But all nine members did agree, contrary to Blount's charge, that the U.S. troops conducted themselves properly and had not become involved in the Revolution.[34]

Morgan Report exonerated U.S. troops

The four Republican senators disagreed with the committee report's exoneration of Blount and President Cleveland. They felt that Blount's appointment and mission were unconstitutional, having failed to get Senate approval, and that the president had far exceeded his powers in attempting to interfere with a government, the Provisional Government, that had been recognized as sovereign by the United States and every other country with interests in the Pacific. The 809-page report contains a wealth of fascinating historical material in its sworn testimony and exhibits.

Today's revisionists ignore Morgan Report

It is in these arguments about Stevens' actions that today's sovereignty supporters commit what many feel is a serious distortion. Their claims are based only on the secretly conducted Blount Report and Cleveland's subsequent vitriolic, one-sided 1893 political statement to Congress on the Hawaiian affair. They ignore the Morgan Report and its voluminous sworn testimony and the ample available statements of the Revolutionists themselves. Their one-dimensional approach to a complex problem unnecessarily fosters questions and dispute. They do not appear to recognize that Hawai'i was caught in a political confrontation that, as might be expected, had two sides. The case for U.S. involvement clearly can be argued either way, and both sides in Washington began to realize that nothing could be done externally to change the situation, whoever was to blame.

Morgan Report shouldn't be ignored

Thurston put it this way in his *Memoirs* regarding one of the key points of the investigations:

"It has been argued, on behalf of the royalists and the Gresham-Cleveland administration, that the revolutionists depended on the American troops, and not on their own strength, to carry the revolution into effect; the royalists cite the request of the Committee of Safety to the American minister to lend assistance. The reply is that Minister Stevens informed the committee, although he was sympathetic with their cause, that he would not assist them against the Monarchy, and he gave specific assurance that troops would be landed for the exclusive purpose of protecting American lives and property. The revolutionists undoubtedly knew that the royalists thought that American troops would be used to support the revolution, but it was not the duty of the revolutionists to inform the royalists that their impression was erroneous. Seemingly the royalists held the theory that it was the duty of the revolutionists to begin a bloody fight; if they did not do so, they were not entitled to take advantage of the situation and the misconceptions of the royalists."

Stevens sympathetic, but did not assist Revolutionists

The Revolutionists were under no such restriction. They seized the opportunity and took full advantage of whatever confusion and lack of determination may have existed in the Queen's camp.

One point is agreed on today by both sides: It was not official U.S. policy to seek control of

Hawai'i. President Cleveland had made this very clear by withdrawing the Annexation treaty that had been before Congress when he took office. In his subsequent denunciation of the Revolution he went even further. He said he regretted any part the United States may have played in it, and demanded that the Provisional Government return the throne to Lili'uokalani. As we have seen, he replaced Stevens with a new minister to Hawai'i to bring this about, but the Provisional Government absolutely refused to yield.

U.S. policy not expansionist at time

The Queen made one futile try at a counter-revolution, knowing that in view of Cleveland's outspoken remarks, the United States would not support the Provisional Government or its successor government, the Republic, this time, whatever its action had been in 1893. In fact, the U.S. government, in what the Republic later charged was a violation of international neutrality law, allowed arms to be shipped from California in late 1894 to the Queen's forces for use in the January 1895 counter-revolution.[35]

U.S. allowed arms shipment to counter-revolutionists

The Hawaiian segment of the population numbered nearly forty thousand in 1893, and seven thousand of these, her office claimed, had signed a petition a few months earlier asking the Queen to promulgate a new Constitution. The 1895 counter-revolution should easily have overwhelmed the few hundred troops of the Republic, if she had popular support and the backing of the seven thousand whom she claimed had signed the petition. It has to be assumed she did not have popular support, as the counter-revolution collapsed in its first skirmish. One member of the Republic forces was killed, Thurston's law partner and close friend, Charles L. Carter. Two members of the Royalist forces were killed and several hundred were captured, tried and sentenced to terms ranging from banishment from the Kingdom to death. All sentences were later commuted—in striking contrast to the Queen's insistence to Minister Willis on death for the Committee of Safety if she were reinstated.

Republic's quality of mercy contrasted with Queen's

Today some would try to make heroes of those who led the effort to re-establish the throne. The Queen herself, who was tried by the Republic for misprision—the knowledge of treason—and found guilty, is portrayed as a martyr. She was sentenced to be confined to a room in the palace for five years but was released after about eight months. In the history of revolutions against the rule of monarchs, the monarch usually has fared far worse. Efforts by King George III to re-establish his monarchical control over America or the French royalists to re-establish the monarchy in Paris would have been dealt with more seriously.

After the Hawaiian counter-revolution, there was a great hue and cry about severely punishing the several hundred persons who were captured in the brief battle and found guilty of treason. All of the court sentences were commuted but Royalists within the government were summarily discharged. And as Russ notes in *The Hawaiian Republic,* "There is record of at least one instance where this policy of getting rid of Royalists carried over into the business world. Others probably occurred."

Royalists in government discharged

He noted that J.O. Carter, who had advised Lili'uokalani during several of her interviews with Willis and had gotten her finally to back off her threat to have the Revolutionists executed, suffered the economic ax as soon as his role became known. He was the much-respected president and manager of C. Brewer and Co., brother of H.A.P. Carter, foreign minister of the Monarchy under Kalākaua, and an uncle of Charles L. Carter. His stockholders, Russ notes, who were for the most part Annexationists, "thought his continued connection with the concern gave to it an evil reputation in annexationist circles. The stockholders removed him, put P.C. Jones in his place, and passed annexation resolutions."

Royalist Carter lost job

The Hawaiian government earlier, on July 4, 1894, had become a Republic. The Republic was a hard-nosed form of government, giving up aspects of civil liberties and the universal voting rights its people would secure later under Annexation, to assure its control until an administration sympathetic to Annexation took over the U.S. presidency. When Republican McKinley replaced Democrat Cleveland in 1897 that opportunity appeared, and the Republic, still under the presidency of Sanford Dole and by this time an independent nation with a four-year history "untainted" by sub rosa ties with the United States, offered again to accept Annexation.

Republic offered to accept Annexation

Caspar Whitney, in his 1899 book, *Hawaiian America*, notes: "At the first election called by the Republic for Senators and Representatives, about 5,000 voters qualified, and all the members of both houses were elected on a platform favoring annexation." Other reports give a lesser number of voters but agree on the description of a "platform favoring annexation." That goal of Annexation was a part of the Republic's Constitution.

Figures in footnotes of Russ' *The Hawaiian Republic* give an interesting picture of the change in the electorate in the first election of the Republic compared with the last one of the Monarchy. In both cases, Americans were in a minority position but exerted power out of proportion to their numbers. In

1892, there were 10,493 votes cast, including by 637 Americans, 505 Englishmen, 382 Germans, 2,091 Portuguese and 6,878 Native Hawaiians. Americans constituted 6 percent of the electorate. In the first election of the Republic, there were only 1,917 registered voters, of whom 466 were Americans, 274 Englishmen, 175 Germans, 362 Portuguese, 509 Native Hawaiians and 131 others. Americans constituted 24 percent of the electorate, though Native Hawaiians still were the largest single bloc.

Voter statistics show Americans in minority but powerful

The Republic Senate, made up of a majority of Caucasians but including a number of Native Hawaiians, unanimously voted its approval of an Annexation treaty in 1897.[36] As detailed in Chapter One, the House, with a majority of Native Hawaiians, did not have to vote on the matter. House Speaker John L. Kaulukou, however, who had been a leading native figure under both Kalākaua and Liliʻuokalani, strongly favored Annexation and the vote undoubtedly would have been unanimous in its favor.

Republic Senate unanimous for Annexation

Several of the Republic's senators had been supporters of the Monarchy. Senator John Kauhane, vice president of the Senate and a member of its Committee on Foreign Relations, was a full-blooded Hawaiian who had supported the Monarchy but played no role in the Revolution. Senator Cecil Brown, married to a Hawaiian, had lived all his life in the Islands. He had favored monarchical government until 1892, when he began to perceive its weaknesses. Not a rabid Annexationist in 1893, he had wished to give the Queen another chance, and had later withdrawn from the Revolutionary movement. But he voted for the treaty. Also Senator H.L. Holstein, a part-Hawaiian member from the Big Island, commented in 1940 in a letter to Russ: ". . . as a Senator from the Island of Hawai'i on Sept. 9, 1897, I voted for the Treaty of Annexation, with the ambition and hope and belief that some day Hawai'i would become a State of the Union . . ."

As historian Russ put it in his 1959 book, *The Hawaiian Republic,* there could be no conviction in questions about whether or not the Republic had the right to seek Annexation:

> "In 1898 no one could say that the United States was receiving stolen goods, for by that time the new Government had secured a good title."

Republic had right to seek Annexation

This time the United States agreed, and Hawai'i became a Territory of the United States, with full citizenship and voting rights for Hawai'i residents beyond what either the Queen or the Republic had allowed. More than two-thirds of the voters after Annexation were Native Hawaiians, and in the first Legislature, in 1901, the Native Hawaiian legislative majority was 73 percent. The records show many non-Hawaiians voted to elect Hawaiian members.[37]

Full voting rights put Hawaiians on top

While no plebiscite was taken then, the plebiscite taken 60 years later when Statehood was achieved showed more than 90 percent of Hawai'i voters, Native Hawaiians and otherwise, in favor of the relationship with America.

While no polls were taken before or after Annexation, it is interesting to note that the territorial Legislature, with a majority of more than 70 percent Native Hawaiian members, voted unanimously in 1903 to seek Statehood, less than three years after Hawai'i became a Territory.[38] It is a fair assumption that they must have liked Annexation, too, although the number who favored Annexation because they disliked the Republic is another unknown that may have been a factor.

Thus one of the benefits to Hawaiians immediately apparent after Annexation was voting power they had never had under the Monarchy, nor for that matter, under the Provisional Government or Republic. All of them became U.S. citizens on Annexation Day, and the male members of the Hawaiian population, like all other male citizens of America, gained the right to vote. The new Territory's first delegate to Congress, elected by the people of Hawai'i, was Robert Wilcox, the Hawaiian activist who had led the Queen's final abortive effort in 1895 to undo the Revolution. (There are those who argue it wasn't "the Queen's effort" because she was never convicted of being its ringleader. However, her own diaries show she was forming committees, had her Cabinet list made out and had signed fifteen royal commissions to take effect after the counter-revolution. There is little doubt that she was well aware of what was taking place on her behalf and approved of it.)

Hawaiian-dominated Legislature voted for Statehood

Annexation brought voting power to Hawai'i natives

The Republican Party drafted Prince Jonah Kūhiō Kalaniana'ole to run against him in the next election in 1902, and Wilcox was defeated. Again, however, it was the Hawaiian vote that carried the day. It was not until Prince Kūhiō's death in 1922 that the power of that Republican Hawaiian voting bloc dwindled. Up to that time Native Hawaiians, representing the majority of voters, controlled the Legislature. They continued until 1938 to be the largest bloc of voters. Further, a greater percentage turned out to vote than was the case with any other racial group: In 1930, among Native Hawaiians, nine out of ten registered voters actually voted.[39]

For more than two decades, the practical effect of the Revolution was to put control of the government in the hands of its Native Hawaiian residents. As late as 1927, Hawaiians held 46 percent of appointed executive positions in the territorial government and 55 percent of clerical and other government jobs. More than half of the judgeships and elective offices were filled by people of Hawaiian ancestry. They dominated law enforcement offices. In 1935, with fifteen percent of the population, the Hawaiians held one-third of public service jobs.[40] With estimates of the part-Hawaiian population today reaching twenty percent, or two hundred forty thousand persons, a tantalizing control potential exists.

Hawaiians dominated government

Another emotional distortion by sovereignty activists is the claim that leaders of the Revolution were motivated by personal greed or personal plans for power. A succeeding chapter discusses these men as individuals, and suffice it to say now that the Revolution was clearly not a grab for personal gain. No member of the Committee of Safety acquired any land or property as a result of its actions and only two members of the Committee accepted what might be called leadership roles in the new government, either in the Provisional Government that lasted for 14 months, or the successor Republic of Hawai'i. They were W.O. Smith, who agreed to serve as Dole's attorney general and stayed in that office until Annexation, and Henry Cooper, who filled in briefly in several key positions when Dole asked him to help.

Revolutionists not motivated by greed

Nine other members of the Committee of Safety along with five at-large members of the Annexation Club were appointed as an advisory council by President Dole, and he drew on several of them, including L.A. Thurston, as envoys to Washington in connection with the Annexation negotiations. Several others from time to time accepted temporary roles in the Cabinet. But the Revolution was not a device for personal gain or power. It truly was a spontaneous effort backed by the people as a whole to correct what had become to them an intolerable situation in their homeland.

Revolution not for personal gain

Chapter Six

The Men Out Front

The thirteen men who masterminded Hawai'i's 1893 Revolution were a cross-section of Honolulu's leading Caucasian residents.

As we learned in the previous chapter, they had been appointed on January 14, 1893, at a mass meeting of residents alarmed about the actions of Queen Lili'uokalani.[41] The thirteen were carrying out community pressure to put a more stable government in charge of the Island nation. Once in place, they planned to ensure that stability through Annexation to Hawai'i's long-time protector, the United States.

Pressure for stable government

The Queen's sudden announcement on January 14, 1893, of her plans for a new Constitution had caught the community by surprise and caused grave concerns, but in retrospect triggered an opportunity for change to something more stable.

Details of the final planning for the Revolution that would bring about that change were assigned to the Committee of Safety. All of its thirteen members were residents and taxpayers of Hawai'i. Most also were subjects of the Island Kingdom, active in the community as businessmen, attorneys and politicians.

Committee of Safety members all residents

It wasn't the first time the community had responded to a crisis in this manner. In 1853, a Committee of Thirteen had been formed at another public meeting to deal with an attempt to remove two members of Kamehameha III's Cabinet, former missionaries Dr. G.P. Judd and Richard Armstrong, over charges they were responsible for that year's devastating smallpox epidemic. The issue was confused by Annexation issues. The committee, and the American community in general, favored Annexation and some believed Dr. Judd, long-time adviser to the King, did not. Judd's statements to American officials indicated he favored Annexation, but opposed violence to achieve it.[42] Efforts to bring about Annexation then did not get very far, but it was a subject always on the minds of those living and working in the Islands. Virtually every U.S. minister to Hawai'i in the fifty years prior to the Revolution had urged his superiors in Washington to pursue Annexation before some other country moved in.

Annexation interest not new

In 1851, the Kingdom itself, through King Kamehameha III, actively sought Annexation to the United States, and over a three-year period a treaty was negotiated to accomplish it. The King, however, died in 1854 before it could be signed, and Kamehameha IV, who favored ties with Britain, dropped the matter.[43]

Forty years later, this new Committee of Thirteen—the Committee of Safety—emerged and its goal again was Annexation.

Many Hawaiians disenchanted with Queen

Its members were supported not only openly by most of the foreign community but more than likely silently by those Hawaiians less than enchanted by the political tactics and policies of Queen Lili'uokalani. Some of those Hawaiians had supported Queen Emma to become monarch at the time of

Kalākaua's 1874 election. Others had resented Lili'uokalani's efforts in 1889 to force out her brother, Kalākaua. It would have been difficult for any Hawaiian to be a recognized participant in the overthrow of a native monarch, but none did much to help her retain the throne in 1893. And again, two years later, when she tried unsuccessfully to mount a counter-revolution, most were silent.

The Committee formed on January 14, 1893, was a combination of subjects of the Queen and men of other national allegiances, but all were residents of Hawai'i with a keen interest in its future as well as their own. All felt that putting their personal futures at risk was preferable to doing nothing. They and their peers agreed that the status quo ultimately would lead to Hawai'i's downfall and loss of independence, most likely to some colonial power. The native peoples, as had happened elsewhere in the Pacific, would not be accepted as equals by the colonizing power. With Annexation, however, Native Hawaiians would become citizens of the United States, with equal rights to every benefit of citizenship in a free nation, including the unlimited right to vote.

Committee keenly interested in nation's future

Annexation would mean equal rights

Let's look at the men who were appointed to plan the Revolution. We'll review what is known today about their backgrounds and aspirations, as well as those of other leaders of the community who were willing to be openly identified as the men out front in this fight against the Monarchy. These men were just those few willing to put their own personal futures publicly on the line. They knew their viewpoint was widely supported among their friends, and once the movement began, they could count on help. But their actions at this point would be interpreted

Revolutionists willing to put lives on line

as treasonous by the Monarchy. Their lives would be in danger.

Lorrin A. Thurston

Thurston, of American descent but a Hawaiian-born subject of the Kingdom, had been the founder of the Annexation Club in 1892 and was at the core of the new Committee of Safety.

Thurston's ties to Hawai'i deep-rooted

At the risk of seeming to favor Thurston, grandfather of this writer, considerable detail follows on his early life and activities. Since "fact-finder" Blount and his boss, U.S. Secretary of State Gresham, labeled Thurston the leader of the Revolution and maligned both his character and motives, it seems only fair to detail his family background and concerns for the people of Hawai'i and let readers judge for themselves.

Thurston, 35 at the time of the Revolution, had a three-generation background in his native land, Hawai'i. He was the grandson of four missionaries to these Islands. His parents, missionary descendants, were not themselves missionaries. Thurston had been married in 1886 to another missionary descendant, Clara Shipman. She had died eighteen months before the Revolution in childbirth with their second child.

Thurstons were fluent in Hawaiian

Lorrin's father, Asa Goodale Thurston, died at 32 in 1859, sixteen months after Lorrin was born. At the time, Asa was the skipper of an inter-island schooner after a stint as a Kona coffee farmer. Like his missionary father Asa, who gave his sermons in Hawaiian, and his son Lorrin, who worked as an interpreter in the courts before completing high school, he was fluent in Hawaiian.

Asa G. was educated at home in Kona because there was not yet a school in the Islands that missionary children could attend. He was sent to the East Coast for further schooling in 1841 when he was 14, coincidentally the year that a school designed for missionary children, Punahou, was founded by the missionaries in Honolulu. He stayed east for ten years. He attended prep school for several years, then entered Yale in 1845 with a cousin from Marlborough, Massachusetts, but graduated from Williams College in 1849, its first-ever graduate from Hawai'i. On the way home he yielded to Gold Rush fever and stopped off for an unsuccessful effort to find gold in California before coming home.

Lorrin's father served as speaker of the House

Four years after his return he was elected to the Legislature and a year later, in 1854, became speaker of the House of Representatives during the last year of the reign of Kamehameha III.

Asa G. had married Sarah Andrews, daughter of Lorrin Andrews and Mary Wilson Andrews, in October 1853, and when he died on December 17, 1859, he left a widow and two small sons and no estate. Lorrin's sister, Helen, was born after their father's death.

Lorrin's only inheritance was Bible

Lorrin's only inheritance was a Bible, which his father inscribed and signed just before his death.

At his death Asa G. was serving as the founding president of the Hawaiian Mission Children's Society, an organization of missionary descendants formed to send further missions to islands in the South Pacific.

His death left young Lorrin to be raised by his mother, the daughter of pioneer missionaries to Maui. Her father, Lorrin Andrews, had written the first Hawaiian dictionary and was the founding principal of Lahainaluna Seminary on Maui, where he introduced the art of copper plate engraving in 1834. He taught engraving to countless Hawaiians who

Maternal grandfather wrote first dictionary

used these skills to record historical views, prepare textbooks and create works of art that today help give a clearer picture of historic Hawai'i. In later years he served as an associate justice of the Hawaiian Supreme Court.

Lorrin's paternal grandfather, Asa Thurston, was winding down a lifetime career as a pioneer missionary to Hawai'i when Lorrin was born. Lorrin was 10 when his grandfather died in 1868, but he knew the story of what had led that grandfather to the church and Hawai'i: His grandfather's older brother had been training for the ministry until a devastating typhoid epidemic in New England in 1817 killed him, his sisters and his mother. His brother's last words to Asa were a plea that he carry on the pledge of mission service, the last thing Asa had in mind. But he left his trade as a scythe maker and life as a party boy—he reportedly had a beautiful tenor singing voice and, in 1816 as a Yale senior, his strength had won him the respected title of Class Bully. Reportedly, he could jump in and out of a hogshead drum without touching the sides. Back to college he went, to the divinity school associated with Yale. Driven by the inspiration of Hawaiian scholar Henry Obookiah, he wound up in Hawai'i in 1820 where his son, Asa G., was born in 1827.

Paternal grandfather became missionary

Lorrin raised by widowed mother

Lorrin's mother, Sarah Andrews Thurston, a "single mom" in today's parlance, became a teacher for nine years in the Royal School in Nu'uanu Valley to support her young family after her husband's death. In 1868 she was offered the job of matron of a new industrial school for boys in Makawao, Maui, known as the Haleakala School, nine miles from the summit of that mountain. Her brother, Robert Andrews, had been appointed principal, and Sarah moved her family—Lorrin, his older brother, Robert, and sister, Helen—to Maui. Lorrin got his early schooling and his first job there. The job paid 25 cents a day, during vacations, at the I.D. Hall ranch. He had to provide his own horse to carry water to workmen on a fence-building job.

His schoolmates included many boys who later were to have considerable influence on his life. Among them were Robert W. Wilcox, the Native Hawaiian "chronic revolutionist," to use Thurston's words. Thurston said he called him that "because it seemed to make little difference to him which side he took, so long as he was heading a fight." They remained friends throughout the stormy years of the Kalākaua and Lili'uokalani regimes, when they usually, though not always, were on opposite sides politically, and during the three years Wilcox served as Hawai'i's first delegate to Congress.

Early education on Maui, friend of Robert Wilcox

Lorrin left the Haleakala School in 1872 to attend a private school in Wailuku. This was a considerable distance from Makawao, and the young student lived during the week with the Rev. and Mrs. William P. Alexander, returning on his horse to Makawao for the weekends.

The following year he was sent back to O'ahu as a boarder at Punahou School and held jobs to earn his way, such as the 50 cents a week he received for caring for the president's horse. Part of the work program he was required to perform as a scholarship student was to drive a wagon along Beretania Street, picking up younger students and delivering them to school. This was to lead the following year to his expulsion from Punahou at the age of 15, "incorrigible" in the strict views of the faculty.

Scholarship work was driving wagon-bus

His older brother, Robert, 19 and in charge of the carpenter shop at Punahou, died earlier that same year of blood poisoning from a coral cut

Coral cut fatal to older brother

incurred in the waters off Wai'anae, another of a series of tragedies for young Thurston.

Three offenses led to the Punahou letter of dismissal received by Lorrin's mother on Maui. The offenses are laughable today, but there probably wasn't much laughter in the Thurston home the day the letter arrived. In sorrowful tones, the letter from Principal Amasa Pratt set forth what caused school authorities to say he must leave Punahou. In earlier months Lorrin had "taken liberties" in quoting scriptural verse reflecting on women as teachers. The major current offense, though, was racing the wagon up Punahou Street in competition with the "Dillingham boys," who lived on the corner of Beretania and Punahou where Central Union Church now stands. The little girls on his wagon screamed and yelled in terror, the letter notes.

Punahou expelled Lorrin

But the clincher, performed the day the letter was written, was an affront to his English teacher. That worthy lady chastised young Lorrin for an essay wherein he had used the ampersand, "&," in place of the word "and." He was ordered to rewrite the essay. He did so, but in every case where "and" appeared, the young rebel wrote it as large as the space between the ruled lines while writing the rest of the composition in very small characters. This could not be tolerated, and Lorrin was out of Punahou—until in an ironic reversal he was invited back two decades later in 1896 as a trustee, a responsibility he fulfilled for the following 34 years.

Watched history in the making

While he was at Punahou, he seized every opportunity to leave the campus and be a part of what was going on downtown. He was a participant in the near-unanimous election of Lunalilo over King Kalākaua in 1873, helping to distribute ballots, and was a witness to the "barracks mutiny" the following

year. He left school another day to watch the tumultuous 1874 election of Kalākaua over Queen Emma
in the old courthouse where Amfac Towers now
stand, and the riot that followed. It had to be quelled
by U.S. troops, the first of four occasions in Lorrin's
early life when troops were landed to protect American lives and property. This desire to be where the
action was stayed with him.

Worked as interpreter, janitor

Lorrin never did graduate from high school.
Instead he went to work as an office boy in the Honolulu law office of Alfred S. Hartwell, utilizing his
fluency in Hawaiian to serve also as an interpreter,
and welcoming the chance to study law. He was paid
$4 a week but got a dollar increase when he also took
on duties as janitor. He earned additional money at
the Fort Street church—$5 a month for pumping the
organ for rehearsals on Fridays and at two services
on Sundays.

Earned money for Columbia University

By his third year, Thurston had priced himself out of Hartwell's market by earning $1,000 for
the year. He had picked up enough knowledge of law,
however, to receive his own license at age 19. He set
up office in Wailuku and augmented the income of
his early practice years with a job as supervisor and
bookkeeper at Wailuku Sugar Company. After 18
months he had brought his total savings to $1,800.

He used this to enroll at Columbia University law school in New York, and two years later, in
1881, returned to Honolulu at age 23, a full-fledged
attorney and again an assistant to Hartwell. He soon
became a partner in a new law partnership with
W.O. Smith and W.A. Kinney, both of whom were
also to play leading roles in the 1893 Revolution
some ten years later.

Elected to Legislature at age 28

Before long Thurston ran for public office at
his partners' behest and was elected to the Legisla-

ture in 1886 at the age of 28. His love of argument and concern for the ethics of government led to some fascinating exchanges on the floor, recorded in the legislative records of the day, regarding the practices and habits of some of his fellow legislators, including in one notorious case the excessive use by one of them of alcohol.

In 1886 he successfully introduced a bill to reverse what he saw as a grave injustice in early Hawaiian law that gave all of a woman's property to her husband on marriage. His bill enabled women to retain their property and also to carry out independent careers as businesswomen.

Married Clara Shipman, a missionary daughter

That same year he married Clara Shipman, a missionary daughter from Hilo, whom he had known at Punahou. Their first son, Robert Shipman Thurston, was born on February 1, 1888, but on May 5, 1891, Clara died in childbirth with their second child, who also died. Lorrin remarried in 1894, to Harriet Potter of Saint Joseph, Michigan, whom he had met at the Chicago World's Fair in 1893 where he was promoting Annexation for the new Provisional Government of Hawai'i. It was a marriage that lasted until his death in Honolulu in 1931. They had two children: Margaret Carter, born in 1895 in Washington as he was lobbying for Annexation, mother of this writer, and Lorrin Potter, born in 1900.

Served as editor of Bulletin

Thurston's political career was in full swing in the period from 1884 until the Revolution. Before he was elected to the Legislature in 1886, he had served as editor of the *Honolulu Bulletin* for four months during the legislative session, espousing points favorable to his party, which in the practice of the times had leased the editorial page for that purpose. He served in the House of Representatives as a legislator from Molokai and Lāna'i, and later in the upper house, the House of Nobles, having been elected on Maui. He was appointed minister of the interior in the Kalākaua Cabinet that followed institution of the Reform Constitution. He was a Hawaiian subject but the lone American in a Cabinet whose other members all were of British origin. He became the King's key supporter in spite of the fact he largely wrote the Reform Constitution that was put into effect in 1887 over the objections of Kalākaua, who was forced to sign it. He served the King honorably and faithfully and came to be viewed as his prime minister, but by the early 1890s became disenchanted with Kalākaua and they parted ways.

Served as Kalā-kaua's prime minister

In 1888 Thurston was the King's commissioner of immigration and made the successful approach to the government of Portugal that brought in the first Portuguese immigrants. Many settled on the lower slopes of Punchbowl, and perhaps by way of tribute, Thurston Avenue in that area bears his name. As commissioner, he once took to task the inspector-in-chief of Japanese immigration, ordering him to stop the practice of charging Japanese men $40 extra to bring in a woman when the Board of Immigration already was paying the $30 fare for wives.

Brought in the Portuguese

During the years of the Provisional Government and the Republic, he sought no public office, serving only as a government envoy to Washington. He spent most of those five years lobbying for Annexation across the country, and when Congress approved it in 1898, spent much of the next two years successfully helping negotiate terms of the congressional action that led to Annexation and territorial status. He was particularly proud of the terms covering transfer of the public lands of Hawai'i, which provided for an approach never agreed to

Thurston proud of public land transfer

145

before by the United States: They were to be held by the United States in the form of a sort of public trust, with the income or proceeds of any sales to be used only for the inhabitants of Hawai'i.

After Annexation, he returned to Honolulu and at the behest of the Castle family, then owners of *The Advertiser*, bought the newspaper for a reported $5,000. He remained its publisher until his death in 1931, enjoying tremendous respect for his editorial efforts but enjoying only moderate success on the business side. He maintained a constant, if not always profitable, interest in helping to found new businesses, however. He was a modest investor and legal adviser to such enterprises as O'ahu Railroad and Land Company, Hawai'i Consolidated Railroad on the Big Island, Honolulu Rapid Transit Company and a number of sugar plantations.

Purchased Advertiser from Castle family

Current efforts to paint Lorrin A. Thurston as one with no love for Hawai'i or the Hawaiians, their culture and their welfare are revisionism at its worst. He kept up his fluency in the Hawaiian language and his love of things Hawaiian throughout his life, continuing to publish a Hawaiian edition of *The Advertiser* until the mid-1920s. As publisher of the paper, he fought unceasingly for the preservation of key portions of the Islands as parks, the protection of vistas, support of the Bishop Museum and the Hawaiian Homes Commission Act, and in support of the pasteurization of milk and the banning of billboards.

Protection of special places

He is credited with the road around Koko Head and for the setting aside of Haleakalā and Kilauea as federal preserves that later became national parks. He fostered the Kilauea Observatory and would rush to the volcano every time it erupted.

He also had a keen sense of history and he

had his own notions of justice. For example, when the ceremonies were being planned for Annexation Day, he noted that the event was to be held in front of 'Iolani Palace, the same place where Blount had peremptorily ordered the American Flag hauled down five years earlier upon his arrival in Honolulu to conduct the political investigation for President Cleveland, who had hoped to use that "investigation" to return Hawai'i to the Monarchy.

Raised flag Blount had taken down

Thurston thought it would be fitting that the same flag now be raised to signify the permanent relationship with America that Blount had sought to block. That flag had been sold at auction after Blount hauled it down, along with other relics of Monarchy days. It had been bought by Lieutenant Lucien Young, the second in command aboard the ship that had landed the troops in 1893, and Young had given it to Thurston.

Ceremonies of this nature normally called for a new flag. It would take permission of the U.S. president to substitute an old one. Undeterred, Thurston got that permission, as the *San Francisco Chronicle* reported on July 28, 1898, in its extensive coverage of the event. Thurston no doubt was quite pleased with the touch of irony as the old flag rose back into the breeze.

Thurston got president's OK to use old flag

Less is known now of the other members of the Committee of Safety, but some general statistics demonstrate it was a group with wide and varied experience. Nine had American ties—four by birth in Hawai'i to American parents and hence automatic subjects of Hawai'i, four born on the mainland but at the time residents of Hawai'i, and a ninth who had been born on the mainland but had become a naturalized subject of Hawai'i. Two of the four non-Americans also were naturalized subjects of Hawai'i.

The members of the Committee of Safety

In total, seven were subjects of the Kingdom, but all thirteen were residents. They had discussed the possibilities of Annexation and survival of the Hawaiian economy in detail over many years, as had the community at large.

Among the approximately 3,000 men who comprised the *haole* community, most of those with American ties favored Annexation to the United States, but many other foreign residents, particularly the British community, did not. It had been acknowledged since 1843 that America was not going to allow any other nation to take over Hawai'i. Many residents with origins from other nations, however, didn't want to see that protection go so far as Annexation to America.

Only three Committee members had mission ties

Much has been made of the missionary influence in Hawai'i, and sovereignty advocates today often erroneously charge it was this influence along with the pressure of sugar interests that brought on the Revolution. But only three of the thirteen Committee members were missionary descendants. A fourth was married to the daughter of a missionary. At least five were lawyers and three had served in the Legislature of the Kingdom. None worked for firms headed by missionary descendants or worked directly for sugar interests, though seven owned minority amounts of stock in various sugar companies.

In alphabetical order, here's what we know of them:

Crister Bolte

Crister Bolte was wealthy member of Committee

A native of Germany, Bolte had come to Hawai'i in 1878 as a merchant and had become a naturalized subject of the Kingdom. He was 41 at the time of the Revolution and was vice president of the firm of M.S. Grinbaum and Co. He was one of the wealthier members of the Committee of Safety. A respected member of the community, it was he the other members sent to talk Dole into agreeing to become president of the proposed new government.

He was one of two members of the Committee, neither an American, to be interviewed by Blount and was critical of Blount's interview process and constant hammering on irrelevant matters, which he told the Morgan Committee later he had objected to several times. He described Blount's questions as leading witnesses toward conclusions Blount had already made. He said he resented Blount's failure to include his objections in the final report.

Bolte criticized interview by Blount

Andrew Brown

Brown was one of the Committee's four non-American members. He had come to Hawai'i from his native Scotland in the latter part of the 19th Century and was a coppersmith with Honolulu Iron Works in 1893. The Iron Works was an English-owned company that made and repaired equipment for sugar plantations.

William R. Castle

Castle, a son of Samuel N. and Mary Castle, missionaries who arrived in Hawai'i in 1837, was one of the three missionary descendants—with Thurston and W.O. Smith—on the Committee. Due to his birth from American parents in Honolulu in 1849, he had ties with America but was a Hawaiian subject. After graduating from Punahou in 1868 he attended Oberlin College in Ohio before graduating from Harvard and Columbia Law School, remaining on the mainland the entire period.

Castle's father original partner of Castle & Cooke

He was practicing law in New York when Kalākaua asked him to return to Hawai'i and become his attorney general in 1876. Castle then spent the rest of his life in his native land. For nearly nine years he was a staunch supporter of Kalākaua and the Monarchy, but by the time of the Reform Constitution in 1887 he saw the need for change if the nation were to survive.

He was one of the five lawyers on the Committee and perhaps its wealthiest member.

His father, S.N. Castle, was one of Honolulu's most prominent businessmen. He had come to Hawai'i as a member of the third missionary company in 1837 as assistant superintendent of secular affairs, but with fellow third-company member Amos Starr Cooke, he left the mission when it began closing down in 1851. The two founded the firm of Castle & Cooke, whose successor companies exist to this day. Their first office was in the depository, a warehouse-like building at the rear of the grounds now occupied by the Mission Houses Museum, and they were employed by the mission as its agents until the final close-down in 1863.

Castle: History of service

William Castle was very active in Hawaiian politics. When Kalākaua appointed him attorney general in 1876, the second year of his term as King, it was the start of Castle's long career in government service. Two years later Castle was elected as a member of the House of Representatives, serving again in 1886, '87 and '88 as a member of the House of Nobles. He was president of the Legislature in the latter two years. (The House of Nobles and the House of Representatives—along with members of the Cabinet until the Reform Constitution of 1887— met together under terms of the constitutions of the Kingdom, and a noble was elected president, as in this case.) He played an active role in bringing about the Reform Constitution that Kalākaua signed in

Active in Reform Constitution of 1887

1887. Altogether, he served four terms in the Legislature, as had his father.

Ralph S. Kuykendall reports in his three-volume history of Hawai'i that Castle in 1878 spoke in favor of an agricultural system that would be comprised of small farmers, "each of whom will own his crops and possess sufficient property to make him a conservative supporter of stable government." Castle was concerned that a few wealthy concerns would crowd out small planters "and our populations will consist of a small landed aristocracy and a restless, discontented population of ignorant and idle workers." He thought the great plantations of the day—those of Claus Spreckels and H.P. Baldwin, for example—should be divided into ten-, twenty- and thirty-acre parcels.

Castle wanted to see a small farm ag system

Following the 1893 Revolution, Castle served as minister to Washington for six months in Dole's 1895 Cabinet. He replaced Thurston, who was recalled in February by demand of U.S. Secretary of State Gresham as a result of their continuing argument over the United States' strained relationship with the Provisional and Republic Governments, including allowing arms shipments to Hawai'i (see Chapter One) that led to the 1895 counter-revolution. Gresham accused Thurston of leaking information from diplomatic communications to the press, which Thurston denied in a lengthy letter published in the *Chicago Times-Herald*.

Castle's role after the Revolution

Castle served as president of the Board of Education in 1896 and as a member of the Annexation Commission in 1898. Interestingly, like many others, he had been a staunch opponent of Annexation until circumstances surrounding Hawai'i's last two monarchs forced a change in opinion.

Castle Family Trust set pattern for community

His mother and father established one of

Hawai'i's first family charitable foundations, the S.N. and Mary Castle Family Trust. It set a pattern that has seen significant portions of Hawai'i profits plowed back into the community, demonstrating the concern of those early families for the welfare of the people of the Islands.

In the business world, Castle was involved in the start of Oahu Railroad and was a principal financial backer of Honolulu Rapid Transit and Land Co. (electric street cars). He established the Honolulu Gas Co. and was a founder of Pālama Settlement.

Henry Cooper

Cooper a respected newcomer

Cooper, an Indiana attorney, came to Hawai'i in 1890 for a few months as a visitor interested in the possibilities of coffee growing. He returned soon to become a resident, founded the Hawaiian Abstract and Title Company, and quickly became a leading member of the community. He was one of the four U.S. citizens on the Committee who, although residents of Honolulu, had not yet become subjects of the Hawaiian Monarchy.

Chaired Committee of Safety

On a motion by L.A. Thurston at the mass public meeting that gathered spontaneously in downtown Honolulu after the Queen's efforts to promulgate a new Constitution on January 14, 1893, Cooper was appointed chairman of the Committee of Safety formed at that meeting and was directed to appoint its twelve other members. He did so on the spot, naming members of the Annexation Club.

After the Revolution he served as a circuit court judge for three years before becoming, in 1895, minister of foreign affairs for the Republic. He held that post until 1899 when President Dole asked him to serve as attorney general during the critical period of negotiating the terms of Annexation.

Queen Lili'uokalani

Photo: © The Hawaiian Historical Society

Lili'uokalani, Hawai'i's last Monarch, was an accomplished woman but her leadership, following that of her brother, Kalākaua, brought the Monarchy to an end.

Princess Ka'iulani

Princess Ka'iulani, pictured here as a school girl in London in the early 1890s, would have been Lili'uokalani's successor. Her parents, right, were Archibald Cleghorn and Princess Likelike, sister of Lili'uokalani.

Photo: © The Hawaiian Mission Children's Society

William Little Lee, who arrived by the same accidental landing that brought Charles Reed
Bishop to Hawai'i, became Chief Justice, worked tirelessly to get land ownership into the
hands of Native Hawaiian commoners.

Some of the Revolutionists

W.O. Smith

Sanford B. Dole

Henry Waterhouse

Charles Lunt Carter

Theodore Lansing

Samuel M. Damon

Peter Cushman Jones

John Emmeluth

Spreckels and Bush

Photo: © The Bishop Museum

Claus Spreckels, the original sugar baron, lent great sums of money to the Monarchy and exerted great influence. Lili'uokalani believed he'd restore her to the throne.

Photo: © The Hawai'i State Archives

J.E. Bush, a Hawaiian leader, a strong supporter of the Monarchy although opposed to Lili'uokolani, turned pro-Annexation.

The Annexation Committee

Annexation commissioners pose in Washington in 1893; left to right, J. Marsden, L.A. Thurston, J. Mott-Smith (Hawai'i minister to Washington), W.R. Castle and C.L. Carter, standing. The fifth commissioner, W.C. Wilder, is not pictured.

Kalākaua spent $20,000 on two crowns while in Europe, part of extravagant spending on coronation.

The Provisional Government

The Provisional Government executive council, 1893-94. Left to right, J.A. King, S.B. Dole, W.O. Smith, P.C. Jones.

The Provisional Government pulled in volunteers for the Citizens' Guard, ranging from boys to bearded patriarchs.

He was held in high regard by Dole and others and served as acting president of the Republic for several months in 1898 while Dole was in Washington helping to achieve Annexation. Cooper became the first secretary of the Territory of Hawai'i in June 1900, the title for the number-two post until the Statehood Constitution labeled it lieutenant governor. He served also as president of the Board of Health. During his service with Dole, aside from his principal role as minister of foreign affairs, he served four terms as minister of the interior and three as minister of finance.

First secretary of Territory

He was one of the five lawyers on the Committee of Safety. Having arrived in Honolulu less than three years earlier, he clearly had no tie with missionary families or long-term sugar interests. He held no shares in any business enterprises at the time of the Revolution.

As secretary of Hawai'i, he telegraphed on January 2, 1903, the first cable message from Hawai'i, to L.A. Thurston's Columbia Law School classmate, President Theodore Roosevelt. "We all believe that the removal of the disadvantage of isolation will prove a strong factor in the up-building of a patriotic and progressive American Commonwealth in these islands," he wrote.

Hawai'i's first cable message

John Emmeluth

Emmeluth was born in Cincinnati and married a resident of the Islands. He came to Hawai'i in 1878 as a tinsmith and plumber and was the owner of two stores in the 1890s. A contemporary report said they offered, among other things, "the new porcelain water closets . . . under such transparent trade names [as] 'Sanitas,' 'Deluge' and 'Washout', aimed at making sloppers and outhouses obsolete."

John Emmeluth, a pioneer in canning pineapples

He was a pioneer in canning pineapples, which he produced both in Honolulu and Kona from 1889 to 1892, preceding James Dole's profitable development of the industry in Wahiawa in 1900. Emmeluth was a partner with Thurston and Captain John Kidwell in setting up, in 1892, the Hawaiian Fruit and Packing Co. in Pearl City.

Emmeluth was an American citizen, a resident of Hawai'i but not a subject of the Kingdom.

He was one of the "extreme annexationists" and was involved in creation of the *Hawaiian Star* in March 1893, two months after the Revolution, to provide a stronger voice for his favorite goal. The *Star* merged about 1912 with the *Evening Bulletin* to bring about today's *Star-Bulletin*, which in later years took up the fight for Statehood.

Emmeluth sent a statement to Blount through S.M. Damon and expected that Blount would call him for an interview, "but never heard anything from him," nor did the statement get published. Emmeluth was part of a long list of witnesses suggested to Blount by the Committee of Safety but ignored. All were eyewitnesses of or participants in the Revolution.

Emmeluth extreme annexationist

Theodore F. Lansing

Another of the American members of the Committee, Lansing also was among the four who had not become subjects of the Kingdom. As an associate of M. Phillip & Co., he organized the Pioneer Building and Loan Company in 1890. He left Phillip in 1898 and formed Gear, Lansing & Co., developers of residential lands. The firm's first project was on ten acres in Makiki that the partners acquired from David Kawananakoa and Kūhiō Kalaniana'ole. Their next project was a 260-acre Kaimuki subdivision.

Lansing not subject of Kingdom

John A. McCandless

McCandless was largely responsible for the development of the ʻEwa plains through his discovery of the artesian basin that underlies that part of Oʻahu. Born in Pennsylvania, he had come to Honolulu in 1881 and with his brother, Lincoln, soon became an important factor in the community. He was an active participant in getting Kalākaua to accept the Reform Constitution in 1887.

Discovery of ʻEwa artesian basin

He served in the Senate of the Provisional Government and the Republic for four years and was the first superintendent of public works under the territorial government after Annexation. At the time of the Revolution he held no sugar shares, although he was an officer of both Oʻahu and Pioneer Mill Cos. and later served as a director of Waialua Plantation.

After the turn of the century he became president of Home Insurance, a director of Bank of Hawaii and president of McCandless Bldg. Co.

F. W. McChesney

McChesney was another of the Americans on the Committee who also was not a subject of the Kingdom. He had come to the Islands in 1885 from his native Iowa with other members of his family to form a wholesale grocery and feed firm.

He told the Morgan Committee that success of the Revolution did not depend on U.S. support. He said he never thought U.S. troops "would fight our battle." He maintained that the number of men the Queen could have fielded was roughly similar to the number of armed Revolutionists. He said this refuted claims by Blount that the Revolution could not have succeeded without help from U.S. troops.

McChesney didn't need U.S. "to fight our battle"

William O. Smith

Smith, 45 at the time of the Revolution, was one of the three missionary-descendant members born in the Islands and of course was a Hawaiian subject with American ties. He was one of nine children of James William Smith, a doctor who came with his wife to Kaua'i in 1842 as members of the 10th company of missionaries. His wife, Melicent, established the Kōloa Girls' School on Kaua'i in 1861. Dr. Smith left the mission when it closed in 1851 but practiced medicine on Kaua'i until his death in 1887.

Smith of missionary descent

A law partner and Honolulu neighbor of Thurston, W.O. Smith also read law with Judge A.S. Hartwell, who had given Thurston his start. Smith married Mary Abbey Hobron and spent much of his early career in politics and government service, starting as sheriff of Kaua'i in 1870. Two years later he became sheriff of Maui, serving until 1874. He spent twenty years intermittently in the Legislature of various Hawai'i governments, from 1878 until 1912, and served for seven years as deputy attorney general under the Monarchy.

Long-time government servant

He was the only member of the Committee of Safety who took an immediate leadership role in the new government and probably was the most active public servant in Dole's Cabinet. He served as attorney general from 1893 until 1899 and was president of the Board of Health during the same period.

He was highly thought of by the royal family, and at her request, handled the disposition of Lili'uokalani's estate as one of her trustees. He also was one of the original Bishop Estate trustees, appointed by Pauahi herself.

"One of the most gratifying experiences of my life was that after the trying period which led up to the overthrow of the Monarchy and the withdrawal of Queen Liliuokalani, the Queen sent for me to prepare a will and deed of trust of her property and appointed me one of her trustees, together with Hon. C.P. Iaukea and Hon. A.S. Cleghorn," he wrote long after the Revolution.

An original trustee of Bishop Estate

Smith continued in the same letter:

"During the reign of King Kalakaua and later of Queen Lili'uokalani there was a gradual and increasing conflict between occupants of the throne and the judgment of responsible elements of the community. Leading citizens, both men and women, endeavored to exercise a restraining influence, but there seemed to be determination on the part of the rulers toward more centralized power invested in the reigning sovereign. The session of the '92 legislature, of which I was a member, continued in session from March to December with an intermission of only three weeks. During this session three cabinets were removed by acts of legislature. Both King Kalakaua and Queen Lili'uokalani had many estimable qualities and it was with a feeling of deep regret that the community was finally confronted with the issue which resulted in the termination of the monarchy."

Smith was friend of Queen

In later years he returned to his law practice and the business world, serving as president of Bishop Trust. He died in 1929.

Ed. Suhr

Smith outlined problems with last monarchs

Suhr replaced H.F. Glade, one of the original thirteen appointees, who had resigned shortly after his appointment. Glade was a senior officer at Hackfeld, a German-owned sugar factor and predecessor company of today's Amfac. He also was the German consul and resigned from the Committee because he decided it was not appropriate for someone in his position to be involved in planning a revolution against the government he was dealing with as a diplomat.

Suhr also was a German national working at Hackfeld and held German citizenship at the time of the Revolution.

Henry Waterhouse

Waterhouse was born in Tasmania of English descent and was a naturalized subject of Hawai'i. He came to the Kingdom in 1851 when he was six years old. He helped press for the Reform Constitution in 1887.

While not a missionary descendant, Waterhouse married Julia Hawkins Dimond, one of the seven children of Henry and Ann Maria Anner Dimond, who had arrived in Hawai'i in 1835 as members of a missionary company. His sister married one of the Dimond sons.

Henry Dimond was a bookbinder by trade and turned out hundreds of thousands of publications in the Hawaiian language. He left the mission in 1850 when his services were no longer needed, and was in the mercantile business in Honolulu until his death in 1895.

Waterhouse was one of the two Committee members to be interviewed by Blount—neither had American ties—and a review of that testimony today shows that Blount had a narrow focus in his interview. He wanted certain things confirmed—and interpreted what he heard as confirming them whether the testimony was clear on the point or not. For example, he interviewed Waterhouse on May 2, 1893, and clearly wanted Waterhouse to say that

Stevens had been premature in his recognition of the new government, that he had recognized it before it had taken control of the police station or the barracks. Waterhouse himself was not positive on the point. In his capacity with the Committee, he may have been unaware of all of the facts. One might expect that as a seasoned investigator with a list in hand of others more closely associated with leadership of the Revolution, Blount would have called for additional witnesses to more clearly resolve the point. He didn't, however. Here's a sample of the sparring with Waterhouse, from Blount's Report:

Blount asked Waterhouse leading questions

> "Q. You were then in possession of the Government building [at the time the Queen's surrender was received]?
>
> "A. We were.
>
> "Q. Any other buildings at the time?
>
> "A. Only the Government building at that time.
>
> "Q. How long after that before you got Mr. Stevens' letter of recognition?
>
> "A. It was shortly after the station house was given over.
>
> "Q. Are you not mistaken about that?
>
> "A. No; I believe I am not. I do not think I am.
>
> "Q. What about the barracks; had they been given up?
>
> "A. They had.
>
> "Q. Who were at the barracks?
>
> "A. Nowlein.(Ed.—Samuel Nowlein commanded the Queen's army of 272 men.)
>
> "Q. Where was Wilson?
>
> "A. He was at the station house.
>
> "Q. And he gave that up before you had notice of the recognition?

"A. According to my best knowledge and belief."

In spite of this confusing testimony, which conflicted with reports he had received from his Royalist witnesses, Blount did not interview other Committee of Safety members to clear up the matter. He merely interpreted Waterhouse's testimony as untrue. On May 6, 1893, after the Waterhouse interview, Blount wrote to Secretary of State Gresham that neither Waterhouse nor Bolte was telling the truth about Stevens' recognition time but that he, Blount, had confirmed that Stevens had recognized the Provisional Government about two hours before it had secured the police station and the barracks, where the Queen's troops were located. Blount added that he was ready to come home.

Blount failed to interview key Revolutionists

William C. Wilder

Wilder was a naturalized subject of Hawai'i, one of the four mainland Americans who was a Hawaiian subject. He owned the ship that Dole's government chartered to make its trip toward Washington on January 19, two days after the Revolution. He was one of the wealthiest members of the Committee.

He was editor of the *Pacific Commercial Advertiser* for a short period in the 1890s and served as president of the Republic's Senate in 1897.

William Wilder was editor, legislator

Charles Montague Cooke

Prominent among other residents of the community who played leadership roles in the changeover was C. Montague Cooke. Though not a member of the Committee of Safety, he and those whose names follow are among the 25 men generally conceded to have been in the forefront of the Revolution. Cooke was the son of missionaries Amos Starr and Juliette M. Cooke. He was born in 1849 at the Chiefs' Children's School, which his parents ran at the request of King Kamehameha III for the education of children of the royal families. When the mission closed in 1851 his father joined fellow-released-missionary S.N. Castle to form Castle & Cooke. Young Cooke attended Punahou and Amherst Agricultural College before returning to Honolulu to join Lewers & Dickson, a lumber importer that eventually became Lewers and Cooke. After the Revolution, he was one of the founders of Bank of Hawaii. He was appointed by Bernice Pauahi Bishop as a trustee of the Bishop Estate, appointed by herself. He married Anna Rice in 1874 and died in 1909.

Cooke was born at Chiefs' Children's School

Helped found Bank of Hawaii and later served as its president

Samuel Mills Damon

Damon, also not a member of the Committee but active in dealing with problems of the day, was a pioneer banker. He served as administrator of finances for both the Kingdom and the Provisional Government. He was 48 at the time of the Revolution and typifies business leaders of Hawai'i who were immensely sympathetic to the Monarchy but who lost faith in it during the reigns of Kalākaua and Lili'uokalani.

He was an adviser to Lili'uokalani and considered himself a close friend. It was Damon who went to her on the final day of the Revolution and advised her to yield. In 1887 he had served as finance minister for Kalākaua and served again from 1889-90 for the Queen. From 1893 to 1900, he served the Republic as finance minister. He was a member of the Privy Council of the Kingdom from 1884 to 1889. Damon also was an original trustee of Bernice Pauahi Bishop's foundation and of the Kamehameha

Damon was pioneer banker, adviser to Queen

Schools. He created Moanalua Gardens on land bequeathed him by Pauahi, and after his death in 1924, his will dedicated it for public use. Because of his close association with the former Queen, he represented her at Queen Victoria's diamond jubilee in London in 1912—she had attended the 50-year jubilee in 1887 with Queen Kapi'olani.

Damon told Queen she lost his support

The night before the overthrow, Damon went to the Queen and told her he had to leave her political party. He told her that while he'd always supported her, her recent actions were not acceptable. Russ reports in his two-volume history of the 1890s that Lili'uokalani urged Damon to take a position in the new government because even though it represented a political viewpoint in opposition to her, he might be able to help her by being involved—a friend in court, so to speak.

Captain James Anderson King

James King important business leader

King was another business leader who played a public role in the Revolution and the new government but did not serve as a member of the Committee of Safety. He was appointed one of the four members of the Executive Council of the Provisional Government and served as its minister of the interior as well as the Republic's. He was a pioneer of inter-island shipping, along with Wilder. His wife, Charlotte, was one-quarter Hawaiian, a descendant of one of the O'ahu chiefs who was killed by Kamehameha I when he conquered that island. The O'ahu chief, from Kāne'ohe, had a daughter, Mahi, whom Kamehameha in the traditions of the time "gave" to an American named Oliver Holmes, whom he favored. Holmes had arrived in Hawai'i in 1793 from Plymouth, Massachusetts, but fought with the losing O'ahu forces against Kamehameha. He switched allegiance after the battle, which Kamehameha approved of by giving him the Kāneʻohe chief's daughter. The son of James and Charlotte, Samuel Wilder King, was elected Hawaiʻi's delegate to Congress in 1934 and was appointed governor of Hawaiʻi by President Eisenhower in 1953; he served until 1957. A grandson, Samuel P. King Sr., is a highly regarded, retired federal judge in Honolulu.

Peter Cushman Jones

Jones, a community leader with ties to the Monarchy, broke off that relationship in dismay in 1893. He was so concerned about the future of his community that he switched allegiance and committed himself to the Revolution, even though he felt that switching in the face of his earlier service as the Queen's finance minister would put him in great personal danger. Asked by Charles Carter and Crister Bolte to take the post of minister of finance in the new Provisional Government, he agreed to do so if Dole would become its president, but not without reiterating his concerns for their safety.

Jones concerned about future of community, overcame fear

He told his wife of his concern: "It is more than probable that the Queen's party will not submit without fighting, and the chances are that I will get shot."

He reported her reply: "If you do get shot I can give you up, for I feel it to be your duty to take part in this move. The country needs you at this time and if you lose your life it will be in the discharge of your duty."[44]

He was born in Boston and arrived in Honolulu in 1857 at the age of 20 with sixteen cents in his pockets. In 1871 he was a partner in C. Brewer and became its president in 1883. He was an extremely religious man. He built Pālama Chapel, out

Wife told him the country needed him

of which grew Pālama Settlement. He was treasurer and a trustee of Punahou for many years.

In his later years as president of C. Brewer, he served at the same time as founding president of the Bank of Hawaii. He and his son also founded The Hawaiian Safe Deposit and Investment Company, predecessor company of Hawaiian Trust Co. and today's Pacific Century Trust. He was a deacon of Central Union Church.

When the mass meeting of 1887 was held to bring about the Reform Constitution that reined in Kalākaua, P.C. Jones was the chairman.

Jones a strongly religious businessman

In 1892 he was appointed minister of finance by Lili'uokalani. His appointment by the Queen as a member of her Cabinet in 1892 along with three other members of the community was hailed by people from all parties as a sound move by the Monarchy. The so-called Jones-Wilcox Cabinet was highly respected and restored needed confidence in members of the community who had serious doubts about Lili'uokalani's government.

Part of respected Cabinet

But when this Cabinet refused to push for the lottery and opium bills and cautioned against her plans to promulgate a new Constitution, she ousted and replaced all four on January 12, 1893, two days before the Revolution began.

Jones was 56 at the time of the Revolution and lived until 1922.

James Francis Morgan

Morgan was another Honolulu community leader who had become disillusioned with the Queen and played a role in the Revolution. He was born in New York City in 1862 and came to Hawai'i at the age of three. He started working at 12 at an auction house, E.P. Adams Auction Co., and eventually became the sole owner. After the Revolution, he served as a member of Dole's Advisory Council. He was in real estate and was an organizer of the Honolulu Stock and Bond Exchange, serving as its president. A grandson, James F. Morgan, Jr., manager of several sugar plantations for Alexander & Baldwin, served nine years as chairman of The Contemporary Museum, guiding it to its Makiki Heights location in 1988.

Morgan was on Dole's Advisory Council

Edward Davies Tenny

Edward Davies Tenney came to Honolulu in 1877 at age 18. He started in sugar at Hilo, came to Oʻahu and by 1880 was a junior clerk at Castle & Cooke. Eventually he became president and general manager of the firm. In 1917 he was president of Matson Navigation while still president of C&C. Dole appointed him to the Provisional Government Advisory Council following the Revolution. Tenney married Rose Williams Makee in 1889.

Tenney was also on Advisory Council

Alexander Young

Young came to Hawaiʻi in 1865 and set up a foundry and machine shop in Hilo. He moved to Honolulu, bought an interest in Honolulu Iron Works and invested in sugar. He was also an interior minister after the Revolution.

Young was born in Scotland, married Ruth Pearce in England and went to America in 1860 before heading for Hilo. He was a mechanical engineer and a member of the Monarchy's House of Nobles from 1887 to 1892. Dole appointed him a member of the Advisory Council of the Provisional Government in 1893.

Alexander Young served in House of Nobles

In 1900, he built the Alexander Young Hotel

in downtown Honolulu. In 1905 he acquired the Moana and later the Royal Hawaiian Hotel, which at that time was adjacent to 'Iolani Palace. He died in 1910.

Young built hotel downtown

These were the kinds of men who ousted Queen Lili'uokalani to achieve a stable government for their Island nation. They certainly weren't radical interlopers out for personal gain. The next chapter, a vignette, gives a picture of their mindsets as they attained their first objective, a bloodless Revolution. With the Revolution behind them, the minds of these former Annexation Club members turned to their long-range goal, Annexation itself. In Chapter

Ultimate goal: Annexation

Eight, we will review the fifty-year road to that objective. Before that, in Chapter Seven, we take a look at the two investigations that attempted to set the record straight on what happened in 1893. They weren't able to do so, at least to everyone's satisfaction.

$\mathcal{T}$he Old Order Changes

tories are told and pictures are drawn for us by critics of the Revolution portraying a bunch of bad guys plotting with malice aforethought to viciously, spitefully overthrow the Queen and seize control of the government. Evil motives are suggested. It is as unpleasant a picture as it is inaccurate. It is a play on emotions, and it stirs unjustified reactions in its viewers.

No malice or spite drove Revolutionists

If you read the proceedings of the Provisional Government, beginning minutes after the proclamation was read announcing the revolutionary takeover of Hawai'i's government, you can draw different pictures.

Imagine this group of men, for they were all men, all white men, we cannot change that. But being men and white, in their time and place, does not mean that they were bad men. They were men concerned with the moral, ethical and economic future of the Islands that were their home.

Jones thought he might be shot

What they did was no lark. Each must have been fearful in his heart. We read in the Morgan Report that P.C. Jones thought the Queen and her supporters would fight, "and chances are that I will get shot." His wife believed that change in the government was necessary. "If you lose your life it will be in the discharge of your duty," she said.

The proclamation was read on the front steps of the government building about 2 p.m. Tuesday in full view of the palace across King Street, and it must have been a tense and frightening moment. Word had gone out through the community that everyone should come out to back this audacious move, but the expected supporters arrived late and in dribbles. Sanford Dole, in his *Memoirs*, recalled only a single volunteer was there when he and the others arrived to take over the building and read the proclamation. It had been drafted that morning by Thurston from his sickbed up in Nu'uanu, where he lay felled, apparently by the same flu-like virus that hit Castle and a number of other members of the takeover team, as well as Stevens and various government workers.

Thurston drafted proclamation from sickbed

Did the paper Henry Cooper read from tremble in his hands? The Revolutionists had heard that the Queen and her Cabinet planned to stop them by force. Did they look this way and that, waiting to be beset upon by men with guns? As it turned out, the Queen's Cabinet did not follow through on its plan to counter the takeover.

Carter asked for help from troop commander

Charles Carter, however, was worried. He went across the street to where the commander of the American troops stood (the troops were out of sight, behind a building, with their arms stacked) and asked for a guard. The commander replied, "I remain passive." This same commander, W.T. Swinburne, had told Carter the day before that if the Queen "calls upon me to preserve order, I am going to do it." Two years later, in the Queen's unsuccessful attempt at a counter-revolution, Carter was to die in the gunfire at Diamond Head.

Samuel M. Damon reported the American

troops were leaning against a picket fence, their arms stacked, not even at ready. This shook him. "I could not imagine why we were there without being supported by American troops . . . . We were not supported in any way."

Following the proclamation, the men of the new executive and advisory councils gathered in the government building. They didn't throw a party or toast each other on their good luck to have made it thus far without incident. There would be no jocular mood. There was no gleeful rubbing of palms. One might imagine them, a sheen of sweat on their brows, dressed in suits appropriate for the occasion but unfit for the climate. Nervous. They might have looked one to the other almost in surprise. Yet the men got down to business, the business of government.

Revolutionists got down to business of governing

Their first acts were out of concern for public safety. Protecting the people of the Islands fell solely on them now. They had a moral obligation to prevent blood from running in the streets. They called for all supporters in the community to bring arms and ammunition to the government building "as soon as possible in order that efficient and complete protection of the life and property, and the public peace, may immediately and efficiently be put into operation."

First concern was for public safety

They didn't want to use guns, but they knew they needed to be prepared. At any moment, a mob could burst through the doors with guns and clubs. It had happened down the street some years earlier when Queen Emma's supporters erupted at the old courthouse against the election of Kalākaua. To prevent trouble from brewing in an unstable moment, these men of the new Provisional Government declared martial law and suspended liquor sales.

A mob could burst in anytime

Sent for former Cabinet

It was still early afternoon. They sent word to the four members of the Queen's most recent Cabinet to come to the government building for a talk. Two, Parker and Cornwell, did so. These two said they didn't intend to offer any resistance but neither would they give up without conferring with the other ex-Cabinet members.

No resistance from Cabinet

As gentlemen would, the Provisional Government officers allowed the men to return to the station house and even agreed to send Crister Bolte, a member of the Committee of Safety, and Damon, a respected longtime adviser to the Queen, with them. Both sides wanted to avoid bloodshed.

Now the two other ex-Cabinet members said they didn't wish to offer resistance either, but didn't want to surrender without "some understanding with the ex-Queen," the proceedings report.

Perhaps while the Cabinet ministers were over at the palace, one of the Revolutionists might have attempted a joke, maybe about Thurston—sick in bed at home. They might have joshed about how Thurston got them into this, now where was he when they needed him. Or maybe there was no pause for even mild humor.

Queen said she was surrendering to U.S.

The former Cabinet members and a few other of her advisers met with their Queen and she agreed to surrender under protest. She ordered her men to give up the station house without resistance. Without negotiation on the matter, because only Damon from the new Provisional Government was present while she met with her Cabinet, and as Dole pointed out later, he had not been sent to negotiate, the Queen was allowed to file a letter stating she was surrendering to the superior forces of the United States. The phrasing did not correctly characterize the situation, but what did it matter—the Queen could write anyone or say anything she wanted to, and they had successfully avoided bloodshed. But her letter would rise to haunt them later.

Meanwhile the new government was lining up the support or acceptance of foreign delegations, including the United States. Of course, these men hoped their Provisional Government would be short-lived and their service as its leaders would be brief. They believed Hawai'i's best interest would come with U.S. territorial protection, Annexation. That would not come for a number of years. That evening, they continued to meet and decided to charter the ship *Claudine* to send a delegation to Washington, D.C., offering that Hawai'i be annexed as a U.S. territory.

Delegation sent to Washington

The leadership of the Provisional Government met again, first thing the next morning. One might imagine that a heavy weight rested on them. Yesterday, despite its tension, had been marked by the euphoria that comes with success. But today, there was a nation to run, agitated and worried people to calm. They borrowed $1,000 from Bishop and Co. because George E. Smithies, who possessed the key and the combination to the government safe, was also sick abed, and they needed some money until he could get up. In those days, in order to forestall more severe illnesses, people took to their beds when flu-like symptoms struck.

Revolutionists borrowed $1,000 to run government

The British minister requested that his dispatches be sent to the United States on the *Claudine*. The Queen requested her letters be carried by the same ship. Both were opposed to Annexation. Imagine the discussion. Might the Advisory Council members all have been in favor, or might one or two have said no, why should we carry the Queen's protest? But the motion was carried, and her request as well

They agreed to carry Queen's letters of protest to Washington

as the British request was granted. These men who are being recast as monsters then voted to allow the ex-Queen to draw her usual amount from the treasury at the end of the month.

Would not take Queen's delegation

But then Damon came and said the Queen wanted permission to send a delegation of her own aboard the *Claudine* to Washington to protest to the U.S. government. One might imagine an outburst from the Council members. This was going too far. "It was moved and carried that this should not be allowed," reads the report.

The Council disbanded the Queen's guards, but provided them with salaries to the end of the month. They sent an envoy to Lili'uokalani to ask her if she desired a guard, and if she did, they'd designate sixteen Hawaiians to serve her.

Concern over Kalaupapa

What about the people of Kalaupapa? The "lepers" they were called then; the name Hansen's disease was not yet in use. The Council sent the president of the Board of Health to Molokai to explain the political changes to the people of Kalaupapa.

It had been another full day of government business. There were no serious problems in the city, although rumors swirled every which way. Things were settling down quickly. The next day, only two days after the Revolution, the Council found it safe enough to reopen the saloons for a large part of the day.

And so the proceedings of the new government go on. They are not vindictive. In every circumstance, they appear to take the higher road.

Royalists agreed resistance was useless

A report came in that Lili'uokalani's closest supporters had decided resistance was useless; that they would attempt a plebiscite among Hawaiians in an effort to get annexed to Great Britain. Rumor had it that the former Queen believed she would be able to get a larger income from Great Britain.

The new government watched the newspapers for inaccuracies or potential trouble. The editor of the Royalist *Bulletin* was called before the Council. A story had run in that paper that said the Provisional Government would allow the Queen's representatives to travel on the *Claudine*. The editor promised a retraction.

Media corrections

Ka Leo o Ka Lāhui, one of the Hawaiian language newspapers, printed an account alleging that a resolution had been introduced by the new government that would require all Hawaiians to be removed from government employment. The newspaper suggested this was the treatment Hawaiians might expect from the *haole*. The Printing Committee was directed to interview J.E. Bush, the Native Hawaiian editor, and "inform him of the falsity of his report." The committee did so, reminding him of the proclamation that had been read and posted, and which clearly stated that only the Queen, her Cabinet and Marshal Wilson had been asked to resign and that all other government workers had been asked to "continue their functions." A retraction was demanded. Instead, Bush wrote further that it was only Dole's vote that had blocked the anti-Hawaiian resolution. Again, Bush was questioned. This time he said the failure to correct the misinformation had been accidental and promised to correct it in the next issue.

And so it went. The Council dealt, day in and day out, with juggling the business of running the governmental affairs of the Islands and keeping a careful watch that no problem would erupt into bloody dispute in the streets. These men believed their job was temporary; they believed their envoys to Washington would send them word of Annexation to that country. They would do the best they could to

Believed Annexation would come soon

keep Hawai'i at peace and move forward until Annexation happened, and then return to their businesses or professions. None of them wanted a permanent government job.

It would be a long wait, but they didn't know that yet.

$\mathcal{T}$he Investigators

mericans were captivated by the Revolution in Hawai'i as both sides sent emissaries to Washington to seek administration backing. Popular opinion seemed to favor the Revolutionists but there were plenty of voices raised on behalf of the Royalists and it made good copy for months in newspapers across the country.

Two U.S. investigations

Washington officials conducted two investigations of the Revolution, both by Democrats. Former Congressman James H. Blount of Georgia was dispatched to Hawai'i in secret in March 1893 by President Cleveland to make an investigation on the ground. The other was ordered by a Senate resolution in January 1894 and was conducted by the U.S. Senate Committee on Foreign Relations, chaired by Sen. John T. Morgan of Alabama.

The Blount Report in the spring of 1893 was based on secret interviews, unsworn statements and Blount's acknowledged arbitrary selection of witnesses. His report charged that U.S. Minister John Stevens and U.S. naval forces had conspired with the Revolutionists in violation of international law, enabling success of the Revolution. That charge, though not supported by any subsequent hearing,

Blount's Report arbitrary, secret

was the basis for Cleveland's efforts in November 1893 to restore the Monarchy through his new minister to Hawai'i, A.S. Willis.[45] Cleveland also made similar charges against Stevens in September 1893 on recommendations by Blount, though the report itself was not released until several months after the president made his charges and did not reach the Provisional Government until December. The Provisional Government was given no time to comment or react before Cleveland made public his charges, a diplomatic breach that was highly criticized by the new Hawaiian government as well as critics of the Cleveland administration.

Dole had no chance to comment on Blount Report

The other investigation, the Morgan Report, was launched in early 1894 after the Blount Report became public. All of the Morgan Committee evidence was based on sworn statements and its hearings were open to anyone who wished to testify. It exonerated Stevens and the U.S. troops by a vote of five to four among the Senate committee members and held out the hope of Annexation.

Both investigations were conducted by politicians experienced in foreign relations and in conducting hearings. Blount had been chairman of the Committee on Foreign Relations of the U.S. House. Morgan was the current chairman of the Senate Committee on Foreign Relations. Testimony in the Morgan hearings hinted that many believed Blount was sent by Cleveland with a predetermined agenda, which Blount denied. He testified before the Morgan Committee that he had been sent only to gather facts and had no contact with the Queen except for two formal meetings, one when he arrived and one when he left, each only several minutes in length. There is no doubt, however, that he made recommendations regarding restoration of the Monarchy and censuring

Two reports, opposite findings

Stevens. And in spite of only the two meetings, his sentiments were carried to the Queen and her reaction was sought by him through others. As an experienced Washingtonian, he must have known that when he talked to her close associates, Cabinet members and friends, reports would be going back to her, and he used these channels. She details many of these messages in her diaries. In the period from his arrival on March 29 to October 16, 1893, Lili'uokalani makes a dozen or more references to assurances coming to her from close advisers who had met with Blount that "he will take care of everything." As early as April 10, three days after Paul Neumann, her attorney and emissary to Washington, had returned to Honolulu, she writes about "good news" he brought, that he spoke personally with Cleveland and "was promised justice. [Neumann] wants to impress on me two things, [that I stress my] love of my people, and [my concern for] their future welfare—that their rights be restored and be maintained. Heard that in two weeks everything will be settled, then he (Ed.—Blount) is going to enjoy a good time. Fraulein (Ed.—her personal psychic about whom more is related in Chapter Three) says between the 21st and 25th I will be restored to the throne."

Ex-Queen's diaries say Blount will help

Fortuneteller predicted return to throne

On May 28, she reports hearing from Mary Carter, wife of her long-time, closest supporter, J.O. Carter, "that Mr. Spreckels said plainly there is nothing for him to do now but to help restore me to the throne, that it would be well for me to appoint a new Cabinet, proclaim a new Constitution, proclaim martial law, etc. Mr. Spreckels will call on me tomorrow morning."

Spreckels expected to help return her to throne

The May 29 entry must have left the Queen in a very good mood. "Mr. [Sam] Parker (Ed.—her ex-minister of foreign affairs) came and [had] breakfast with me, informed me that Mr. Spreckels would be the means of putting me back on the throne (Ed.—through various moves that she outlines). Mr. Claus Spreckels called at quarter to 12 noon and told me all that Mr. Parker had stated and proposes to have Mr. Antone Rosa as Attorney General when I go back . . . he said he will stay until everything is settled. Says that when he draws money from them they will fall to pieces (Ed.—the Monarchy government had incurred a huge debt to Spreckels that was coming due, but Dole and his advisers managed to raise the money privately and paid him off, thus thwarting this maneuver.) **They will not require guns—he and Blount will do everything** (Ed.—emphasis added). They must suffer those missionaries for overthrowing my government, and their property must pay for all."

Spreckels advised ex-Queen Blount would restore her

Spreckels obviously was reflecting more than a casual conversation with Blount when he discussed whether guns would be needed or not. And the Queen, with her reference to the missionaries, was reflecting the erroneous political propensity for blaming everything on the missionaries. We know there were no missionaries involved in the overthrow—just three descendants of missionaries on the Committee of Safety and an additional handful of descendants among the hundreds of volunteers.

Further evidence of an open and informed relationship between Blount and the Queen's supporters is confirmed in diary entries for May 12 and 22 dealing with a petition opposing Annexation, which was made a part of the Blount Report.

On May 12, the Queen notes that "Mr. Blount asked Mr. Parker what we were doing among the people. He knew there was a memorial [petition] being got ready but why are they so long about it. He was aware of the untruthfulness of the statements of the other side."

On May 22, she notes that "Mr. Parker brought news that Mr. Claus Spreckels was taking a memorial around amongst the principal firms in town to take their signatures expressing their opinion against annexation . . ."

Blount encouraged ex-Queen

Blount himself had told her, she notes on April 24, that "he had no authority to act in anything." In the same entry, however, she notes he told her he had withdrawn the troops and raised the Hawaiian Flag, and she adds cryptically, "but whatever we did for ourselves he had nothing to do with."

In between her comments about encouragement from Blount, she makes many references to signing commissions, discussing Cabinet appointments, making other preparations for becoming Queen again "after the restoration." She knew where Blount was headed.

Blount recommended ministers to Lili'uokalani

On August 5, after Blount's second official— and farewell—meeting with her, she notes that "He wished I would select such men as J.O.C. (Ed.—J.O. Carter) and E.C. Macfarlane to help me in the administration of the government.

"When I told him that the P.G.s (Ed.—Provisional Government people) had threatened to take my life, should news be received of my restoration, what ought I to do? He said is not Admiral J.S. Skerrett here, and also the British and other commissioners."

James H. Wodehouse, British commissioner and consul general to Hawai'i and a vocal opponent of U.S. Minister John Stevens and Annexation to the United States, was a frequent visitor to the Queen and a frequent social contact with Blount during his stay. He is mentioned many times in the diaries with

British agent was emissary between ex-Queen & Blount

comments on the restoration theme and her personal safety. She writes on June 5, after recording details of a visit from Wodehouse, "[He] said he and Blount would act together." The context seems to be in terms of protecting her.

Her entry for September 20 appears to confirm this. She writes about the concern of various of her friends for her safety, then adds, "I have such confidence [in] what Mr. Blount said when he went away that I have no fears."

Lili'uokalani got messages from Blount

On another subject, on August 15, the Queen was visited by Archibald S. Cleghorn, father of Princess Ka'iulani, a close family friend and brother-in-law whom she had appointed governor of O'ahu. She writes: "[He] asked why I did not make arrangements for E.C. Macfarlane to go to the United States as such had been the instructions from Mr. Blount. I told him I was not aware that Mr. Blount had said so. We then made arrangements for his trip." Macfarlane arrived in Washington on September 10 and met secretly with Blount and Secretary of State Gresham. Blount actually came to Macfarlane's hotel and warned him not to tell anyone about it.

Macfarlane makes secret mission to Washington

The reason for Macfarlane's secret mission to Washington becomes clear in the Queen's diary entry for October 10, Macfarlane having just returned. (At this date in Washington, Gresham had completed his study of the Blount Report and had privately told several people that the Queen must be restored to her throne, but Blount's recommendations were not made public until over a month later, November 16. The Provisional Government did not get a copy until late in December). Macfarlane obviously had a very good relationship with Gresham. The Queen writes:

"Mr. E.C. Macfarlane called to pay his

respects. He reached Washington 10th Sept. Mr. Blount called on him and spent two hours—was told not to let any one know that he had seen him except J.O. Carter. Asked how everything was in Hawai'i—was told everything was in peace & quiet. He was glad to hear it, he was much afraid disturbance would arise, but it was wonderful what power the Queen had over her people, and it was the best thing for us. It has been the main chance of our success. He (Ed.—Blount) said within five or six weeks from now Mr. Willis & Mr. Mills will be [in Hawai'i] and Mr. Willis will have his instructions. They will first call on you and Mr. [J.O.] Carter."

Macfarlane relayed messages

This was well before the Willis mission became public. Ellis Mills, about to be appointed new U.S consul general in Hawai'i, took the notes for Blount's interviews as well as Willis' crucial later interviews with the Queen.

The diary entry continues: "He (Ed.—Blount) must not be seen or known to have called on Mr. M (Ed.—Macfarlane). That next day he (Ed.—Macfarlane) should call on Mr. Gresham and say nothing about him (Ed.—Blount). He (Ed.—Blount) would advise him not to stay long in Washington, for himself he would immediately leave as his steps were being dogged, and he must go back to Georgia. He was annoyed the P.G.s should mention his wife's name." (Blount, who did not interview Dole but who met formally with him to present his credentials— which said nothing about his mission—also had several arguments with Dole while he was in Honolulu, most of them over minor or technical matters. One was a serious disagreement involving freedom of the press and the powers of the Provisional Government

Blount kept mission secret

Blount didn't interview Dole

versus those of the U.S. representative, Blount. In that case, the Provisional Government had charged Charles Nordhoff, a reporter with the *New York Herald*, with libel for publishing a totally erroneous story claiming several members of the Provisional Government Advisory Council had signed the lottery petition during the last legislative session. The government wished to banish him. Passage of the lottery bill had been one of the reasons for the Revolution and the Provisional Government had repealed it as one of its first actions. Nordhoff, who was a staunch supporter of the Royalists, was trying to paint the "P.G.s" as hypocrites. Blount, who had spent many hours with Nordhoff during his investigation, intervened and Dole backed off.)[46]

Erroneous story in N.Y. Herald

The Queen's diary entry for October 10 continues: "Macfarlane met Secretary Gresham. Was immediately ushered into his presence while all the others had to wait. From one to five their interview lasted. Mr. M. was allowed to say all he had to say without interruption. Found Mr. Gresham a man of great shrewdness and broad mind & great intelligence. He found that Mr. Gresham seemed to have great interest in our cause, asked about the Queen & her capability, again about taking an election, whether there would be equal voting. (Ed.—Gresham apparently was wondering about a popular election for a new monarch.) Mac said no, it would simply end in the Queen & no other, and why no other: because we would have no other . . . Mac met Mr. Mills & dined with him."

Gresham shrewdness

These events suggest pretty clearly that Blount, if he ever had been a neutral "fact finder," had become deeply committed to the effort to reinstate the Queen—she knew a lot more about U.S. strategies than did the Provisional Government.

The Queen's diary entries disclose little for the critical period of November 16 to December 23 when Willis was engaged in his secret meetings with her, trying to bring about the restoration of her throne. He had first to get her to agree to comply with Cleveland's demand for amnesty for the Revolutionists, which she turned down flatly on November 16. According to Willis and Mills, who was taking notes behind a screen, she said she would have the Revolutionists beheaded. With no cable to discuss this enormous problem with Gresham, Willis was not able to get back to her until December 16. By then he had new instructions that Cleveland would withdraw his support if she did not agree to amnesty.[47] J.O. Carter was present at the December 16 meeting, and again she refused to bend. On December 18, however, she met again with Willis and Carter and had changed her mind completely. Now she was offering amnesty. But it was too late. Cleveland had already turned the matter over to Congress. Willis, however, did not yet know of this and on December 20 he met with leaders of the Provisional Government and presented Cleveland's extraordinary demand that they restore the Monarchy. An entire plan, new Cabinet, new Constitution, the signing of eleven commissions for new ministers, etc., had been worked out by the Queen and her advisers, although Willis did not agree with all of the names she had submitted as new Cabinet members and officers. It never became a problem because on December 23 the Provisional Government said no to the entire matter in the "extraordinary correspondence" detailed in Chapter Five.

For several months the Provisional Government wrangled with the United States over the breaches of diplomatic protocol involved in Willis

Lili'uokalani said she'd behead Revolution leaders

Cleveland turned matter over to Congress

Queen had plans ready for restoration

Provisional Government did not yield

183

clandestinely operating within the boundaries of a recognized foreign country, plotting the downfall of its government. Meanwhile, the Queen for several months in her diaries continued to write of her developing plans for Cabinet members, meetings with Wodehouse, the British consul, etc., but her brief association with Blount, Willis, Gresham and Cleveland was over.

Going back to the Blount Report as a research source about the Revolution, it's obvious he cared little about events that had led to its happening. Kuykendall described his report as a "lawyer's brief, making the best possible case for the queen and against Stevens." The historian said the Morgan Report "presented an equally effective case for the Provisional Government and Stevens, and against the Queen."

Blount's Report described as lawyer's brief

Blount's interviews with the only two Committee of Safety members he chose to include, neither an American, show his questions were directed toward determining when Stevens had recognized the new government, not what had caused the community to revolt. Blount steered clear from formally interviewing anyone who might be construed as a U.S. citizen, but nevertheless he managed to blame the United States for the Revolution's success.

Blount's Report wrong on Cabinet's actions

His report, too, was put together in a less-than-neutral manner, quite aside from his one-sided selection of witnesses. He stated, based on interviews only with the Queen's Cabinet members, that they had been approached by L.A. Thurston to get their help, rather than the other way around. The Provisional Government did not get a copy of the report until December, after which Thurston wrote a letter explaining that the Cabinet had approached him, giving the Queen her first knowledge of her

Cabinet's treasonous idea. It is a measure of her confidence in the parties that she wrote in her diary that day that Colburn and the Cabinet were the treasonous men—she did not question Thurston's account.

Blount also referred to American members of the Committee of Safety as persons of "foreign origin," and in the case of the Hawaiian-born members such as Castle, Smith and Thurston, "Hawaiians of foreign origin." Here he was gathering facts for his American president and he fails to inform him that most of these key figures were of American origin, the children of U.S. citizens, or U.S. citizens themselves.

One of the most influential, concerned and knowledgeable members of the community about the background that led to revolt was P.C. Jones, who had been finance minister in the Cabinet ousted on January 12 by the Queen.

Jones went to see Blount when Blount arrived in Honolulu and told him that as he was intimately acquainted with the government during the last two months of the Monarchy, "I may be able to give some information in regard to our affairs, and I shall be pleased to give my statement if you desire it." Blount told Jones he'd be pleased to have an interview with him, and would let him know when he would be ready to do it. In fact, Jones had a statement drawn up and sworn to, but Blount never contacted him, "though [I am] informed and believe that other persons suggested to Mr. Blount that he secure the statement."

Jones' statement ended up being submitted to the U.S. Senate Committee on Foreign Relations, the Morgan Committee. Unlike many of the statements accepted by Blount, and his interviews, every statement accepted by the Morgan Committee was sworn

Blount gave president skewed information

Blount didn't interview key Cabinet ministers

Jones statement submitted to Morgan group

to and every witness testified in public and under oath.

Jones wanted it clear that the roots of the Revolution were not shallow, but dated back to the beginning of Kalākaua's reign. Extracts from his testimony follow:

"No King ever had better prospects for a peaceful and successful reign than did Kalākaua, and if he had made a proper use of his right and powers he might have made his reign a prosperous one.

King was corrupt

"He seemed to be wholly corrupt, and his influence was one which had its effect on the mass of the native people. Not satisfied with [his ability to appoint] (Ed.—before the Reform Constitution) the House of Nobles, he interfered in the election of representatives by using liquor which was taken from the custom-house duty free and promising offices under his patronage.

"He dismissed more than one cabinet for nothing, and in some instances sent messages to their houses in the middle of the night asking for their resignations, while others whom he assured had his implicit confidence he discharged a few hours after.

Kalākaua always in debt

"Kalākaua surrounded himself with men of bad character and gave himself up to habits unbecoming a King. He was always in debt and resorted to measures for raising money that were wholly dishonorable for any man, much more a King.

"The Legislature of 1890 paid up his debts and issued bonds to the amount of $95,000 to meet his obligations, pledging the income of the Crown lands at the rate of $20,000 a year to meet these bonds, but when his sister came to the throne she immediately repudiated the pledge given by her brother, and now this debt has to be born by the

State, only $5,000 being received on this account.

"When he died the country had much hope for the better state of things from his sister Lili'uokalani [but] she evidently had not profited by the Revolution of 1887 and thought herself to be sufficiently strong to get back the power taken from her brother . . . . She was more cunning, more determined, and no coward as he had been."

Jones felt the time for him to break with the Queen had come. In his affidavit, he told the Morgan Committee: "I was fully convinced that if ever it was necessary to take a decided stand for representative and responsible government it was at this time. While the Queen had professed to take back all she had said and done about a new constitution I felt it was only to gain time to make better preparations to carry out her designs and . . . I felt it was my duty . . . to do what I could to assist in putting down a form of government that was oppressive and corrupt . . . ."

Jones saw need for responsible government

Jones detailed in his affidavit the bribery and other tactics of the Queen and her cohorts in bringing about passage of the lottery and opium bills, removing the Jones-Wilcox Cabinet from office and appointing a new group of four to replace them. The new Cabinet members, all opposed politically to the Jones-Wilcox Cabinet, were expected to support the Queen in her efforts to gain new powers. They did back her in her successful efforts to pass the lottery and opium bills, but after much thinking and discussion, they decided to oppose her attempt to promulgate a new Constitution. Inasmuch as they represented various elements of the Hawaiian community opposed to the Annexation Club membership, it is clear she did not have the full support of her own people in her quest for new powers for the Monarchy.

Jones detailed bribery

Queen didn't have full support

Blount apparently failed to get this insight. There is no doubt that he made his recommendations and assessments about the character and intentions of leaders of the Revolution without talking with them or listening to their testimony. Committee members' relationships and conversations with Stevens would seem to be critical to making a finding of conspiracy, as he charged. His failure to interview key individuals is a fairly obvious indication he had already decided that Stevens and the Republican administration of President Harrison were to bear the blame. At the very least, he failed to secure information and evidence that normally would be the basis for such a finding.

Blount failed to get key information

A generally favorable essay on Blount contained in a carefully researched 1988 work, *The New South Faces the World*, by the noted southern historian Tennant S. McWilliams, indicates Blount approached his task with a bias built-in by his upbringing and political background.

McWilliams, professor and chairman of the history department at the University of Alabama, had this to say about Blount and his mission to investigate America's role in the Hawaiian Revolution:

Blount: condemnation of Revolution

"One of the first scholars to examine Blount's mission, Julius W. Pratt, suggested that the special commissioner—a former Georgia congressman and former Confederate—acted in a most peculiar way. Instead of reflecting the 'southern' racial and economic support for expansionism characteristic of the loud-talking Senator Morgan, Blount recommended that the president condemn Americans involved in the Hawaiian Revolution and reinstate Queen Lili'uokalani as the rightful royal authority over the Islands. An assessment of the Georgian's developing career, however, and a close analysis of his Hawaiian investigation suggests that Blount and many other southerners could hardly have thought any different-ly." They were simply opposed to expansionism and intervention by the U.S. government in any fashion.

McWilliams agrees it was Blount's known sentiment against Annexation—and the support of three of his southern friends in Cleveland's Cabinet who were similarly disposed—that was perhaps the most important factor in his selection for the mission. He did not disappoint, though as McWilliams insightfully points out, his report apparently went too far even for Cleveland.

Writes McWilliams:

"Blount's document did not find overwhelm-ing applause in Washington, D.C., nor in many other places in America. For the 'paramount' special com-missioner had done more than nail a conspiracy on the Republican foreign policy of 1893. He had docu-mented the case against *any* American administra-tion . . . ever annexing Hawai'i. This was not neces-sarily what Cleveland had had in mind."

When credibility of the Morgan Report is weighed, its supporters are influenced favorably by the more than 800 pages packed with testimony and information from more than 50 witnesses: Hawaiian historians, leaders of the Revolution and leaders of the military forces landed by the United States, most of whom testified in line with the findings of the committee. Supporters feel the sworn testimony of that many persons before a committee composed of interrogators from both sides of the question should be given more weight than the findings of a single individual with a known bias.

The Morgan Report has been criticized because the chairman asked leading questions at times, as the record shows, and the report did not

Blount went too far, even for Cleveland

Credibility of Morgan Report enhanced by 800 pages of information

receive the unanimous agreement of all nine committee members. In testimony at the Morgan hearings, Blount, too, was accused of asking leading questions. But because Blount's questioning was done in secret, no one knows the extent of such questioning practices. We know from other testimony that he did not seek the opinions of those in favor of Annexation, or with American connections, or involved in the leadership of the Revolution. We do not know for sure what testimony he received but did not include in his report nor even what questions he asked. There is no explanation either as to why he excluded witnesses whose commitments to Annexation were well known or who had firsthand knowledge of decisions made by the Revolutionists or causes for the Revolution itself.

Valuable witnesses excluded

He interviewed one former member of the revolutionary military force, Fred W. Wundenberg, who told Blount that without the support of U.S. troops the Revolution would not have been successful. Blount accepted this as fact without interviewing anyone on the other side. Wundenberg, a part-Hawaiian, resigned from the revolutionary force a few days after the Queen's surrender and when his testimony to Blount became known in December, he was branded a liar and a traitor.[48] The *Star* labeled him a "perjured and lottery-besmirched" Royalist spy. He was fired from his position as clerk of the Supreme Court after a public outcry. The *Star* said he had withdrawn from the revolutionary movement because he was disgruntled at not being appointed marshal. Blount treated him as though he had been in the high command of the revolutionary force and made no mention of his having been a turncoat.

Wundenberg called perjurer

The Blount Report had one signature, his own. The Morgan Report was the signed opinion of nine senators, with two minority reports split along party lines and covering disagreements on only a few points, detailed later in this book.

Witness after witness at the Morgan hearing testified about faults in the Blount Report. Either he had failed to talk with them or he disregarded facts they had presented to him. In the case of Crister Bolte, a German citizen and one of the two members of the Committee of Safety whom Blount did talk to, Blount's questions were challenged as leading or unfair. As Bolte stated, ". . . during this interview, on several occasions, [I] objected to the method employed by said Blount, and remonstrated with him that he did not put his questions fairly. . . . Said Blount asked his questions in a very leading form, and . . . on several occasions when [I] attempted to more fully express his meaning, said Blount would change the subject and proceed to other matters."[49]

Criticism of Blount Report

Strangely, as noted above, Blount did not interview any of the leaders of the Committee of Safety although all offered to meet with him. As mentioned earlier, he labeled its three missionary-connected members, Thurston, Smith and Castle, "Hawaiians of foreign origin" without mentioning the American citizenship of their parents. He made his charges that they and the other Committee members had conspired with Stevens without input from any of them, although all were readily available to him. In an affidavit filed with the Morgan Committee, the entire Committee of Safety, under oath, stated:

Blount ignored leaders of Revolution

"That we are the persons appointed as a citizens' committee of safety, at Honolulu, in January last.

"That neither prior to nor after our appointment as such committee, did we or

Sworn statement denied complicity of Stevens

either of us, individually or collectively, have any agreement or understanding, directly or indirectly, with the U.S. minister, Mr. Stevens, or Captain Wiltse, that they or either of them would assist in the overthrow of the Monarchy or the establishment of the Provisional Government.

"That at no time, either before or after such appointment, did Mr. Stevens ever recommend or urge us, or either of us, to dethrone the Queen or establish a Provisional Government.

Troops not used in overthrow

"That at no time, either before or after such appointment, did Mr. Stevens or Captain Wiltse promise us, or either of us, that the United States troops would be used to assist in the overthrow of the Queen or the establishment of the Provisional Government, and such troops, in fact, were not so used.

"That the forces that rallied to the support of the Provisional Government were ample to overthrow the monarchy and establish the Provisional Government, and such action would have been taken by the Committee regardless of the presence or absence of the American troops.

Supporters of movement organized

"That the reason of the confidence of the committee in its ability to accomplish its object was that the same men who were supporting the movement had carried through a peaceful revolution in 1887 and suppressed an armed uprising in 1889. The armed supporters of the movement were not a disorganized body, as has been represented, but were composed largely of the volunteer white militia which was in existence and formed

the effective strength in the conflicts of 1887 and 1889 (Ed.-emphasis added), and which, although disbanded by the Royalist Government in 1890, had retained its organization, and turned out under the command of its old officers, constituting a well drilled, disciplined, and officered military force of men of high character and morale, with perfect confidence in themselves, and holding in contempt the courage and ability of those whom they have twice before overawed and defeated."

"Revolutionists men of high character and morale"

In a separate statement filed with the Morgan Committee, L.A. Thurston, at the time Hawaiian minister to the United States, replied to what he called "personal attacks [by Blount in published extracts from his report] upon me and those associated with me in the Provisional Government, impugning our veracity, good faith, and courage, and charging us with fraud and duplicity. I deem it proper, therefore, to make a personal reply to such charges, confining myself to statements of fact . . .

Thurston took issue with Blount

"First, before stating such facts, I desire to call attention to Mr. Blount's method of constructing his report. Although he, in several places, states that I was the leader of the revolutionary movement, he has never asked me a question concerning the same, nor given me opportunity to make any statement, although I have at all times been ready and willing to do so. The same is true of a large number of other men who took a leading part in the movement of January last.

"In the second place, his evidence consists exclusively of prepared affidavits or of answers to leading questions put by himself, at private interviews, no one else being pres-

Blount offered no cross-examination

ent but the stenographer. In no instance has there been any cross-examination of witnesses or opportunity given to contradict or explain evidence given or present other evidence."

Blount also came in for some harsh words from Sanford B. Dole, president of the Hawaiian government at the time. Dole formulated a stinging indictment of American diplomacy in his January 11, 1894, letter to Blount's successor, Minister Willis, who had been sent under secret orders to Hawai'i to demand its government turn the nation back to the Monarchy. In the letter, he had these comments to make about Blount:

Dole had harsh words for Blount

"Upon the arrival of Mr. Blount in the country he did not communicate or in any manner intimate to the Hawaiian Government that his investigations were to be directed toward the right of existence of the Government to whom he was accredited. All of his investigations and examinations were private, and such persons only were examined as he chose to call.

"An examination of his report since published, shows that there are statements by approximately sixty Royalists and twenty supporters of the Provisional Government.

"That he obtained no statement from the four members of the Cabinet voted out before the revolutionary attempt of the Queen, although he has obtained exhaustive statements from their Royal successors.

"That he has examined only two of the thirteen members of the Committee of Safety, one of the original four members of the Executive Council of the Provisional Government, three of the original fourteen members of the

Advisory Council, two of the eight speakers who addressed the mass meeting called by the Committee of Safety on the day prior to the establishment of the Provisional Government, and but one of the eight field and staff officers and none of the eleven line officers in command of the forces of the Provisional Government, and none of the five commissioners sent to Washington, although all of such men . . . were eye witnesses and active participants in the overthrow . . . and all [are] men of character and standing in the community, while a number of those examined on the royalist side are irresponsible characters.

Blount ignored eyewitnesses

"Although Mr. Blount's Report is official in character, vitally affects this Government, is distinctly hostile to it in tone and conclusions, no request to this Government for explanation of the charges therein made was received, nor opportunity to reply thereto, or notice of its contents given prior to its publication."

Provisional Government not asked to comment

The Hawaiian government read extracts of the report in American papers, dated November 20, 1893, but did not receive a copy of the report until December 22, "only after several applications therefor to the State Department," Dole wrote.

Thurston's statement to Morgan continued:

"A brief examination of the published portions of the [Blount] report shows numerous incorrect statements. I shall endeavor for the present, however, to answer the more salient points only. "First, Mr. Blount charges that the American troops were landed under a prearranged agreement with the committee of safety that they should so land and assist in the overthrow of the Queen. In reply I hereby

Thurston disputed points of Blount Report

state that at no time did Mr. Stevens or Captain Wiltse assure me or the committee of safety, or any subcommittee thereof, that the United States troops would assist in overthrowing the Queen or establishing the Provisional Government; and as a matter of fact, they did not so assist."

No witnesses said Stevens would support Revolutionists

Thurston went on to say there were witnesses "in overwhelming number" who could testify in support of that statement, "but Mr. Blount has rendered it unnecessary to do so." Thurston cites the testimony of Wundenburg and Damon in the Blount Report as proving his point. Neither gave testimony directly stating that Stevens had said he would support the Revolutionists. Their testimony inferred that Stevens' avowed support of Annexation could lead to an assumption he would have been supportive of the Revolutionists had fighting broken out.

"Second," Thurston continued, "Mr. Blount charges that the Queen had ample military force with which to have met the committee, and but for the support of the United States representatives and troops the establishment of the Provisional Government would have been impossible."

U.S. troops not essential

Thurston said the U.S. troops were not essential and did not assist in the overthrow. "The result of the movement would have been eventually the same if there had not been a marine within a thousand miles of Honolulu." (Incidentally, the term "marine" has been used loosely by all sides in accounts of the Revolution. In fact, the marine members of the U.S. force were divided equally between the American legation and the American consulate, nowhere near the palace grounds. Bluejackets were the troops positioned near the palace, albeit across the street and out of sight.)

Thurston cited this evidence the U.S. troops were not necessary:

"1. The troops did not land till Monday night, the 16th of January, after the revolution had been in full progress since the afternoon of Saturday, the 14th, during which time the committee of safety was openly organizing for the avowed purpose of overthrowing the Queen." (Ed.—Stevens and Captain Wiltse and the ship *Boston* were in Hilo for the previous ten days, returning to Honolulu at noon on the 14th with obviously no up-to-the-minute knowledge of developments until they reached Honolulu Harbor, there being no inter-island phones.)

Revolution in full progress before Stevens got back

"2. There was absolutely no attempt at concealment from the Government of the objects and intentions of the committee.

No attempt at concealment by Committee

"3. The Queen, her cabinet, and their supporters were utterly demoralized, suspicious of one another, and devoid of leadership."

As evidence that there was no concealment from the government of the intentions of the Committee, Thurston stated:

"On the afternoon of Saturday, the 14th, in reply to the request of the Queen's cabinet for advice as to what they had better do, the Queen then still insisting upon the proclamation of the constitution and supporting it by force, I advised them to declare the Queen in revolution and the throne vacant, and at their request and at the expressed approval of two of them and the tacit assent of the other two, then and there drew up a form of proclamation to that effect.

Queen's ministers well aware of revolt plans

"At half past 4 in the afternoon of Saturday, the 14th, at a meeting of about 200 citizens at the office of W.O. Smith, the Queen was denounced in the strongest terms, armed resistance and a counter-revolution were openly advocated, and the Queen's minister of the interior, John Colburn, addressed the meeting, asking [citizens'] armed support against the Queen. The Queen's attorney general, Mr. Peterson, and her personal attorney, Paul Neumann, were both present taking part in the meeting. The committee of safety was publicly then and there named and proceeded forthwith to organize.

Queen's men requested 24 hours

"At 6 o'clock on Sunday morning, the 15th, I told Mr. Peterson and Mr. Colburn, two members of the Queen's cabinet, that the committee intended to depose the Queen and establish a provisional government; that if they would take charge of the movement, well and good, otherwise the committee intended to take action on its own account. They asked for twenty-four hours in which to consider the matter. I declined to wait, stating to them that the committee intended to proceed forthwith.

Committee met openly, Queen's police watched

"The committee met openly that morning at 10 o'clock, with the full knowledge of the Government of the place of its meeting. It remained in session during the greater part of the day, while several [of the Queen's] police kept watch of the building from the street.

"On Monday morning at 9 o'clock the committee, without attempt at concealment, met in my office, within 200 feet of the police station, Marshal Wilson's headquarters, where the entire police force was stationed. While the meeting was in progress Wilson came to the office and asked to speak to me privately, and we went into an adjoining room."

Wilson tried to stop revolt

Thurston stated Wilson wanted the Revolution stopped and said he could control the Queen. Thurston told him it was too late, and they were going to "settle it now, once and for all."

"Wilson left the office. He has since stated that he immediately reported to the cabinet and advised arresting the committee, but the cabinet was afraid and refused to allow it.

"At 2 o'clock on the afternoon of Monday, the 16th, a mass meeting of 3,000 unarmed men was held within a block of the palace. The meeting was addressed by a number of speakers, all denouncing the Queen. The meeting, with tremendous cheering and enthusiasm, unanimously adopted resolutions declaring the Queen to be in revolution, and authorizing the committee to proceed to do whatever was necessary . . . . While this meeting was in progress, another was being held by the Royalists in the streets, within a block of the armory, which adopted resolutions in support of the Queen.

Mass meeting declared Queen to be in revolt

"Never in the history of Hawai'i has there been such a tense condition of mind or a more imminent expectation of bloodshed and conflict . . . . Mr. Blount's statement that the community was at peace and quiet is grossly inaccurate. It was at this juncture, two hours after the adjournment of the above meetings, that Captain Wiltse and Mr. Stevens, acting upon their own responsibility and discretion, and irrespective of the request or actions of the Committee, landed the troops, which were distributed in three parts

Community not at peace

of the city, instead of being massed at one point, as stated by Mr. Blount."

Thurston's statement goes on to detail efforts of the Queen's Cabinet to gain support from the community to overthrow the Queen themselves, the signing of a petition of support of their proposal by more than 80 persons at the meeting in Smith's office, and details of the previous two revolutions, in 1887 and 1889.

Troops discussed as safety measure

A sworn statement by William R. Castle, an attorney, former legislator and a member of the Committee of Safety, pins down to Monday morning the Committee's first request to Minister Stevens for the landing of troops. He said it was not thought of until that morning's meeting of the committee when discussions began about possible rioting, fires and threats to American lives and property.[50]

"The request was therefore made to Minister Stevens for exactly that kind of protection. It was put in writing, signed by the entire Committee of Safety, and taken to Minister Stevens by Mr. Thurston and myself after the mass meeting . . . . The troops landed about 5 o'clock . . . . Monday night was one of suspense and terror throughout the entire community. A riotous uprising of the mob element was feared at any moment; no confidence was felt in the ability or disposition of the Queen's Government to cope with the same.

Riot was feared

"It is my belief, which I think is shared by nearly every one, that the mere presence of United States troops exercised a restraining influence . . .

"At this point I desire to state that if there had been any plan or conspiracy by which the United States troops were to land and assist the Revolutionists in overturning the Government, I should most certainly have known it. There was no such plan, and I utterly repudiate the attempt to impugn the character and actions of both Minister Stevens and Captain Wiltse, and state here that it seemed to me at the time, and I believe now, that they would have been perfectly justified in giving a quicker and more open support to the Provisional Government than was finally accorded . . . and that they still would have been within the requirements of international law upon that subject."

Castle defended Stevens

One can sense the frustration in the statements of these three leaders of the Revolution, learning belatedly of Blount's misstatements, knowing that Cleveland had depended on the Blount Report for his own message to Congress and charges against the Revolutionists. They believed it was unconscionable for Blount not to give a balanced report, particularly on the following key points:

Leaders found Blount unconscionable

1. He relied totally on Admiral Skerrett for the damaging and erroneous viewpoint that the troops were placed at Arion Hall so as to block the Queen's possible retaliation, thus implying deliberate United States intentions to defeat her. Skerrett was not even there. Lieutenant Young and Captain Wiltse were, and Blount did not seek their statements, which would have been a complete refutation of the Skerrett opinion. Admiral Skerrett, in his May 23, 1893, letter that Blount included with his report, told Blount that the troops in that Arion Hall location were "distantly removed from the business portion of the town, and generally far away from the United States legation and consulate-general, as well as being distant from the houses and residences of Unit-

Skerrett not even there

ed States citizens." The admiral was mistaken: they could hardly have been closer to downtown—a scant two to three blocks away. There were sixteen marines at the legation and also the consulate. Residential Honolulu surrounded all three locations as shown on a map in the Morgan Report.

Troops out of sight of palace

2. Blount, too, said all of the troops were massed in one spot, which he said was ill-conceived and by implication, sinister. Actually, as mentioned earlier, sixteen marines were at the U.S. Consulate, another sixteen at the American legation, and the balance of one hundred thirty troops, no marines, at Arion Hall, out of sight of the palace.

3. Blount's source for his statement that the Revolution would not have succeeded without the U.S. troops was Fred Wundenberg, but he did not mention in his report that Wundenberg was a turncoat who had resigned from the revolutionary group two days after the event. Nor did he get any statements to the contrary, though the entire Committee of Safety was available and would have testified otherwise.

Only three of thirteen members missionary descendants

4. He did not mention that the U.S. troops at Arion Hall had stacked their arms, stating instead that they were armed and ready to face the Queen's troops.

5. He referred to the Revolution and the Provisional Government as operations by "missionary descendants" without stating that only three of the thirteen members of the Committee fit that description and only two of the leaders of the government, Dole and Smith.

6. In perhaps the worst exaggeration of all, Blount included fifteen affidavits from the Queen's Cabinet, her officers, her attorney and other advisers attesting to their version of peaceful conditions in

the city on January 16, 17 and 18, the placement of troops, the timing of Stevens' recognition, etc., but none from the other side. If there had been nothing but peace and quiet, as Blount stated, in Honolulu on those days, Captain Wiltse would not have dispatched one hundred sixty-two officers and men to protect American lives and property.

And then there is the later argument that if it was bad for Stevens to land troops and sympathize with the Revolution—an act of war, said Cleveland, although there was no documentation regarding either of these allegations—what was one to make of the documented U.S. effort to secretly subvert the Provisional Government, which the United States had recognized? The Committee of Safety had been completely open, fully advising the Queen through her Cabinet of its intentions. Blount, Gresham, Willis and Cleveland tried in secrecy to overturn a foreign government, deliberately lying to Dole in the process. Cleveland's message to Congress was cloaked in noble sentiments; the subversion was not mentioned until the Morgan hearings.

Cleveland et al secretly tried to overturn government

Chairman Morgan and the other four Democrats, as well as the four Republicans, all agreed on one key point: They disagreed completely with Blount's "finding" that U.S. troops were part of a conspiracy to overthrow the Queen. The committee unanimously exonerated the officers of the forces landed by the United States. All members supported the finding regarding those officers, enunciated by the chairman: "There was no irregularity or want of authority to place the troops on shore." The report added: "In this view of the facts, there is no necessity for inquiring whether Minister Stevens or Captain Wiltse [commander of the troops] in arranging for the landing of the troops, had any purpose either to

Morgan Report exonerated U.S. officers

aid the popular movement against the Queen that was then taking a definite and decisive shape, or to promote the Annexation of the Hawaiian Islands to the United States.

"But justice to these gentlemen requires that we should say that the troops from the *Boston* were not sent into Honolulu for any other purpose than that set forth fully and fairly in the following order from Captain Wiltse to the officer in command of the detachment:

"'...You will take command of the battalion and land in Honolulu for the purpose of protecting our legation, consulate, and the lives and property of American citizens, and to assist in preserving public order...'"

Blount decided without officers' testimony

Blount, as indicated earlier, without listening to testimony from the officers involved and based mainly on the comments of another officer not present at the time, decided that the troops had taken up a position that was not in keeping with the above order; in other words, he felt they had taken a position near the palace that was not just for the preservation of peace and order. Blount's Report, silent on troops in other locations, indicates he may not have realized they had taken three positions that were central to American interests.

Republicans blamed Blount, not Stevens

The Republicans agreed with the chairman that Stevens was not to be blamed. They went even further. They felt Blount, Willis and Cleveland had all acted without authority and unwisely.

Their minority report stated:

"The question of the rightfulness of the revolution, of the lawfulness of the means by which the deposition and abdication of the Queen were effected, and the right of the Provisional Government to exist and to continue to exist was conclusively settled, as the report so forcibly states, against the Queen and in favor of the Provisional Government, by the act of the administration of President Harrison recognizing such Provisional Government, by the negotiation by that administration with such Provisional Government of a treaty of annexation to the United States; by accrediting diplomatic representation by such administration and by the present administration to such Provisional Government; therefore, it incontrovertibly follows that the President of the United States had no authority to attempt to reopen such determined questions, and to endeavor by any means whatever to overthrow the Provisional Government or to restore the monarchy which it had displaced."

U.S. President had no authority to overthrow Revolutionists

The four Republicans also signed their approval of the rest of the committee report.

The Democrats felt that Stevens had gone beyond his authority and that "his conduct as the public representative of this Government was directly conducive to bringing about the condition of affairs which resulted in the overthrow of the Queen, the organization of the Provisional Government, the landing of the United States troops, and the attempted scheme of annexation . . . and [he is] deserving of public censure."

Democrats felt Stevens deserved censure

Two of the Democrats added that they were in favor of Annexation. All signed their approval of the rest of the committee report.

Contrary to criticism by some who belittle the Morgan Report, the findings of the majority of the full report were approved by all nine committee members, with a five-to-four finding that the United States did not play the key role in the overthrow. The

Blount Report was signed only by its one-man com-
mittee-investigator, Blount himself.

Blount's final statement in his July 31, 1893,
letter to Gresham accompanying his report is reveal-
ing of his attitude—and not a great compliment to
his prescience:

*Blount forecast
fell short
of mark*

> "The condition of parties in the islands is one
> of quiescence . . . . The present Government
> can only rest on the use of military force, pos-
> sessed of most of the arms in the islands, with
> a small white population to draw from to
> strengthen it. Ultimately it will fall without
> fail. It may preserve its existence for a year or
> two, but not longer."

An unbiased consideration of the two reports
cannot help but reach the conclusion that at the very
least, each of the two viewpoints of this matter has
some validity. At the very least also, the question of
U.S. involvement in 1893 is a gray area in the history of Hawai'i, though this writer feels the evidence
against any conspiracy outweighs the evidence that
there was one. Subsequent events make clear that by
the time of Annexation, there were no gray areas
about U.S. involvement in Hawai'i's affairs.

*Hawaiian
government
stood on its own*

Despite Blount's assessment of its strength,
the Hawaiian government still stood on its own in
1898, with five years as an independent Republic on
its record. Its citizens included any and every Hawaiian who swore allegiance to it. That included many
Native Hawaiians, as we will see in the next chapter,
which details the long road to Annexation.

$\mathcal{T}$he Road to Annexation

he fifty-year-long road to Annexation began formally for Hawai'i in 1851 when Kamehameha III, responding to concerns of foreign intervention, executed and delivered to the American minister a provisional cession of Hawai'i to the United States. At the time, the United States was a democratic power with no colonial aspirations, barely seventy-five years old.

King offered cession to U.S.

It was the first of many moves by the small Island Kingdom to seek the power of America as protection against the challenges of colonial empires. In every case but one, the record shows that Native Hawaiians through their Hawaiian leaders wanted Annexation to the United States, including the final effort by the Republic of Hawai'i that succeeded in 1898. The one case where we cannot be sure there was Native Hawaiian support for the association with America was the unsuccessful effort in 1893 by the Provisional Government to gain Annexation in the months following the Revolution. While it might or might not have been approved in a plebiscite or a legislative vote, it was never tested and remains an unknown.

Native Hawaiians backed Annexation

Three months after the King's offer of cession early in 1851, on June 21 of that same year a joint resolution by the two houses of the Hawaiian Legislature—one appointed, one elected—authorized the King to place the Kingdom under the protection of a foreign state, and negotiations began for Annexation to the United States.

By February 1854 things were so far along that the U.S. consul in Honolulu, Benjamin Franklin Angell, was able to write an attorney friend, John H. Jones, Jr., in Moscow, New York:

Formal treaty for Annexation completed by King and U.S. minister

"In my judgment these Pacific Islands will be made a Territory of the United States in less than a year; a treaty of cession is now in progress of negotiation and I am hurrying it forward with all my power."

The first formal treaty to annex Hawai'i to the United States was completed by the King and U.S. Minister to Honolulu David L. Gregg later that year, under the instructions of U.S. Secretary of State William L. Marcy. A final draft was agreed upon, but the King died before it could be signed, and his successor, Kamehameha IV, withdrew the agreement.

Nineteen years later, in a February 17, 1873, dispatch to U.S. Secretary of State Hamilton Fish, the resident U.S. minister in Honolulu, Henry A. Pierce, analyzed thinking of that period:

"Annexation of these islands to the United States and a reciprocity treaty between the two countries are the two important topics of conversation and discussion among Government officials and foreign residents.

"A large majority of the latter favor the first-named project, while the former advocate reciprocity. All are convinced, however, that some measure should be taken by the Hawaiian Government to effectually stay the decline in prosperity of the country, evidenced in decreasing exports, revenues, population, whale fishery, and an increasing public debt."

Earlier U.S. minister foresaw Revolution

In a statement in a sense twenty years ahead of its time, Pierce commented further:

"Annexation of the islands to the United States will never, in my opinion, be adopted or presented as a Government measure [by the Monarchy] however much the people as a whole may desire it. The glitter of the crown, love of power, and emoluments of office have too many attractions . . . . Should the greater interests of the country, however, demand that annexation shall be attempted, the planters, merchants and foreigners generally will induce the people to overthrow the Government, establish a Republic, and then ask the United States for admittance into its Union."

Reciprocity Treaty gave U.S. link

The Reciprocity Treaty followed two years later, in 1875. While it did not provide for Annexation, the seven-year treaty did provide an exclusive link between the United States and Hawai'i. In return for duty-free trade agreements, the Kingdom pledged to make no similar deals with any other country nor to allow any other foreign government to lease, own or develop any ports or portions of the Islands. When the many-times-extended treaty was to expire in 1887, the "Pearl River Clause" was added by Hawai'i to secure further extensions. In that clause, King Kalākaua granted exclusive rights to the United States for the use and development of Pearl Harbor, tying the two countries together even more tightly.

In 1884, the community seemed to be more

in favor of a strong, independent Kingdom than Annexation, as summarized in an editorial in the *Bulletin* by its then-editor, Lorrin A. Thurston. In an editorial on August 27, 1884, Thurston wrote:

In '84 Thurston favored King-dom over Annexation

> "For many years there have been a few residents here who have desired the annexation of these Islands to the United States . . . . some believing that under that great Government the permanent interests of the islands would be best secured; others that more money could thus be made . . . . But the majority of intelligent foreigners, and especially those born here of foreign parents, have contended for the independence of the Government. They have believed it to be far more for the interests of the native race that they should maintain an independent Government and a distinctive national existence . . . . It is well known that the United States Government does not desire the annexation of these Islands; the accession of foreign territory is contrary to its policy; but it is certain that Government will not permit its interests here to be sacrificed, nor permit any other foreign Government to control here. When these Islands cease to be self-governing the United States Government will take possession."

Queen's attor-ney said many natives desired Annexation

Interestingly, Kuykendall notes that the Native Hawaiians, with a few exceptions, were known to have been strongly opposed to Annexation. But he points out that Lili'uokalani's attorney, Paul Neumann, during a visit to San Francisco in November 1889, was quoted in the *San Francisco Examiner* as saying, "A great many natives want annexation to the United States, and it is only their innate loyalty to the King that represses the feeling."

Events and statements after the Revolution in 1893 show continued wide-ranging feelings within the Island community supporting abolition of the Monarchy and a move toward unity with the United States. Native Hawaiians and Caucasians were listed on both sides of the issue. The side supporting the Queen and the other side supporting the move toward Annexation each had Hawaiian and Caucasian supporters. Creation of a constitutional form of government in the mid-19th Century had softened the absolute power of the monarch and given Hawaiians the ability to express their personal beliefs as individuals. They expressed this variety of individual views as members of the Legislature or through one or another of the political parties and newspapers that existed in the Hawaiian community. Not all Native Hawaiians were found to be supporters of any particular monarch or even the concept of monarchy itself. Moreover, as the century was drawing to a close, not all were opposed to Annexation.[51] As indicated earlier, whenever a proposal for Annexation or ties with the United States came before the Hawai'i Legislature, it was approved wholeheartedly, including in 1897, with no dissension from Native Hawaiian members.

Constititional Monarchy allowed subjects to express opposition

By the 1890s, the Queen's party was certainly the largest and the strongest of the Hawaiian political groups, and according to reports of the time, she kept a very firm grip on her followers. After the Revolution, she and her closest supporters were accused by members of the Liberal Party, which maintained a running criticism of her during the early 1890s, of keeping a "powerful system of terrorism" over her former subjects, threatening them with speedy punishment if they were disloyal to her cause of rein-

Queen reportedly had firm grip on her followers

statement. Her inner circle of supporters, as might be expected, deplored loss of the Monarchy and opposed Annexation as a concept, though many, including the ex-Queen, found some good in being connected to the United States once it happened.

Lili'uokalani, for example, said in her diary on Sunday, September 2, 1900 (in the context of commenting on her overthrow, explaining why she had consented to being serenaded by the "old Royal Hawaiian Band, now the Government-led band", on the occasion of her 62nd birthday):

> "Tho' for a moment [the overthrow] cost me a pang of pain for my people it was only momentary, for the present has a hope for the future of my people."

A long-time political supporter and military commander of Kalākaua's, V.V. Ashford, whose family opposed the Revolution and played an active role in the unsuccessful counter-revolution, was another who withdrew his support of the Monarchy. Ashford was a complicated political figure, one of the few Royalists who was for Annexation, as he said, "both from a Hawaiian and American standpoint" and in the days "when [being for] annexation meant treason."[52] He was quoted in newspapers of the day as saying that the situation regarding the royalty had become so bad by the time of Lili'uokalani's assumption of the throne in 1891 that she didn't get the traditional welcome from Hawaiians as she made her initial tour about the Islands. Her retainers, he said, couldn't get enough supplies of food from the Hawaiian people and "had to get it from the whites."

Ashford was one of the founders of the *Hui Hawai'i Aloha'āina* (Hawaiian Patriotic League) formed in March 1892 by him and several hundred disgruntled Native Hawaiians to overthrow the Queen and seek Annexation to the United States at a time when Dole and others were against it. When he recounted to Blount his view of Hawaiian politics and the perceived shift away from a belief in the Monarchy, he had this to say:

Ashford saw a shift in Hawaiians' view of Monarchy

> "Of the most stable class of natives, the following sentiment, related to me by one who, under Kalakaua, had held in succession all the most distinguished positions in public and political life, is a sample of the then prevailing thought:
>
> "'I have been trained from childhood to love and obey my alii; no one would more gladly give his very life for them. But the days of the alii are past; they are no more; their successors are unworthy of the name; my aloha for them has withered. I weep for Hawaii. The Kingdom must come to an end; and who can say what will be best for our country—annexation or a republic.'"

"Kingdom must come to an end"

Ashford was a Canadian who had become a voluble Hawaiian subject. He wrapped up his statement to Blount with the ringing statement: ". . . monarchy is now dead, and Hawai'i knocks for admission to America's door. Give us not an oligarchy. Give us democratic government. Give us a government of the people, for the people, and by the people."

"Give us democratic government"

There were many Native Hawaiians at the time of the Revolution who supported the move toward more democratic government, including J.E. Bush, editor of the Hawaiian language newspaper, *Ka Leo o Ka Lāhui.*

Historian William De Witt Alexander, a missionary son testifying under oath before the Morgan

Committee in 1894, spoke to the great dissatisfaction among Native Hawaiians, first with Kalākaua and then Liliʻuokalani:

"The most intelligent natives, those of the best character, independence of character, were on the side of the Provisional Government. I think two-thirds of the native preachers and those members of the legislature who had independence enough to vote against the lottery bill, and many of those of whom I consider the best natives, are on that side. It required a good deal of moral courage on their part, because they were called names, traitors, by their fellow-countrymen, and were threatened in case the Queen came back that it would go hard with them . . . that element of the natives has been ignored by some writers on the subject."

Hawaiians dis-satisfied with Kalākaua and Liliʻuokalani

Indeed, that element continues to be ignored by most writers on the subject more than 100 years later. Also pretty much ignored today are Hawaiians who do not support sovereignty but keep quiet because it is politically incorrect for them to speak out against it.

Politically incor-rect opinions kept quiet

It would be easy to dismiss Alexander's comments, reading them 100 years later, because he appears to take a superior tone toward the "natives." But Alexander and other like-minded people of the day took a morally superior view also of the "lower class of whites" who came to Hawaiʻi and lived a "debauched life" of sex, drinking and gambling. He and his friends among the missionary element measured people by religious, moral and ethical standards, not along racial lines. Once a person became a Christian, he was accepted as a friend and associate regardless of race.

The Monarchy was in trouble with many thoughtful members of the community when King

Kalākaua began the abuses of power that led to imposition of the Reform Constitution in 1887. It was a move that would take the Hawaiian Monarchy along the path of British royalty, ironically much admired by Kalākaua as well as later members of the Kamehameha dynasty. Over time, British monarchs have been divested of all but ceremonial duties, with no real ruling powers remaining. There are parallels worldwide. Monarchies that survived into the 20th Century were pretty much guided by constitutional mandates and hobbled by laws that forced them to be more democratic.

Constitutional monarchies can survive

It is interesting that while the ways and lifestyles of British monarchs were much admired by Kalākaua and Lili'uokalani as well as the last two members of the Kamehameha dynasty, the Hawaiian monarchs could not accept the kinds of restrictions on their power that British monarchs had learned to accept as necessary for survival of their way of life.

Monarchy needed to accept change

If Kalākaua and Lili'uokalani had been willing to live within such restrictions for the common good, many residents of Hawai'i would have preferred, as did men like Charles Reed Bishop, to maintain the Monarchy.[53]

Hawai'i differed from other 19th-Century countries mostly because the conflict between Monarchy and democracy here involved mixtures of races. Caucasians, in the eyes of international politics of the time, were much less willing to believe in the divine right of kings if they weren't already subjects of a benign monarchy, such as Britain. The majority of Hawai'i's Caucasians, Americans, were not enamored of the idea of monarchical rule. Japanese immigrants, who in the late 19th Century probably were more accepting of the dictatorial powers of

Rejection of divine right

a strong monarchy, were viewed as threatening by all of the foreign national groups in the Islands, as well as by the Native Hawaiians.

Kalākaua's capricious acts and the resultant disruptions to business and government caused concern among people of all races. His reputation for immorality, the rumors of orgies, the dealings with men like Spreckels and Gibson that called for bailouts from the Legislature angered more than just his political opponents.

Residents concerned by King's behavior

While the 1852 and 1864 Constitutions authorized the ruling monarch to appoint and fire his Cabinets at will, there had been a nice working balance between the King and his Cabinet, which under both of those Constitutions was required to approve of actions of the King. Kalākaua, with his strong ego and desire to dominate, broke this pattern. He would change Cabinets on whim, sometimes in the middle of the night. Both the Reform Constitution and a ruling from the Hawai'i Supreme Court finally brought this practice to a halt by requiring legislative approval of a Cabinet's dismissal. Interestingly, he had sought the ruling from a Supreme Court he himself had appointed.

King changed Cabinets on whims

Within the Native Hawaiian political community, there were leaders who early on thought his successor, Lili'uokalani, was heading in the wrong direction with her efforts to expand the powers of the Monarchy and oppose Annexation.

One of the most outspoken was J.L. Kaulukou, who was speaker of the House of Representatives for the Republic at the time of Annexation but who once had been a strong Royalist in favor with both Kalākaua and Lili'uokalani. He is credited with giving her the description "*'onipa'a*"—"steadfast"— which she adopted as her personal motto and which

President Cleveland's special commissioner, James Blount, right, poses with his wife and secretary, Ellis Mills, who later replaced John Stevens as U.S. minister to Hawai'i.

Ali'iōlani Hale, the government building where Revolutionists read proclamation deposing Lili'uokalani.

The Cabinet of the Republic

Left to right, S.M. Damon; J.A. King; S.B. Dole;
H.E. Cooper; B.L. Marx, secretary; W.O. Smith.

The Palace

'Iolani Palace as it appeared in 1893, viewed from atop Aliʻiōlani Hale, the government building, 200 yards away, across King Street.

U.S. troops marched along King Street, dipped their colors to the Queen at the palace, stopped briefly at Mrs. Hopper's house, right, to see if a campsite had been located.

Dole transfers Hawai'i to the United States on August 12, 1898.

These forty men wrote the Constitution of the Republic in 1894, setting Annexation as a goal.

Photo: © The Hawai'i State Archives

Prince Kūhiō Kalaniana'ole, wearing his campaign hat in this photo, served the Territory of Hawai'i in the U.S. Congress. He and all other Native Hawaiians gained the right to vote as the American Flag rose on Annexation Day, pictured below, and dominated the government until WWII.

Photo: © The Hawaiian Mission Children's Society

is widely used today by sovereignty activists. Kaulukou, in his then-capacity as marshal of the Kingdom, presented the motto idea to her "on behalf of the whole nation" at her 48th birthday party in 1886.

"I regard Annexation," he told the *San Francisco Chronicle* in an interview published July 28, 1898, "as the best thing that could happen for Hawai'i, both for the native and foreign population. I have advocated it ever since it became an issue in practical politics and I rejoice heartily that it has come. For years I have looked upon it as being, if not inevitable, at least as the only way in which the best interests of Hawai'i could be protected and advanced."

Kaulukou saw U.S. tie best for Islands

At the time, Kaulukou was a twenty-year veteran of Hawaiian public life. He represented a district in Windward O'ahu that was heavily dominated by Native Hawaiian voters and in which he had earlier served as a district judge, appointed by Kalākaua in 1877. He served until 1884, one of many appointments he was to receive from the King. He was first elected to the House from the district in 1880 and again in 1882.

Veteran of public life

In 1884 he was appointed sheriff of the Island of Hawai'i, and while in that office was appointed tax assessor for the district of Hilo. In 1886 he was elected to the House from Hilo and while in the House was appointed postmaster general by the King. A few months later the King appointed him marshal of the Kingdom and for a brief period later, attorney general.

While serving as marshal it fell to him to proclaim the 1887 Reform Constitution, which by custom required the marshal to ride through the streets. Stories of the day report he rode a "superb white horse" as he promulgated the new order.

Kaulukou resigned as marshal in 1888 to pursue the practice of law on Oʻahu. In 1890 and again in 1892, he ran for the House from his original Koʻolau Poko district and was defeated both times.

He told the *Chronicle* he first began to swing toward Annexation after the 1890 defeat and his feelings intensified during the next campaign.

Kaulukou leaned toward Annexation after 1890 defeat

"The Queen and some of her partisans were then striving for an entirely new Constitution. . . . The platform upon which I went before the people was that an attempt to replace the then Constitution with an entirely new instrument was, in the condition of affairs that existed at that time, dangerous both to the Queen and to the Native Hawaiians.

"I urged that the better way was to secure the changes that seemed desirable by amendment (Ed.—as provided in the Constitution itself). I told the people that the country was in no mood to submit to the Queen's notions of unlimited power, and that if the effort to entirely overthrow the constitution and replace it with a new one were persisted in, there would be an end of monarchy.

Queen's notions of unlimited power would end Monarchy

"I said that the interests of the natives and of the foreign residents were identical; that both wanted a stable, efficient and well-administered government, and that the way to this lay through representative government, and not through unlimited monarchy.

"I said that what the Hawaiians needed was better schools, better public improvements and more of them, an equitable assessment of taxes and an honest administration of the revenues for public purposes, and not more power in the monarchy and more . . . display and ostentation in the [royal] court."

Kaulukou, representative of other Hawaiians who agreed with his views, did not take part in the overthrow but did support the Provisional Government when it was established.

Kaulukou urged friends to take oath of allegiance

"With the establishment of the Provisional Government and [subsequently] the Republic, I advised my people to take the oath of allegiance, to take part in public affairs and to join with the haole, among whom were many of their best friends and very many of their best advisers, in securing good government and that advance in material and intellectual prosperity which our race pride made us believe was within our power . . ."

He noted in the *Chronicle* article that the "achievements of some of our people have demonstrated that it is so."

In Annexation, he believed he saw ". . . stability of government and [a] constant source of influence and association in governmental, social and educational affairs which would enable the Hawaiian people to develop and advance to the plane of the highest civilization."

Annexation to bring stable government

He was a strong proponent of education and foresaw

". . . a university in these Islands giving the broadest culture anywhere attainable. I expect to see the intellectual, the social and the material life broadened and quickened through our political union with the United States and the consequent blending of interest and thought. We have now become a part of a great people [and] the influence[s] of thought and progress will reach us more directly now than they did before.

"I am not insensible to that feeling of

attachment to the land of one's birth and the pride in one's race which is touched, and which brings a sentiment of sadness when that land ceases to be a nation among the nations, her flag blotted from the firmament of national ensigns, and the race name ceases to be synonymous with nationality.

Sadness over loss of sovereignty

"I, too, am an Hawaiian. These islands bear in their bosom the bones of my ancestors to the remotest generation. I am proud of my race. I am proud of my nationality. But in annexation I see a larger place for my race, and the stream of national life merging in a still larger national life will flow in deeper and wider channels . . .

Race not synonymous with nationality

"I shall, as I have done in the past, urge my people to take part in public affairs, to cultivate both individual and civic virtues, to be Americans in that enjoyment and exercise of liberty which is the birthright of an American, as it is the greatest guarantee of race progress and national perpetuity."

It is interesting to note that with the acquisition of full voting rights under their new U.S. citizenship, Hawaiians kept control of the government by dominating the Legislature for more than a generation after Annexation.

Hawaiians kept control of government after Annexation

Chronicle writers also recorded viewpoints from two who deplored the loss of sovereignty. The two were Princess Ka'iulani and Prince David Kawananakoa, both relatives of Kalākaua and Lili'uokalani and named by Lili'uokalani as next in order for succession to the throne had the Monarchy continued.

Ka'iulani, who died not long after at the age of 24, was portrayed as particularly distressed at the "loss of her country." She was said to be contemplating a move to England, where she had spent four years while in college and whose association she favored over the association with the United States.

". . . Lili'uokalani and I are the last of our race," she said.

"When the news of Annexation came it was bitterer than death to me. In us the love of race is very strong—stronger than anything else. It was bad enough to lose the throne, but infinitely worse to have the flag go down . . .

Ka'iulani saw aunt ill-advised, obstinent

"I was sorry, of course, that trouble came to my aunt, but I realized that she had been obstinate and ill advised. It is so bitterly hard for a woman. If there had been a single man among all her advisers to stand by her in her hour of need and to have arrested that Committee of Safety, all this would never have happened . . .

"I would have liked to be Queen. Had the monarchy ever been restored it would have been my aunt or me, of course, and while there was an independent government in Hawai'i there was always hope, but now everything is ended . . ."

On the night of the Revolution, Prince David Kawananakoa had assisted the new government with the paperwork involved in gaining recognition from the other foreign missions in Honolulu. At the time of Annexation, however, he told the *Chronicle* he felt he would "take no part in public affairs. I shall hold myself a private citizen, seeking to do my duty in my social and business relations, and advising no one as to their political duties."

Kawananakoa withdrew from public affairs

A great grandson, Quentin Kawananakoa, is

back in Island politics, in 1997 a Republican member of the state House of Representatives and candidate for the U.S. House. He continues to favor some kind of sovereignty for Hawaiians and no doubt will play a significant role in defining the form it might take.

In the background of all discussions of Annexation in the 19th Century was the high probability that other foreign powers would make a grab for Hawai'i.

U.S. minister concerned by strategic moves by other countries

Even as Minister Stevens was bringing U.S. troops ashore at the time of the Revolution, he was voicing concern over possible strategic moves by Japan and Britain and urging his Washington superiors to place Hawai'i under the formal protection of the United States. When the Provisional Government was established he immediately expressed concerns for its vulnerability to British forces. A British warship was reportedly due to arrive "and the English Minister here, thus aided, might try to press unduly the Provisional Government," he noted.

"With the Islands under our protection, we think the English Minister will not attempt to insist that his government has the right to interfere . . . ," he added.

Foreign intervention possible

William M. Morgan analyzed Stevens' actions in detail in his 1980 Ph.D. dissertation at Claremont Graduate School. He believes this concern over British interference quite likely reflected Stevens' primary motive in his relationship with Hawai'i. "If Stevens had intended to use bogus fears of foreign intervention as an excuse for American occupation," Morgan notes, "he could have established the protectorate immediately after the Revolution.

"Not until the possibility of foreign intervention seemed to increase in the latter part of January, however, did Stevens put Hawai'i under American protection . . .

"To prevent meddling by Japan or Britain, Stevens needed additional naval forces. Currently only the cruiser *Boston* was in port. Stevens thus asked for 'the most powerful American ship available' to bolster the protectorate. Hawai'i must be protected, he believed, or it would fall [into wrong hands]," Morgan writes.

Stevens feared other nations would pluck the "Hawaiian pear"

"The Hawaiian pear is now fully ripe," Stevens told Secretary of State John W. Foster in a Feb. 1, 1893, dispatch, "and this is the golden hour for the United States to pluck it." He argued that either Japan or Britain would be delighted to acquire the Islands if it could be done without antagonizing the United States.

An editorial in the *Honolulu Daily Bulletin* on March 21, 1893, put it succinctly: "So long . . . as the United States maintains any claim to ascendancy in these islands, it is safe to assume that there will be no interference from any other quarter. If that claim should be withdrawn, it is exceedingly doubtful whether Japan would withhold her hand any longer from the 'Hawaiian Pear.'"

If U.S. backed off, Japan would move in

Morgan notes further in his thesis that "On balance, given Hawai'i's value to American security and the strong possibility that withdrawal of the annexation treaty [by Cleveland] had been mistaken for abandonment of the islands, the United States was understandably fearful of British or Japanese intervention."

Blount's precipitate action in removing Stevens and his failure or unwillingness to appoint a successor before his departure in late July 1893 worried the Provisional Government. Listening to the concerns of its leaders, Blount realized the need for a

Blount warned Japanese

final precaution against Japanese intrigue. At Dole's request, Morgan states, Blount, in the form of a letter to Dole, issued a stern warning to Japan not to attempt anything rash.

The pressure by local and national officials in Japan for Japanese suffrage in Hawai'i was very much before the Provisional Government at that time. A few months later, Japanese petitioners formally protested to their Imperial Government their inability to vote. Morgan notes they decried the fact that Americans—"the most influential element"—"have control of nearly the whole of the Islands. . . . We are far from satisfied with this state of affairs."

Japanese felt they should be dominant

The petitioners hoped the Imperial Government could provide redress, for "we should be dominant as we are the most important element in these Islands."

Morgan notes that from this petition and other Japanese activities, the white oligarchy inferred that the Japanese intended to obtain through the ballot box the political dominance that the whites currently enjoyed. Moreover, the petition offered an opportunity for the Japanese government to involve itself further in Hawaiian politics and it immediately seized on that opportunity.

Japan requested voting rights

In December 1893, the Japanese warship *Naniwa* returned to Honolulu Harbor, and in March 1894 Japan formally requested that the Constitution being prepared by the Republic of Hawai'i grant Japanese nationals the same voting rights given to other foreign nationals, particularly Americans. Because Japanese subjects outnumbered American citizens of the Republic more than ten to one, allowing both groups to vote foretold Japanese control of the Legislature at a time before Japanese residents of Hawai'i had become American citizens, Morgan points out. This concerned the Provisional Government, which had come about because its Revolutionist founders were looking toward closer ties with the United States, not some other foreign power.

Certainly the Republic also realized that Japanese voting rights probably would preclude Annexation to the United States.

Congress, meanwhile, also was expressing concern about foreign intervention. Resolutions were introduced giving warning to the world against outside interference in Hawai'i.

The Cleveland administration no longer could ignore the situation, and in early 1894 it sent Admiral John Grimes Walker to Honolulu as commander of American naval forces in the Pacific. Walker, like most military officers of the day, had spoken strongly in favor of Annexation on earlier occasions. His assignment to Hawai'i clearly indicated a realization within the Cleveland administration, though it never came out for Annexation itself, that Hawai'i could not be allowed to fall into foreign hands. Blount's departure, the withdrawal of warships, the removal of the U.S. Flag and surrounding events had given the world almost an opposite impression.

Further, the administration had removed its commanding military officer in Hawai'i, Admiral Skerrett, in October 1893 for alleged Annexation sympathies. This background made the appointment of Admiral Walker even more striking.

The admiral moved quickly to bolster U.S. forces in Hawai'i. He had written in an earlier report of his concern over the small size of the American presence: "We are equaled in strength by the English and surpassed by the Japanese . . . . We ought to have the controlling force here—stronger than that of any other foreign power and equal to any two of them combined."[54]

Japanese pressures reached their peak about that time with efforts by the Imperial Government to gain suffrage for the nearly 20,000 Japanese males in Hawai'i, but at least two events quickly brought about a reversal. Dole's government stood firm in refusing suffrage and made it clear that its refusal to give Japanese nationals voting rights was permanent by adopting a new Constitution for the Republic that restricted voting rights to Hawaiian-born or -naturalized citizens. Since only the United States and a few other largely Caucasian nations had naturalization treaties with the new Republic, the Japanese were blocked. There was no block, however, to their ability to negotiate for a naturalization treaty, a diplomatic point that could be interpreted under international law as not singling them out for discrimination.

Japan's war with China ended pressure

The principal reason for Japanese withdrawal, however, was Japan's war with China that began in 1894. Japanese warships were withdrawn to their home ports, and nothing was heard further on Japanese government protests over the new Constitution.

U.S. backed off Hawaiian issue when Japan left

The Cleveland administration felt it was safe to back off the Hawaiian issue again and withdrew both Admiral Walker and American warships, relying on the Japanese withdrawal and an agreement by the British to replace their minister to Hawai'i with one less sympathetic to the Royalist cause. In addition, the new Republic was being recognized by every country that did business with Hawai'i and appeared stable and in control, particularly after it put down the counter-revolution sanctioned by Lili'uokalani in 1895.

For the remainder of the Cleveland administration, it was Congress that continued to express concern over Hawai'i's strategic importance to the United States. In a memorable eight-week debate on foreign policy in 1895 in the wake of the Sino-Japanese War, it became clear that all it would take to bring about Annexation even under a Democratic administration was one more outbreak in the Pacific. Japan had demonstrated its sea power during the war with China, and Congress felt the United States could not afford to let down its defenses.

Henry Cabot Lodge Sr. warned about Japan

Sen. Henry Cabot Lodge Sr. during the debate warned that Japan endangered American control of Hawai'i.

"Remember that they [the Japanese] are a new people," he said. (Ed.—Setting aside that their civilization predated America's by centuries, they certainly were in 1895 a new force in international affairs.) "They have just whipped somebody," he continued, "and they are in a state of mind where they think they can whip anybody," he said.

Strong U.S. fleet needed to deter attack

"It is a very dangerous state of mind for any people to be in, dangerous for themselves and for others.

"The surest way to prevent such a war and avoid such a danger at Hawai'i or upon our Pacific Coast is to have a fleet" strong enough to deter attack, he said. He warned that the Japanese must be carefully watched, for they are "our nearest neighbor on the Pacific," with Hawai'i halfway between.[55]

The congressional debates went on for weeks, almost every speaker calling for substantial increases in the U.S. Navy presence to meet pressures from both Japan and Great Britain, all of which helped the cause of Annexation.

Republic waged public relations war for U.S. ties

The Republic, meanwhile, was waging a public relations war to bring about a mood in the United

States that would lead to that Annexation. In a personal letter from Washington dated November 19, 1893, to President Dole, Lorrin A. Thurston, then Provisional Government minister to Washington, set forth the course for the revolutionary group in its quest for Annexation.

Secretary of State Gresham had just made public his report denouncing the Provisional Government, demanding it return the Kingdom to the Queen and announcing that another Cleveland special emissary, Albert S. Willis, was already in Honolulu to bring this about. Nothing was known in advance by the new Hawaiian government or its Washington representative, Thurston, about this or how it was to happen, and the men in Hawai'i wouldn't find out for another ten days or so. Willis' orders were secret and not revealed by Gresham. But Thurston did know the Cleveland position did not sit well with the country at large.

Gresham denounced Provisional Government

"The outburst of denunciation of the proposed policy by the press of the country, regardless of party, has . . . been something wonderful. With the exception of one here and there, the papers, secular and religious, condemn it in the severest terms," he wrote after word of the Gresham position was released.

Administration clearly against Annexation

He noted he had mailed the accounts of his two interviews with Gresham, during which it became clear that the administration was against the Provisional Government and opposed to Annexation. In a move denounced later by Senate Republicans as an abuse of international law, the Cleveland administration demanded that the Provisional Government, which the United States earlier had recognized as the government of the Islands, return Queen Lili'uokalani to the throne. Thurston also sent a 580-

word telegram covering the same points to Dole via San Francisco, where it would catch a steamer.

He wrote "The *N.Y. Sun* sounded the key note on the day after Gresham's report was published, with an editorial entitled, 'The Policy of Infamy', and has kept it up ever since, with three or four editorials every day, and on two days during the week, devoting the entire editorial page, with the exception of a few squibs, to a discussion of the subject in its various phases."

Thurston reported newspapers condemn Gresham plan

Thurston went on to note similar support from the *Outlook*, an influential publication of the day, and *The Washington Star*. He wrote, "The *Star*, usually a neutral noncommittal paper, has out-rivaled Dana [editor of the *N.Y. Sun*] in the use of every condemnatory adjective and phrase at his command—Mr. Noyes, the editor, was at Honolulu this summer and knows his ground.

Whole country awaits news of Willis action

"The feeling throughout the country was intense, and, as one of the newspaper correspondents put it, 'the whole country is holding its breath awaiting the arrival of the *Australia* [to find out what Willis was doing in Hawai'i].'" The *Australia* was known to be the first ship to leave Hawai'i after Willis' arrival and it was expected to be carrying dispatches reporting his meetings with Dole.

After explaining why he didn't think it would be fruitful for him to make a formal reply at this point to Gresham, because, among other things, the administration obviously wanted to deal directly with Dole, Thurston added,

"We must not lose sight of the fact that even though we may not hope to secure annexation through this Administration, we still must try in every possible way to keep on their good side, so long as such position is not a surrender of essential principles.

"I do not therefore consider it sound to engage in any more controversial correspondence with them than is absolutely required. I am rewriting my letter, toning down the English in its more vigorous positions, and have about made up my mind to first submit the draft of it to Gresham before formally presenting it, if I present it at all.

Must not give up hope on Annexation

"In my last interview with him, his manner was more than usually agreeable, and he several times reiterated his personal friendly feelings. Although things look rather blue so far as getting anything from this Administration is concerned, I do not give up hope that all will come out right. It is darkest before dawn.

Harsh Gresham report made friends for Hawaiʻi

"Arbitrary monarchy never seemed so firmly seated in power as on the 13th of January last, and yet it was standing on the verge of its self-dug grave. So I believe that the arbitrary harsh course proposed by the Gresham report has raised us up a host of friends who did not before exist, and by stimulating interest in our affairs has given us a vantage ground which we could have reached in no other way. I believe that it will be a strong factor in favor of the ultimate success of the annexation movement."

This 12-page letter of November 19 was written over a period of days, and meanwhile the *Australia* had reached San Francisco with reports that Willis' initial meetings with Dole had been friendly enough.

Thurston's letter continues:

"It was an intense relief to us, and to the whole country, to learn upon the arrival of the Australia, that Willis had taken no radical steps. Of course there is still the uncertainty as to what he may yet do; but after his presentation and personal expressions of regard to you, it will be a difficult thing for him, after the lapse of so many days, to change and adopt a policy of open hostility, with the acknowledgment that he has under cover of fair word and smiles been concealing a bludgeon in his clothes with which to batter your brains out when the occasion seemed opportune.

Was Willis concealing a bludgeon?

"It fills me with wrath when I think what a fever of excitement you are going to be plunged into upon the arrival of the now outward bound steamer [with the Gresham report], even if Willis has not previously exploded his bomb.

"But I am pinning my faith upon my trust in the courage and steadfastness of you who know what we have come through and what odds we have already overcome and what we would have to go through again if monarchy were restored. You may be assured that the American public are overwhelmingly on our side—There are numerous proffers to go down and help you fight if necessary.

"American public overwhelmingly on our side . . ."

"I hope to God that under no circumstances have you consented to give up your organization, and that if you have been forced out that you will by force go back again as soon as possible. It is an unpleasant alternative, but we might as well have it out now as to let the boil fester along, keeping the whole body politic in a fever.

Thurston urges Dole to hang on

"The Royalists will not be satisfied until they are once more thoroughly beaten. Even if Willis takes no radical action, it seems to me altogether probable that Mr. Gresham's letter will so stir up and encourage the Royalists that it is altogether probable they may take some overt action which will warrant your . . . proclaim[ing] martial law . . ."

Thurston went on to say that if this happened, he favored arresting and deporting the Queen and her most prominent supporters.

Queen and supporters seen as menace to public peace

"Until you get rid of them they will prove a constant menace to the public peace . . . there will sooner or later be an outbreak which will result in the loss . . . of lives . . . .

"I believe the time has fully arrived for change to a permanent form of government on the lines previously indicated. Keep the control for as long a time as it is reasonably probable that it will be required. I favor not less than 5 years for a readjustment and settling down period, before elections take place. I would not rush the formation of the new government. Take time to carefully consider and reconsider the different provisions of the constitution.

"There is much in a name— call it The Republic . . ."

"There is much in a name—call it 'The Republic of Hawai'i'. It will not be a full exponent of the republican principle but that is the central thought around which it is gathered and into which it will develop in time."

The outbreak by the Royalists did come, though not until 1895. Also, Willis did "drop his bomb," demanding the return of the Kingdom, but the long delay in his making the demand, because of the Queen's adamant stand against amnesty, enabled Thurston to arrive back in Hawai'i as the demand was made. Over a period of several days Thurston,

Dole and the Cabinet put together a clear and firm position in the form of a letter. In this remarkable letter from the Provisional Government to the United States, President Dole denounced the demand and announced the new government would stand fast and fight the United States, if necessary. The new Republic of Hawai'i was formed and it did keep a tight grip on things in Hawai'i for the next four or five years, subverting a few democratic principles to maintain control until Annexation. Thurston did send his letter to Gresham and it so riled the secretary of state that he demanded of Dole that Thurston be withdrawn from continued service as minister from Hawai'i.

Thurston forced to withdraw

His official status removed, Thurston spent most of the five years between the Revolution and until Annexation on the mainland, speaking, visiting newspaper editors, writing articles for the cause. His 84-page pamphlet on the subject, *A Handbook on the Annexation of Hawai'i*, is a masterpiece in its summary of the background of Annexation, and was widely circulated.

Five years spent on Annexation campaign

This was Hawai'i's fourth formal effort to annex itself to the United States, the pamphlet notes. It makes much of the strategic values for Annexation, the differences between the vast Pacific and the Atlantic, approximately half its width:

"One of the first principles in naval warfare is that an operating fleet must have a base of supply and repair (Ed.—this being in the days of coal-operated ships).

Naval supply and repair in strategic location

"Without the possession of Hawai'i, all of the principal countries possessing interest in the Pacific, are so far away that the distance is practically prohibitory of hostile operations against the Pacific Coast. For instance, the nearest English station is forty-six hundred miles distant from San Francisco. The nearest French station is thirty-six hundred miles distant. The nearest Spanish station is forty-seven hundred miles distant. Russia is forty-seven hundred miles away; Japan forty-five hundred miles, and China fifty-five hundred miles."

Pearl Harbor attack evidenced Hawai'i's strategic value

Hawai'i, of course, is about twenty-five hundred miles off the Pacific Coast, and in the hands of any of the other countries would provide a jumping-off place against the United States. Less than fifty years later, the Pearl Harbor attack gave evidence of Hawai'i's strategic value.

Commenting on the decline in Native Hawaiian population, the pamphlet states: "It is no longer a question of whether Hawai'i shall be controlled by the Native Hawaiian, or by some foreign people; but the question is, 'What foreign people shall control Hawai'i.'"

Pamphlet detailed Hawai'i imports

Great emphasis also was put on the trade benefits to the United States. For example, Hawai'i imported more West Coast wine than any other single country in the world; was its third biggest purchaser of salmon—more than all the countries of the world combined, leaving out England, Australia and New Zealand; the third largest consumer of West Coast barley, and so on. The pamphlet listed some 200 items of import in detail—in 1896, 132 carriages, 362 bicycles and 1,560 saddles, for example—all in exchange for providing a free market for Hawaiian sugar, rice and bananas.

The pamphlet points out that all of this "astonishing" commercial activity derived from a population of only 109,000 people, with a foreign trade per capita of $208, "a record almost unparal-

leled in the history of the world." Tantalizingly, it
adds that Hawai'i could easily support a population
of a million, which would "place its commerce in the
front rank of American export trade."

The pamphlet also discusses "twenty objections to Annexation with replies thereto." Many
were questions of unconstitutionality, all of which
the pamphlet declares not true.

It discusses at some length the possible objection on a racial basis. After explaining the many similarities between United States and Hawaiian laws,
customs, infrastructure and lifestyles, the pamphlet
states:

*Islanders called
energetic people*

> "The people of Hawaii as a whole, are
> energetic and industrious. They are annually
> producing and exporting more per capita
> than any other nation in the world . . . . No
> people who are leading the world in the per
> capita export of manufactured products can
> be truthfully characterized as lazy, worthless
> or unreliable. As a matter of fact, there are no
> poor-houses, paupers, beggars or tramps in
> Hawaii."

The pamphlet then deals directly with arguments regarding the habits and lifestyles of each
racial background present in the Islands.

*Hawaiians have
struggled
against
retrogression*

About Native Hawaiians, it has this to say:

> "Only 33,000 in number, [they] are a
> conservative, peaceful and generous people.
> They have had during the last twenty years,
> to struggle against the retrogressive tenden-
> cies of the reigning family; but in spite of
> that, a very large proportion of them have
> stood out against such tendencies, and are
> supporters of the Republic and Annexation.
> The majority of the present House of Repre-

sentatives, the first under the Republic, consists of pure-blood Native Hawaiians, and the Speaker of the House is a Native Hawaiian.

"There is not, and never has been any color line in Hawai'i as against Native Hawaiians, and they participate fully on an equality with the white people in affairs political, social, religious and charitable. The two races freely intermarry . . ."

There has never been color line against Hawaiians

The argument that no popular vote was taken or was contemplated regarding Annexation and that this is "un-American" is dealt with at length.

After noting that "this is the argument most resorted to by the ex-Queen Lili'uokalani and her supporters" and that "their objection is not based upon opposition to the American Republic, but upon opposition to any Republic," the pamphlet adds: "They are selfishly seeking the restoration of the Monarchy for their own benefit, and as long as Hawai'i remains independent, they hope for some internal discord or foreign complication which will restore them to power.

Restoration of Monarchy would be for personal gain

"The reply to [this] objection is that no Hawaiian voters have been disfranchised, and that it is not un-American to annex territory without a vote of the inhabitants." The vote of the legislatures of the various territories annexed earlier was sufficient, as was the case in Hawai'i.

The seven annexations of the previous one hundred years are described in detail: Louisiana, Florida, California, New Mexico, Arizona, Alaska and Texas. Thurston notes that in none of these cases was a popular vote taken on the question of annexation. "All that was done or lawfully required to be done, was the agreement of the two [elected] Governments, and the act was completed without reference to either the people of the United States or of the territory proposed to be annexed," the pamphlet states.

Popular vote not required for Annexation

"There is, therefore, no precedent, in any of the annexations of the past, for taking a popular vote upon the subject. Why, then, is it un-American to annex Hawai'i without a popular vote?" the pamphlet asks.

The Constitution of the Republic contained an article directing its president, "by and with the consent of the Senate, to negotiate and conclude a treaty of annexation with the United States." The pamphlet argues this means that in a very real sense "there has been a practical vote in Hawai'i upon the subject of annexation, for every person who is now a voter in Hawai'i has taken the oath to the Constitution of Hawai'i, thereby ratifying and approving of annexation to the United States." The Hawai'i Senate, with a number of Native Hawaiian members, voted unanimously for Annexation. Property requirements for election to the Senate were the same as those in the 1887 Constitution for election to the House of Nobles, which made it a fairly exclusive club.

Many Hawaiians approved of Annexation

In summary, the pamphlet says:

"1. Neither the Constitution nor laws of the United States nor of Hawai'i require a popular vote.

"2. During fifty years, there have been four annexation treaties negotiated by Hawai'i with the United States, viz.: in 1851, 1854, 1893 and 1897, in which neither under the Monarchy, Provisional Government, nor the Republic, has any provision been made

Four annexation treaties negotiated by Hawai'i

for a popular vote, either in the United States or Hawai'i. (Ed.—Of course, the 1893 and 1897 attempts were made under auspices of the Revolutionists, who did not want to take a chance with a popular vote on the matter.)

"3. Six annexations of inhabited territory by the United States during the past 100 years, have been made without a popular vote being taken. (Ed.–The seventh, Texas, also did not enter with a popular vote, but its elected legislature, as did Hawai'i's, approved annexation.)

Six annexations made without popular vote

"4. The Constitution of the United States, in general terms, and that of Hawai'i specifically (Ed.—that of the Republic), authorizes the respective Presidents and Senates to conclude a treaty of annexation. If the theoretical philanthropists of America who are lifting up their voices against annexation through sympathy for the native Hawaiian could descend out of the clouds long enough to ascertain the facts, they would learn that every native minister of the gospel; most of the better educated natives; almost without exception, all of the white ministers of the gospel; the representatives of the American Board of Foreign Missions; the Hawaiian Board of Missions; the practical educators; those who have for years contributed their time, their money and their lives to the Hawaiian people; who feel that their welfare is a sacred trust—all of these are working, hoping and praying for Annexation as the one last hope of the native Hawaiian."

"Annexation . . . one last hope of the Native Hawaiian"

The public relations war went on, and finally, the event the Republic had been waiting for occurred: a new administration was elected to Washington in 1898. President Cleveland was out and

President McKinley was in, bringing with him an administration that favored Annexation. Nevertheless, Annexation was not a shoo-in. McKinley's first efforts to bring it about failed as congressional debate swirled around arguments that years later were sounded over and over again in the sixty-year fight for Statehood: Hawai'i's offshore geographical position and its polyglot population. In the midst of this, the Spanish-American War broke out and the battleship *Maine* was sunk in Manila Bay. With American troops being sent across the Pacific in goodly numbers, Hawai'i's strategic position took top billing in the debate over Annexation.

Anti-Annexation arguments same as anti-Statehood

Still, the administration did not have the votes to put a treaty through the Senate that customarily would have been the vehicle to bring about Annexation. Congressional strategists passed instead on July 7, 1898, a joint resolution directing Annexation. A similar process had been used to bring Texas into the United States, but in spite of the historical precedent there are sovereignty activists today who insist Hawai'i's Annexation was an illegal action. It has yet to be challenged in any court of law and it is doubtful it ever will be. The vast majority of Hawai'i's residents obviously are happy with the end result.

Our Annexation was legal, happy action

All that remained was negotiation of the Organic Act, the enabling legislation that finally passed on April 30, 1900. It made Annexation official and created the Territory of Hawai'i. Negotiators for the Republic did a masterful job with the Organic Act, and in an unprecedented action, Congress accepted Hawai'i without taking its government lands into the federal land bank.

Chapter Nine

*L*and is the Key

"*T*he United States stole our lands."

"The *haole* stole our lands."

"The missionaries stole our lands."

It's the mantra today for many Native Hawaiians.

"The haole stole our lands"

Maybe sovereignty should be spelled l-a-n-d. It's certainly the key element in nearly all forms of the sovereignty movement.

What's the basis for these constant claims of theft? What makes a sovereignty activist think Native Hawaiians are entitled to state lands?

It's hard to believe, but many sovereignty advocates want to take public lands from the state government and give them to the 4 percent of Hawai'i's residents who have more than a 50 percent measure of Hawaiian blood. They want to go beyond their mandated one-fifth share of income from these lands and acquire actual title. Some say these lands should go to *all* calling themselves Native Hawaiians, about 20 percent of Hawai'i residents. Other activists even say private lands should eventually be taken over by the Hawaiian minority.

Some advocates say public lands should go to 4 percent of Hawai'i's residents

Their claim is based on what they maintain is the "inherent right of Native Hawaiians" to the lands of these Islands, at least the public lands. They contend, erroneously, that Native Hawaiians owned the public lands before the 1893 Revolution, that the lands were taken from them at the time—"stolen"— and the Hawaiian people were not compensated. As we'll see in this chapter, the native people never did own them. They were government lands at the time, and have been since the Great *Mahele* in 1848. All the Revolution did was transfer control of those public lands to a successor government. The beneficiaries, all of the residents of Hawai'i, remained the same after Annexation and continue to be the same under Statehood.

Revolution transferred control, not benefits of land

For the Native Hawaiian claims for transfer or compensation to become successful, history would have to show that the lands were formerly owned by Native Hawaiians and their descendants. The activists are at work distorting and rewriting history to make this seem true. The revisionism has already gained acceptance in some circles not familiar with the real history of Hawai'i or its lands.

For example, "whereas clauses" in the congressional apology resolution of 1993 state that government lands were ceded to the United States at the time of Annexation "without the consent of or compensation to the Native Hawaiian people."

Misleading statements cloud the issue

They add that Hawaiians "never directly relinquished their claims to . . . their national lands."

Both of these statements are misleading— and erroneous—in their implications. Unfortunately, no public hearing was held by Congress to examine the truths of the whereas clauses. In a resolution such clauses don't become law anyway, but today activist writers would have us believe they do have the force of law, and since Congress adopted the resolution, the same writers state Congress has thus decreed or agreed that the lands were once owned by

Native Hawaiians. The fact is, Native Hawaiian people as individuals never owned those government or so-called ceded lands, nor until recently expressed any claims to them. Along with the rest of us, Native Hawaiians continue to get government benefits that are financed by revenues received from ceded lands. Recent legislative acts have given them a larger share of state income than is received by any other racial group. On what basis should they now expect to get ownership of the lands in addition?

Ceded lands were never owned by individuals

Since the ceded lands weren't stolen, there is something inherently unfair in the concept of taking away land now owned by the government and being used for the benefit of all of the residents of these Islands—and giving it to a minority of those residents. The process would undermine the land and economic policies of today's Hawai'i.

This effort by a few to get compensated for something neither they nor their ancestors ever owned needs to be put into perspective. And perhaps more importantly, any expectation by those being given these false promises needs to be laid to rest before unfulfilled expectations lead to problems and potential violence.

Undermining land and economic policies

By way of background, this chapter will present a brief history of land in old Hawai'i, how it was held, how it was worked, and how it was affected by contact with the Western world. An understanding of this background will help make clear that today's government lands belong to all in Hawai'i, and not just to those with some measure of Hawaiian blood.

The ancient Hawaiians arrived in these Islands from Polynesia in prehistoric times. In keeping with the prevailing attitude toward land in those days, they did not consider ownership of the Islands in the sense we do today. A feudal system prevailed.

Land was something for everyone to use. Of course, someone had to exercise control, and at any one time, that someone was whoever had become the most powerful member of the community. As a chief or a king, he told the rest what to do and when to do it and governed as though he owned the land itself. Sovereignists argue that in effect he was holding it in trust for his people. That argument wouldn't have carried much weight with Kamehameha I or any of the earlier chiefs who took control by conquest. The only time they would agree that "title" changed hands was when a more powerful chief came along.

Titles changed hands through conquests by chiefs

Archeological studies indicate there were people here at least on some of the Islands before the people we now call Hawaiians arrived. The differences between stone implements found on Kaua'i and those found elsewhere in the Island chain, for example, suggest artisans from different backgrounds and experiences and therefore probably from different points of origin.

Recent archeological thought is that for hundreds of years there was two-way travel between Hawai'i and several of the more southern source areas, such as Tahiti and the Marquesas. Several colonies could have been established on what are now the Hawaiian Islands and their founders could have traveled back and forth, staying within their own land areas both in Hawai'i and south at their starting point. The Marquesans, whom some archeologists in the 1960s and 1970s thought may have been the first visitors, for example, could have maintained a base in Hawai'i for centuries that would have been visited only by other Marquesans. The residents of such an established base in Hawai'i would not yet think of themselves as Hawaiians.

Differing colonies could have been established in Islands

Later, the thinking goes, the two-way travel

slowed down and the warriors from one colony in Hawai'i moved to conquer another Hawai'i colony. The end result would have been the designation of the combined colonies as Hawaiians rather than occupants of a Tahitian or Marquesan outpost.[56]

Two-way travel slows, warfare begins for land

Legends tell us also of the presence of "little people," the *menehune*, even before the first Hawaiians, Tahitians or Marquesans. Marvelous stonework in ancient fishpond walls is attributed in legends to the workmanship of these unknown craftsmen. They may have been descendants of Japanese fishermen who drifted here the way Japanese net floats do now, and remained stranded on these Islands, though the volume of *menehune* work seems to negate that possibility. More than likely they were early, successful colonizers from a different source to the south.

Whoever they were, they worked the land while they were here and left signs of their skill and culture. They were wiped out by whoever came next. Whether those first inhabitants were strangers of a different race or Marquesans who in turn were wiped out by the first arriving warlords to become Hawaiians, or whether they were just the first elements of the Hawaiian migration, wiped out by later arrivals, we do not know for sure.

Menehune probably early colonizers

The early Western visitors noted a difference between the leaders, the *ali'i*, and the common people, the *maka'āinana*. A Russian explorer, Otto von Kotzebue, noted during his voyages of 1823 to 1826 that this difference in appearance and bearing in Hawai'i was very similar to what he had noted in Tahiti. There are those who believe this indicates the final winners in the battle for control of the colonies in Hawai'i were *ali'i* from Tahiti.[57]

Westerners noticed difference between ali'i and commoners

What is clear from Hawaiian legends and oral

history is that the prevailing chiefs of each island controlled the land of their valley or their island and thought of themselves as owning it, even though they did not own it in the Western sense. They got it by conquest in the frequent tribal warfare and "owned" it until it was taken from them by someone more powerful.

The word "owned" misused

Common usage of the word "owned" shows up throughout the literature. One instance, over the signature of Lili'uokalani in the Washington, D.C., *American-Examiner*, in 1898 is particularly interesting in view of current activist claims that the early monarchs didn't really "own" the lands but simply held them in trust for everyone else.

The Queen wrote, in the context of discussing Hawaiian land practices, "Let me turn back, then, to Kamehameha III, who made the Great Division [the Great *Mahele*]. He was an enlightened monarch. As Lord of All, he ruled absolute, **owning in his own right every acre of the Islands. It was a typical feudal system, not unlike that which existed in Europe during the Middle Ages . . .** (Ed.—emphasis added)."

Lili'uokalani had sophisticated grasp of Western culture

Among other things, this writing by Lili'uokalani demonstrates her sophisticated grasp of Western culture. She may have lacked certain skills as a ruler, but she was well educated, possessing highly developed talents and demonstrated skill in music. Those who would argue that she was a naive native who was taken advantage of by the *haole* are clearly wrong.

When Captain Cook arrived in 1778 and the written history of Hawai'i began, the feudal practice Lili'uokalani discussed was in place and a score of chiefs were in control of the lands of their private fiefdoms. They allowed the common people to work

246

the lands under a system of tribute, the kind of thing practiced over the centuries in nearly every part of the world. Unlike some European feudal systems, however, the early Hawaiian commoners were not tied to the land.

Common people worked lands under system of tribute

The chief collected as taxes a share of whatever was produced on the land he controlled—agricultural crops, pigs, dogs, fish, anything that lived there or that individual enterprise could grow or raise. In return for these taxes, the chief organized defense of the area from neighboring tribes, dealt with the gods and dispensed justice. He also called his farmers into battle as warriors whenever he wanted to, and at other times forced them to perform team labor such as building new fishpond walls or temples of worship and sacrifice.

Over time, a few farsighted chiefs gave their people considerable latitude and encouraged them to stay within the areas the chief controlled. Obviously a contented work force could produce more of the necessities of life and had the time and the skills to develop ways of living and using the lands that made sense for the future as well as the present. Under the ancient Hawaiian system, though, the commoners seldom were treated this generously.

A few chiefs gave people more freedom

By modern standards, most Native Hawaiian common people were treated poorly by their chiefs. In fact, by the standards of the missionaries and their children, the treatment was often deplorable.

William De Witt Alexander was born in the Islands in 1833, the oldest child of missionaries William and Mary Ann Alexander, who had arrived the year before. In his sworn testimony before the Morgan Committee in Washington in 1894, he was recognized as a historian and told the committee:

Commoners not well treated by early chiefs

"When I was a child, natives were abject

slaves to their chiefs. They had no rights that the chiefs were bound to respect. They were tenants at will. They could be turned off their land at the word of a chief. Sometimes the whole of the inhabitants of a valley could be evicted at the change of the landlord—at the order of a higher chief. The country was full of natives who were dispossessed, looking around for a place, another home. They were very poor . . .

Natives were slaves to chiefs

". . . They were subject to forced labor by their chiefs. Previously to [my childhood] the sandalwood was exhausted. While the sandalwood lasted they suffered a great deal of oppression; they had to spend months in the mountains cutting sandalwood for their chiefs. [They had to carry it from the mountains] on their backs in [very heavy] bundles. It was a mine of wealth for the chiefs . . . ."

Ahupuaʻa part of feudal land system

The *ahupuaʻa* approach to use, division and control of the land developed in ancient times from the feudal experiences. An *ahupuaʻa* considers the land as a whole entity and any one *ahupuaʻa* usually includes land stretching from the ocean to the mountain top. Those living in the *ahupuaʻa* had access to the sea for fish, to fertile portions of the lowlands for growing (and later, grazing) and to the mountains for water and big timber for canoes. Rarely did those living in the *ahupuaʻa* of one chief or *konohiki* (landlord or sub-chief) have anything to do with a neighboring *ahupuaʻa* under control of another chief. In the days before Kamehameha's reign commenced—for the most part in 1795 although he didn't control Kauaʻi until 1810—none were free to wander to a strange chief's lands. It is doubtful that ordinary natives ever had a right to wander until, perhaps, the Great

Mahele in 1848, which revolutionized the system of land titles. The constant warfare mentality that had prevailed before Kamehameha I, however, tapered off under his overall rule and an individual was no longer subject to instant death for trespassing on the lands of some other chief. Meanwhile, the *ahupuaʻa* form of division made a lot of sense in describing land on an island, and when Western practices took over description and organization, the *ahupuaʻa* structure became a formalized part of the lexicon.

Ordinary natives not given freedom to wander on own

A few farseeing chiefs in times of stability could see the interdependence that was necessary to ensure a future and orderly life for all of their people. Thus they enforced respect for the land and its uses, putting into effect bans on fishing, for example, when overuse threatened to deplete the supply.

Some chiefs saw interdependence was necessary

There were problems, of course. One constant concern for an idyllic lifestyle was the threat of invasion from other Hawaiians, be it from one valley to the next or from one island to another.

Warfare was normal in ancient Hawaiʻi and it meant families were constantly undergoing change. When the chief wanted to invade neighboring lands, he drafted warriors from among the farmers, and the savagery of their battles meant many did not return. When a neighboring chief defeated your chief, you were subject to new rules and could be taken, for example, to a new area to accomplish something the victor wanted done, such as building a new *heiau* or fishpond wall or water supply system.

Warfare normal for Hawaiians

The system was undergoing change when Captain Cook arrived. A new and powerful Hawaiian leader was emerging. The man who would become Kamehameha I envisioned himself as ruler of all the Islands. After Cook brought that first contact with the West, Kamehameha saw the advantages of Western methods and sought the help and advice of foreigners like John Young, who had jumped ship at Kawaihae Harbor on the Big Island in 1790 to take up residence on land instead of sea. With his help, Kamehameha put together an armed force that included ships, guns and European tactics. He began conquering and killing off other chiefs on his own island, Hawai'i, in 1782; by 1795 he had conquered in bloody warfare all of the Islands except Kaua'i.

System changing as Cook arrived

By 1810, that island's chief surrendered and the Kingdom of Hawai'i was formed for the first time in recorded history. The lands of the entire Kingdom thus became controlled by one king. Of necessity he exercised control through appointed governors of each island and chiefs under them.

The common people continued to work the fields, take care of the livestock and catch the fish, all under the eyes of these sub-chiefs and with the payment of tribute. They were happiest when their landlord left them alone.

Feudal system did not give freedom

This feudal system did not give the people freedom but it did provide the possibility of stability and a means of self-sufficiency. The Hawaiian Kingdom under Kamehameha I had the ingredients for survival as an independent nation because the threat of civil war was much diminished under his central and inspired rule. Farming and commerce, without the threat of constant warfare, might have continued uninterrupted and contributed to a buildup of the economy by a population that was held together by common aims. But four things prevented this from happening.

One was the decimation of the population from Western diseases that caused the number of Native Hawaiians to drop drastically from the three to four hundred thousand estimated to be here when

Captain Cook arrived in 1778, to about one hundred thirty thousand when the missionaries arrived in 1820. They took a census shortly after their arrival, which produced that first factual record of the extraordinary net loss in population numbers.

Incidentally, estimates of the pre-Western-contact population range up to eight hundred thousand and even higher, though three hundred thousand to four hundred thousand are more widely accepted numbers. It is astonishing enough to think of a population plunging from four hundred thousand to one hundred thirty thousand in forty years, much less twice as big a drop.[58]

Hawaiians saw astonishing population drop

While better medical practices under the missionaries slowed the process, population numbers continued to decline in the years that followed. The net loss of two hundred thousand to three hundred thousand in those first forty years meant a yearly population net loss of five thousand to seven thousand five hundred, a catastrophic annual decrease of about 1.5 percent. The drop of another ninety thousand in the next seventy years leading up to the Revolution calculates to an annual net loss of a little over twelve hundred, or less than 1 percent annually after the missionaries' arrival. Only a little over forty thousand were still alive in 1893 and Native Hawaiians already were less than a majority in their own homeland. Their number dropped to thirty-three thousand by Annexation, and some observers were forecasting their disappearance.[59]

Missionaries slowed decimation

The second factor that had a devastating effect on farming and food production was the mass movement of the remaining natives away from their farms and fishing preserves to towns building up around harbors where westerners could land and engage in trade and other Western practices.

Mass movement devastated farming and food production

The third factor that brought change to the Kingdom was the result of the new pressure on Kamehameha I, both in his lifestyle and his life itself. In order to strengthen his grip on the Kingdom, he needed Western weapons and ships, which required money. The conservation practices of old had to give way to immediate demands for barter and money.

Conservation practice not the best

Kamehameha's desire for sandalwood, a prized item of barter, led to his ordering intensive harvesting practices that continued after his death into the middle 1820s to the extent sandalwood, a tree that can take a hundred years to mature, barely survives today. This and his acceptance of cattle from the British explorer Vancouver in 1793 wiped out forest lands, birds, and flora and fauna on a major scale.

The King died in 1819 and a new era began with the fourth factor that profoundly affected the Hawaiian lifestyle. Hawaiians had noticed that westerners had violated various of the many ancient *kapu* (taboos) without suffering the drastic consequences forecast over the centuries by the *kāhuna*, the priests whose fear-based control rivaled that of chiefs. Kamehameha had named his favorite wife, the strong-willed Ka'ahumanu, as regent to support his 22-year-old son, Liholiho, known as Kamehameha II.

Young King challenges the kapu system

Based on her skepticism of the ancient taboos and her advice, Kamehameha II took on the well-entrenched *kāhuna*. In a giant step toward the inevitable Westernization of Hawai'i, the young King banished the old pagan religion and taboos that had guided the native people. This led to one last major battle, in Kona in January 1820, where the new rule was threatened by Kekuaokalani, a cousin of Liholiho's and a chief who wanted to go back to the old ways and taboos. The uprising was defeated, both Kekuaokalani and his wife dying in the battle, and the taboos were gone forever.[60] The religious void left Hawaiians with no controlling force in their lives.

The American missionaries arrived in the next couple of months, astonished to find the taboos and pagan practices they had feared were already gone. They took it as God's miracle. Liholiho, after considerable debate, allowed the missionaries to land and start the spread of Christianity. Within months he recognized the value of their teachings and directed that all of his people learn to read and write.

Breaking of kapu system was huge step

Liholiho died a scant five years into his reign during a trip to London to visit King George IV. In a sidelight of early Hawaiian history, Kamehameha I, intrigued with the strength of Western powers, had made a casual deal with the British Admiral Vancouver to cede his nation to Britain.[61] It is likely Liholiho was visiting England to see what life would be like as a British subject. With Liholiho's death, the cession was never pursued.

Liholiho visit to England led to his death

Liholiho was succeeded by his brother, who took over as Kamehameha III. In his long and productive rule, Kamehameha III adopted more and more of the Western ways he could see were necessary for the survival of his people in a different world than that of his forefathers.

Kamehameha III exhorted the dwindling number of his subjects to work harder and more effectively on the small farms they were letting go idle, hoping this would bring economic strength to his nation, but the forces of change adversely affecting the Hawaiian people were too powerful. The Kingdom needed to look to other means of commerce with the Western world.

Kamehameha III encouraged investment in Hawai'i

This required the introduction of conditions that would encourage investment in Hawai'i. In 1840 Kamehameha III promulgated the first written laws of Hawai'i, designed to bring order and stability to living and doing business. The Constitution and the constitutional Monarchy he proclaimed brought enormous and beneficial changes even as the dwindling native population threatened its existence.

Arguments broke out over use and ownership of land, and his foreign advisers, mostly English at the time, urged the King to embrace Western land systems. He and his key supporters were motivated by a belief that widespread ownership of land by individual Hawaiians would strengthen their agricultural efforts, which they and the King thought were critical to their long-term welfare. His advisers also strongly believed economic development and hence prosperity for the Kingdom would not occur unless investors could be assured of the opportunity to own the land they were developing, and the King and his chiefs accepted this.

Advisers urged land use and ownership by individuals

In 1848, Kamehameha III took the action that was to change Hawai'i perhaps more than any other single event: the Great *Mahele*, or division of lands, gave his people for the first time a chance to own land in their own names.

The man who more than any other worked to push toward widespread land ownership by Native Hawaiians was a young Harvard graduate who came to Hawai'i by accident. The accident changed the course of Hawaiian history, and its ramifications demonstrate the ability of Native Hawaiians to sift out the good in Western advice and capitalize on it.

William L. Lee pushed for native land ownership

The man was William L. Lee. He and another recent Harvard student, Charles Reed Bishop, neither of them missionaries, had set sail from Newberryport, Massachusetts, on February 23, 1846, on the Brig *Henry*, bound for a new life in Oregon. The ship's captain chose the long tack from New England to the Azores and downwind around the Horn. It turned out to be a fearsome voyage—"The old brig bounded and pitched like a wounded bison, and sicker than death, we were cooped up in our narrow berths without the least hope of escape. For thirteen days we were knocking about in the wildest confusion without making a single knot on our course. The raging waves swept our deck continually . . ."

Harrowing passage for Lee & Bishop

Young Lee, in a letter home dated April 16, 1846, handed off to a passing ship, continued, "Our sufferings were intolerable, and everyone except the Captain & crew vowed a sacred vow that if they ever planted feet on 'terra firma' again, there they would remain."[62]

In his next letter, bearing a Honolulu dateline, January 20, 1847, we learn that in another difficult tack on the way up the coast to Oregon, fate stepped in. The mainmast broke in strong tradewinds just short of their destination, and the only course available to the stricken ship was to turn downwind for Hawai'i. True to their pledge, Lee and Bishop got off and settled down.

Accident led to landfall in Honolulu

Bishop met and married a Hawaiian princess named Pauahi, a great-granddaughter of Kamehameha I. Bishop was extraordinarily generous, one of the great community leaders of these Islands. He and Pauahi were the leading philanthropists of 19th-Century Hawai'i. No doubt his own views as well as the training Pauahi received from the missionary teachers of the Chiefs' Children's School influenced her to create the Princess Bernice Pauahi Bishop Estate. She endowed it with about 11 percent of Hawai'i's land and directed that most of the income from her estate be used for the education of Island children. Contrary to widespread belief today, she did not specify in her will that the income devoted to the Kamehameha Schools be used only for the education of children with Hawaiian blood. The will reads:

*Bernice Pauahi
Bishop's will
was act of
generosity*

". . . to erect and maintain in the Hawaiian Islands two schools, each for boarding and day scholars, one for boys and one for girls, to be known as, and called, the Kamehameha Schools."

Note there is no mention of race, though Kamehameha has always limited acceptance to children with some measure of Hawaiian blood. The confusion may have arisen because later in her will she also directs her trustees "to devote a portion of each year's income to the support and education of orphans and others in indigent circumstances" and, in this section only, adds, "giving the preference to Hawaiians of pure or part aboriginal blood . . ." The fact that she makes a distinction in this later section emphasizes her clear intent earlier to provide schools for all children, regardless of race.

*Kamehameha
Schools not
specified for
children with
Hawaiian blood*

There is an interesting contrast between what happened to her estate and its vast lands and what happened to an estate of about the same land size left by King Lunalilo. He, Queen Emma and Queen Lili'uokalani also were influenced by their missionary training to set up large charitable trusts.

Emma's established the Queen's Hospital. The hospital thrives in 1998 and lands of the estate, including 18.5 acres in Waikīkī, are beginning to be developed significantly. The Queen Emma Foundation and its 12,618 acres will be a growing influence in the Islands.

The Lili'uokalani Trust helps needy Hawaiian children, and its six thousand three hundred acres, some in Waikīkī and some in north Kona, are growing in value.

The Lunalilo Estate is a sad example. The King set aside some four hundred thousand acres, a holding larger than that of the Bishop Estate, to establish facilities to benefit aging members of his race. His trustees, anxious to fill the need of the moment, sold off the lands, built a home for aged Hawaiians and invested the remaining proceeds in conservative investments such as Santa Fe railroad bonds. Today just one Lunalilo Home exists and income of the trust barely meets its needs.

Lunalilo Estate a sad example of land policy

The trustees of the Bishop Estate were directed to avoid the sale of lands—to lease it instead—unless they deemed a sale absolutely necessary for the operation of the schools. Assets of the trust today have been valued as high as $10 billion. In recent years the argument that there is an overriding societal benefit in the fee simple ownership of individual homesites has brought a change in estate policy over the objections of its trustees. The U.S. Supreme Court has approved a fee conversion process with no tax implications to the estate. It has resulted in the sale of thousands of homesites in fee simple.

Bishop Estate avoided land sales

In spite of these greatly different results in usage of the royal lands and the mixed results of the move to make landowners out of individual natives, the King's Great *Mahele* in 1848 has to be viewed as an act of great generosity. He kept less than a third of the lands for himself, about one million acres called the "King's lands" (later the "crown lands"). He turned another third, 1.5 million acres, over to the government. He specified that this land be used for the benefit of all of the residents of the Islands. A final third, another 1.5 million acres, was set aside to be given to his chiefs and the common people, who could get their share by applying for title to lands they and their families had worked over the years.[63]

King's Great Mahele

The reformation of the land system began on December 10, 1845, about three years before the *Mahele* itself, with the passage of an act establishing the Board of Commissioners to Quiet Land Titles. Its five commissioners were appointed by Kamehameha III to act on all land title claims by private individuals and it was this review process that Lee was urging Hawaiians to pursue. The *Mahele* itself, the division between the chiefs, *konohiki* and the King, began in January 1848 and solved the problem of determining the undivided interests of those parties, about 240 in number. Defining those interests was beyond the purview of the Land Commission, meaning it could not proceed to award title of *kuleana* to the *kanaka maoli* or the sale of fee ownership to foreigners until the *Mahele* was completed in March 1848. The *Mahele* gave the chiefs and *konohiki* claims to specific land areas that were quitclaimed to them by the King at the time. Those claims had to be presented to the Land Commission before the chiefs and *konohiki* could get actual title.

Provisions of the land division

Lee, by that time chief justice of the Monarchy's Supreme Court, undertook an all-out campaign on the King's behalf to get Hawaiian commoners to apply to the Land Commission for fee title to the lands they had been working. He wrote many letters to the missionaries heading the sixteen mission stations spread throughout the Islands to get them to help members of their congregations file claims under the new opportunity. The missionaries helped put together thousands of claims from individual Native Hawaiians who otherwise probably would not have filed, much less successfully.

Letters to missionaries helped promote native land title

In a typical letter dated January 12, 1848, to the Rev. C.B. Andrews on Molokai, Lee wrote:

"My dear sir,

"Many thanks to you for your letter in answer to mine . . . and the bundle of land claims accompanying it. I trust you have imbibed the true spirit in reference to the present landed system of Hawai'i, and feel as I do, that these mixed and uncertain rights of Chiefs, Konohiki (Ed.—landlords) and Tenants are a curse to the land and the people.

"It weighs upon the poor mass of the natives like a mountain of lead crushing them to the very earth, nay, into the very earth. The common Kanaka, not knowing what, or how much to call his own has no incentive to raise anything beyond the immediate wants of himself and family. Oppressed by the Konohiki, the great mass toil on, as I learn, from year to year with a bare living.

Oppression by native landlords

"Our great object is to put an end to this system by separating and defining the rights of the tenants, and giving them what they have, absolutely, if it be no more than a patch of 10 feet square.

"The idea of common Kanakas sending in their claims is not so popular with the chiefs as it should be, for they say, as I am informed, that the Konohiki can send in their claims and the tenants still hold their lands the same as ever . . .

Lee felt feudal system worked against commoners

"Before the people of Hawai'i can prosper and thrive I am firmly convinced that this feudal system of landed tenants must come to an end. Perchance the people are not prepared for so great a change, and will remain a long time insensible to its blessings, but I say let us at least offer them every advantage, though they spurn the gift."

In a similar letter to the Rev. R.A. Walsh of Kōloa, Kaua'i, Lee wrote, "In my humble opinion no greater evil exists at the present day . . . than the ill defined and uncertain rights of the people to the land they till, and the fruits they produce. My heart, and I trust yours also, is enlisted in a reform of this evil, and though the work may be heavy and slow, let us not weary in well doing."

He added that "Should the tenants neglect to send in their claims, they will not lose their rights if their *Konohiki* present claims, for no title will be granted to the *Konohiki* without a clause reserving the rights of tenants. But to preserve the rights of the tenants in their lands is not all we seek—we seek . . . to give them such form and shape that they may always know what they possess."

In addition, Lee wrote letters in Hawaiian to influential associates in each district, asking them also to help process claims.

". . . Spare no exertion . . ."

In other letters he mentions he is seeking to get an extension of the time for filing claims and urges the various missionaries to press forward: "I hope and trust you will not slacken in your good labors."

In a January 14, 1848, letter to the Rev. E.W. Clark in Wailuku, Maui, after thanking him for the receipt of a bundle of claims, Lee notes: "Claims are now coming in at the rate of from one to two hundred each day, and [I am] hoping that you will spare no exertion to have all in your district sent in."

On January 19, 1848, he wrote the Rev. I.S. Green in Makawao, Maui:

Natives needed right to the soil

> "I am happy to hear of your anxiety to have the people become possessed of lands in fee simple. In my humble opinion, this nation can never prosper until they have an absolute and independent right in the soil they cultivate . . . it is to my mind as clear as a sunbeam, that unless Hawaiian Agriculture be

fostered and promoted by the liberal distribution of lands among the people, and in other ways, this nation must gradually sink into oblivion. There must grow up a middle class, who shall be farmers, tillers of the soil, or there is no salvation for this nation. . . .

Lee saw need for a middle class

"We now have upwards of four thousand claims pending before the Land Commission, and hoping that you will continue your good labors and send us many more."

This was approaching half of the families at that time, but all was not rosy, particularly on the Big Island, as he notes in a January 20 letter to the Rev. Asa Thurston in Kailua, Kona:

"I feel greatly obliged to you, my dear Sir, for the information your letter contains, and the trouble you have been to in getting the natives of your district to send in their land claims. I am sorry to say, however, that notwithstanding Hawai'i is the largest Island . . . yet it is the least in the number of its claims. We have received 300 claims per day for sometime past, but very few of them are from Hawai'i."

Big Island claims were slow

The Kona district of the Big Island had special problems: fewer farm lands, a larger drop in population caused by the royal court's move from Kailua to Honolulu, and greater distances between settlements. Entire shoreline villages were abandoned. Apparently Thurston, grandfather of the Revolutionist, urged Lee to get an extension of time because Lee notes it is possible and will have his immediate attention. Ultimately, extensions were granted that kept the Land Commission in action until 1855, ten years after it had started its work.

Mahele didn't work perfectly

Getting title to the lands into the hands of the people was a great idea, but it didn't work entirely the way the King and his advisers had planned, not only because many awards were subsequently sold but because not all *kuleana* were actually awarded. Today, before such an undertaking, an educational program would precede the distribution to help prevent many of the failures that occurred. At the time, the common people were not sophisticated in the ways of Western land ownership. The devastating sicknesses that wiped out their will to work continued to wipe out entire families. Their lands often had been simply abandoned and there were no family members left to file a claim.

Commoners received significant land

Hawaiian activists belittle the effort, arguing that only a low percentage of the *maka'ainana* actually received title to the lands they had been working and received pitifully small amounts of land in the process. In actuality, the percentages were surprisingly high and the amounts of land were significant to the individual applicants, in most cases constituting all of the lands they had been working.

Activists misinterpret Mahele results

One of the most critical has been Lilikalā Kame'eleihiwa, a Hawaiian scholar and active sovereignty spokesperson at the University of Hawai'i, who tends to see something sinister in almost everything the *haole* helped do. In 1992 she produced a monumental work entitled *Native Land and Foreign Desires*. On Page 295 she begins an analysis designed to demonstrate how badly the *maka'ainana* fared in the *Mahele.* Using her own figures, one can demonstrate that instead of suffering, they fared well.

She says that in 1848 there were about 88,000 Hawaiians but only 14,195 applications were filed for *kuleana* awards and only 8,421 were actually awarded a total of 28,658 acres. She estimates

there were 29,220 males over 18, and uses these figures to show that only 29 percent of eligible males
received awards, that less than 1 percent of the total
acreage was awarded and that the average award was
only three acres, belittling all of the numbers to make
it look as though the *Mahele* was a rip-off.

Actually, as she acknowledges on Page 296,
there is another way to look at these numbers.
Arguably, each *kuleana* was being worked by a family, not independently by a series of males over 18.
Using her figure of 10 or 11 for the size of the extended family living on each *kuleana*, the 88,000 people
break down into eight or nine thousand families.
Using a family size of six or eight instead of her ten
or eleven raises the number of families working
kuleana to about the same as the number of claims
filed, stripping out multiple claims and claims by
konohiki or foreigners. It thus is likely that nearly
three-quarters of Native Hawaiian families in 1848
received their *kuleana* in fee simple as a result of the
Mahele. So far as area goes, three acres is about all
one could expect a family to be farming without
modern equipment. And one should not overlook
that the *kuleana* lands generally were the best farm
lands in the Islands.

It's possible three-quarters of Hawaiian families received lands

But perhaps the biggest reason why more
kuleana lands aren't in the hands of the *maka'ainana*
today is simply that the new owners of these lands
frequently sold them rather than endure the rigors of
farming. Once your ancestor has sold the family
land, your lack of land is no longer the fault of the
Great *Mahele*. It is something your own ancestor did
and you must live with it.

Commoners sold off their new lands

A thoughtful study made recently is the 1995
book, *Surveying the Mahele*, by Gary L. Fitzpatrick
and Riley M. Moffat. The authors note that in addi-

tion to the *Mahele* as a means of getting land into the hands of the common people, the kingdom stood ready to sell government lands to any Native Hawaiian who did not have a *kuleana* to claim. They note advertisements and editorials in the government newspaper, *The Polynesian*, promoting this program and that the volume *Index of all Grants and Patents Land Sales* lists the individual grantee, the location and the acreage for all such transactions. "Clearly," they note, "the overwhelming majority of the personal names appearing on this list are Hawaiian," though they note many of the larger sales went to people without Hawaiian names.

Mahele overall impact better than expected

"When the quantity of government land sold [at less than $1 per acre] to *maka'ainana* is included, the impact of the *Mahele* may take on a different light than if looked at solely in terms of *kuleana* awards. A total of nearly 400,000 acres in grant sales were recorded between 1846 and 1860 but no analysis of the amount that went to Hawaiians is available."

The authors conclude that further study must be made of these early sales to find out who the buyers were—*maka'ainana, ali'i or konohiki*—and where and what kinds of land were purchased before a definitive conclusion can be reached about the fairness of the *Mahele* to the Hawaiian people.

"King's lands" not owned by individuals

While the move to spread ownership was only partly successful in its effort to make individual landowners out of most Hawaiians, the gift of one-third of the lands to the government clearly benefited all of Hawai'i's residents. The government lands were to be "managed, leased, or sold, in accordance with the will of [the] Nobles and Representatives, for the benefit of the Hawaiian Government, and to promote the dignity of the Hawaiian Crown."[64] Income from leases and sales of this third of the nation was the principal source of monies for the Kingdom and even today provides significant funds for the government, and hence Hawai'i's people.

The lands retained as the King's lands also provided income for the royal office of the Monarchy itself, though members of the royal family viewed them as privately held. Kamehameha IV's widow, Queen Emma, took to court the question of private ownership of the King's lands, which she wanted as her dower right. In 1864 the Kingdom's Supreme Court denied her claim, maintaining they were lands owned by the King as sovereign and not as an individual.

Two Queens sought title to crown lands

The Legislature in 1865 passed an act renaming them the "crown lands" and preventing further sale or disposition of them by any ruling monarch.

After Annexation, Queen Lili'uokalani tried to claim private ownership of the crown lands, but the territorial Supreme Court denied her claim, and in a subsequent appeal to the U.S. Court of Claims in 1910, she lost again. **Until current claims by various sovereignty activists, no one else has tried in the courts to claim these lands are anything but government lands.**

They continued to be government lands after the Revolution, though control passed to the Provisional Government. Later that control became the responsibility of the Republic, but at all times the income went to the government for the benefit of the people.

The ceded lands totalled 1.75 million acres

Various lands in both the crown and government segments had been sold off over the years by the King and the Legislatures of the Monarchy and the Republic so that by the time of Annexation about 1.75 million of the original 2.5 million acres remained.[65] That 1.75 million-acre combination of crown and government lands became known as the "ceded lands" as a result of their cession by the Republic to the United States at Annexation in 1898.

The 1898 Joint Resolution of Annexation led to passage of the Organic Act in 1900 and territorial status for the Islands, but the day the resolution was adopted, August 12, 1898, is marked as Annexation Day. Formal transfer of sovereignty and transfer of title to the ceded lands took place on that date.

Some land was set aside for federal use that Hawaiʻi still enjoys

The joint resolution made clear that these ceded lands and any lands subsequently acquired by exchange were to be held in a trust to benefit the inhabitants of Hawaiʻi. It spelled out that the income and proceeds from any sale of these lands were to be used in Hawaiʻi for the benefit of its residents, and only for "educational and other public purposes."

Clearly there was no theft from the people of Hawaiʻi and thus no reason for them to expect compensation from the United States. The lands were still government lands after the Revolution in 1893, still under the administrative control of the Hawaiian government and the beneficiaries were still the people of Hawaiʻi.

During the subsequent fifty-nine years until Statehood, a few more changes occurred. About four hundred thousand acres were removed from the trust by acts of Congress for military posts, national parks and other federal purposes. Hawaiʻi's people obviously continue to share in the benefits that accompany those uses.

Hawaiʻi land transfer unique in American history

When Statehood occurred in 1959, title to the remaining lands was transferred to the new state with special provisions for their use, a process unique to Hawaiʻi in American history. Again, they remained government lands and do so to this day.

The Admission Act spelled out that the lands

transferred and the income from them could be used in only five ways:

"(1) a public trust for the support of the public schools and other public educational institutions,

"(2) for the betterment of the conditions of Native Hawaiians, as defined in the Hawaiian Homes Commission Act, 1920, as amended (Ed.—50 percent blood quantum),

"(3) for the development of farm and home ownership on as widespread a basis as possible,

"(4) for the making of public improvements, and

"(5) for the provision of lands for public use."

Hawaiians not identified as specific beneficiaries in Organic Act

Native Hawaiians had not been identified as specific beneficiaries of the ceded lands in the Organic Act at the time of Annexation—they shared in the total income, as did all other residents. The Admission Act's language that designated one of the five uses for ceded land revenues as support for Native Hawaiians with more than 50 percent blood level soon led to pressure for further legislation making certain public revenues available for the use of Native Hawaiians of lesser blood quantum.

The 1978 Constitutional Convention under the drive of soon-to-be Governor John Waihee and his "*palaka* power" slogan spent considerable time developing amendments designed to improve the financial lot of Native Hawaiians of whatever quantum. One amendment provided that one-fifth of state revenues, including those from ceded lands, would go to a newly created Office of Hawaiian Affairs for the benefit of Native Hawaiians, who were described in the amendment in much broader terms than the

Office of Hawaiian Affairs

Hawaiian Homes description that had been used in the Admission Act. OHA provides a wide range of benefits for Native Hawaiians, who under OHA terms are defined as "any descendants of the aboriginal peoples inhabiting the Hawaiian Islands which exercised sovereignty and subsisted in the Hawaiian Islands in 1778, and which peoples thereafter have continued to reside in Hawai'i." Because of the federal limitation on the use of ceded land revenues to Native Hawaiians with 50 percent or more native blood, the use of OHA's overall revenues requires complicated bookkeeping, which was under study at the state level in 1997.

Ceded land revenues restricted to those with 50 percent native blood

Other amendments included one creating a "Native Hawaiian Rehabilitation Fund," which gets 30 percent of state receipts from lands previously cultivated as sugar cane lands and from water licenses. Those receipts, before Statehood, had been designated for loans to lessees of available lands.

In 1997, discriminatory provisions based on race were being questioned. Aside from their effect on the state's financial condition, these provisions were being challenged as unconstitutional because of their racial discrimination.

Classification as Native American difficult

An impressive analysis of the implications of present practices termed discriminatory and what will be required of Native Hawaiians to qualify as beneficiaries of government largesse was published in December 1996 in the *Yale Law Journal*. The writer, Stuart Minor Benjamin, holds scant hope for current benefit programs to hold up if challenged. And the road to qualification is difficult and strewn with obstacles to Native Hawaiians who would seek to be classified as Native Americans and thus possibly receive the federal benefits now awarded Native American tribes.

Attorney John W. Goemans, local representative in 1997 of the Campaign for a Color-Blind America, which is working toward the elimination of racial discrimination in America, summarized Benjamin's positions:

"1. Recent Supreme Court cases (i.e., Croson, Adarand) establish that all government programs containing racial or ethnic classifications are presumptively invalid and must be subject to 'strict scrutiny' (i.e., must meet a compelling governmental interest by means that are narrowly tailored to meet that interest).

Strict scrutiny of government acts granting racial or ethnic preferences

"2. That test requires a showing of (a) past discrimination and (b) the lingering present effects thereof which require remediation.

"3. The strict scrutiny test must be applied to all governmental acts which grant preferences to groups by race or ethnicity. Congress may grant preferences if a particular group has a "special relationship" with Congress...[under the Congressional] power to regulate commerce with the Indian tribes and only to federally recognized Indian tribes.

"4. The states have [limited] power to legislate such special relations [and then] only as derived from a Congressional Act . . .

"5. Neither native Hawaiians generally or any group thereof have such a special relationship as a federally recognized Indian tribe. Thus all Federal or State legislation granting preferences to persons designated racially Hawaiian is subject to strict scrutiny and, without a showing of (a) past invidious racial discrimination (i.e., pervasive, systematic, and obstinate discriminatory conduct) and (b) the lingering present effects thereof, is unconstitutional.

Hawaiians do not have special federal relationship

"6. There is not now nor has there ever been any reasonable argument that native Hawaiians as a race have been so discriminated against. (In fact, during the first thirty years of the Territory of Hawai'i, native Hawaiians constituted the single largest voting bloc, effectively controlled the territorial Legislature, and elected Hawaiians successively as Hawai'i's first two delegates to Congress.) Consequently, legislation establishing the Hawaiian Homes Commission, the Office of Hawaiian Affairs [or any other legislation] providing privileges and rights based on race will ultimately be struck down as unconstitutional."

Hawaiians not victims of discrimination

Other attorneys, referring to the Kaho'olawe legislation amended by U.S. Senator Daniel Akaka to provide preferences for Native Hawaiians, argue that its language also is not enforceable.

It will take years for these matters to be straightened out in Hawai'i and U.S. courts, and obviously patience is called for in this delicate area.

The path for Hawaiians to gain status comparable to Native American tribes is described in detail by Benjamin. It would require many difficult maneuvers. Suffice it to say here, given the relationships between the various Hawaiian groups, the process looks very difficult indeed. Once Native Hawaiians become aware of the not necessarily beneficial limitations on Native American tribes included in current legislation, there may be even less interest in pursuing this course.

Years before legal matters sorted

Chapter Ten

The Congressional Apology: A Travesty

O n October 27, 1993, the U.S. Senate passed a joint resolution to "acknowledge the 100th anniversary of the January 17, 1893, overthrow of the Kingdom of Hawai'i, *Apology to Native Hawaiians* and to offer an apology to Native Hawaiians on behalf of the United States for the overthrow of the Kingdom of Hawai'i." It passed 65 to 34, with only one hour of debate on the Senate floor during which serious questions were raised that went unanswered. On November 15 it passed the House in even less time, with no debate and no objections. There were no public hearings or input. It was a triumph for sovereignty activists. It is an insult to the rest of Hawai'i's taxpayers and to the American people.

While resolutions do not have the force of law, some sovereignty groups already are using it as the basis for their proposed creation of an independent nation and for efforts to get reparations. Each *Resolutions do not have force* sovereignty group, regardless of its individual goals, *of law* sees the apology resolution as providing some kind of legal basis for proposed actions. It seems incredible that a simple resolution presented as a good-faith reconciliation effort by Hawai'i's two senators, Daniel Akaka and Daniel Inouye, could now be billed as having such authority and meaning.

Senator Inouye stressed that it did not seek special treatment for Native Hawaiians nor imply consent for independence or reparations. Senator Akaka, however, appeared to view it as the opening move toward recognition and reparations, and it's now being used for that purpose. Perhaps more startling, it surfaced in September 1997, that the sovereignty movement views it as resolving by compromise the long-standing differences in interpretation of the events surrounding the revolution. Daviana MacGregor, a professor in the University of Hawai'i Department of Ethnic Studies and the person credited with having written the resolution, said in an article in *The Advertiser*, September 7, 1997:

Senators see apology differently

> "[The resolution] has closed the chapter on the role of the U.S. government in the overthrow. . . . The U.S. Congress and the president . . . recount and agree upon the key historic events leading up to and following the overthrow of the Hawaiian monarchy. . . . They finally admitted and accepted blame for injustices committed . . . with the participation of agents and citizens of the United States."

Resolution not history, not law

As indicated later in this chapter, the resolution appears to be totally derived from the Blount Report and hence in no way represents a compromise between Blount and Morgan's findings. No public hearings or public input were sought by our Senators, who doubtless were astonished to read about this conclusion by MacGregor.

On September 18, 1997, H.K. Bruss Keppeler, a middle-of the-road activist attorney, admitted to an audience at The Pacific Club that MacGregor and others are wrong with this interpretation. He said the apology resolution provides neither history nor law; "it's just a resolution."

Only five senators participated in the debate. Three were opposed and two—Hawai'i's two— argued in favor. Senator Inouye stated several times that it was a "simple resolution of apology" and had "nothing to do" with whether Hawaiians are Native Americans or with the question of Hawaiian homelands. The three senators who spoke in opposition, Slade Gorton of Washington, Hank Brown of Colorado and John C. Danforth of Missouri, however, foresaw problems with the ambiguity of its limited operative language—justified concern given subsequent actions of sovereignty activists.

Little debate on resolution

The opening argument was made by Senator Akaka, who was allowed fifteen minutes. He didn't take that long but he raised more than half a dozen points whose validity is questionable. In his first sentence, for example, he said this resolution concerns "U.S. policy toward its native peoples." Hawaiians, while natives of the former Kingdom, and in many cases citizens of the nation governed by the Republic at the time of Annexation, never were native peoples of the United States. They were native peoples of the Republic of Hawai'i, and along with all of its residents became citizens of the United States on Annexation. Native Hawaiians thus never were Native Americans. Most sovereignty efforts are based on the unfounded assertion that Hawaiians *are* Native Americans, a technical description that opens a number of legal doors. This description of Hawaiian natives has not been accepted by any administration or by Congress. In fact, U.S. Solicitor General Thomas L. Sansonetti issued a lengthy opinion in early 1993 that Hawaiians are *not* Native Americans, a point reviewed later in this chapter. The opinion

Validity of Akaka's points questionable

Hawaiians not considered Native Americans

was withdrawn later that same year for political reasons by the Clinton administration, but no contrary opinion has been issued in the ensuing years.

More to the point that the issue of Native American status was not under consideration during debate over the apology resolution, Senator Inouye, wrapping up the debate, said:

> "As to the matter of the status of Native Hawaiians, as my colleague from Washington knows, from the time of statehood we have been in this debate. Are Native Hawaiians Native Americans? **This resolution has nothing to do with that** (Ed.—emphasis added)."

Senator Akaka earlier, however, had argued for several minutes that Hawaiians *are* Native Americans. He said, "Too often, when the American public and U.S. policy makers think about Native Americans, they mistakenly consider only Native American and Alaska natives as native peoples of the United States." He must be aware of the continuing unresolved debate on this point referred to by Senator Inouye, but he goes on to say:

Akaka: Hawaiians are Native Americans

> "This misperception is based on a lack of knowledge of events surrounding the 1893 overthrow . . . and the current status of Native Hawaiians in our nation's political system.
>
> "Long neglected by the United States, Native Hawaiians have literally fallen through the cracks when it comes to a comprehensive federal policy towards Native Americans. . . . Native Hawaiians are, indeed, Native Americans. . . ."

The senator overlooks several striking differences between Hawaiians and Native Americans. The Native Americans lived in areas conquered by troops of the United States in bloody warfare and their lands were directly seized by the United States to become federal lands until some were set aside as Indian reservations. It's logical that North American Indians are considered Native Americans: They controlled their lands and were living on them when those lands were seized by U.S. soldiers under a clearly stated U.S. policy of expansion and wiping out Indians and their control. Native Americans were long denied citizenship. They deserve compensation for this treatment and this has been recognized for over one hundred years. Alaska natives, too, did not become citizens of the United States at the time of acquisition—or of Russia, from whom the United States bought the lands.

Striking differences between Hawaiians and Native Americans

Not so with Native Hawaiians. Hawai'i was neither conquered nor bought. Hawai'i was acquired by Annexation from the Republic of Hawai'i, which offered itself and its people for that purpose, with the unanimous approval of its Legislature.

Hawai'i was not conquered or bought

Hawaiians were native residents and subjects or citizens, in succession, of the Kingdom, the Provisional Government and the Republic. They, along with all other citizens of the Republic, became citizens of the United States at the time of Annexation. They continued to get the same benefits from their government lands after Annexation as they had before, and continue to do so today, although, as indicated earlier, most sovereignty activists are seeking extra, special benefits for Hawaiians alone.

Hawaiians got same benefits as all citizens

Since the conquest of Kamehameha I, Native Hawaiians have not been treated as a conquered people. Not by the Provisional Government, not by the Republic, not by the United States.

The Republic had existed for more than four years at the time of Annexation and was recognized as an independent nation by the United States and every other foreign government interested in the Pacific. Association with America was something Hawaiian leadership sought over the years. Sovereign kings several times in the 19th Century had offered the Kingdom to the United States for Annexation or Statehood, Kamehameha III going so far as to negotiate a formal Annexation treaty, though he died before it could be signed. These Hawaiian monarchs believed that the association would benefit their people by stabilizing the struggling Island nation in friendly hands with fair treatment under a strong government.

Hawaiian leadership sought association with America

The natives of Mexico who were in the Texas area and the natives of Spain and Mexico who inhabited California before those areas became part of the United States, on the other hand, received discriminatory treatment. Their personal status at the time their lands were being considered for Annexation was similar to the personal status of the natives of Hawai'i: Native peoples of the district, they were living on land controlled by themselves or their independent local government when it became a part of the United States. But as individuals they were not treated similarly when they became part of the United States. None of the residents of Mexican or Spanish ancestry qualified as American citizens when those in control of their independent countries joined the American Flag. None became Native Americans. None retained any interest in the land whatsoever. None got the right to vote until much later.

Hawaiian monarchs sought to stabilize nation

Hawai'i's Annexationists fought long and hard to make sure the Hawaiian people would enjoy the full benefits offered by the United States to its people. The Native Hawaiians did not become second-class citizens.

The vast lands of Texas and California at Annexation and the lands seized from Native American tribes went into the federal land bank. The Republic of Hawai'i, on the other hand, through a three-man committee headed by L.A. Thurston, was able to negotiate a transfer of its lands to the United States in the form of a sort of trust whose income could only be spent for the welfare of all of the residents of the Islands.

Annexationists fought for Hawaiians

Senator Akaka stated that "While the primary purpose of [the] resolution is to educate my colleagues on the events surrounding the 1893 overthrow, the resolution would also provide the proper foundation for reconciliation between the United States and Native Hawaiians." No foundation was laid for the need for reconciliation nor what it might mean. He hinted he had reparations in mind. Our other senator stated just the opposite: The resolution was not a step toward reparations or Native American designation for Hawaiians.

Akaka: Basis for reparations Inouye: Not a basis for reparations

Later Senator Akaka referred to another event not based on any factual evidence and subject to much debate: "In recognition of the complicity of some members of the church" (the United Church of Christ, whose American Board of Commissioners for Foreign Missions sent missionaries to Hawai'i between 1820 and 1850), the church offered a public apology in 1993 to Native Hawaiians. It is true that the national office of the church did make such an apology. But any Hawai'i church members who might have participated in the Revolution were not involved in it on the basis that they were members of the church. Yes, there were two second- and one third-generation descendants of missionaries among the thirteen members of the Committee that spearheaded the Revolution. But they were there as subjects of the Kingdom, concerned for its future, and not as representatives of a missionary viewpoint. In 1893, the church was not asked to take a position on the Revolution and it did not do so.

Church not asked to take a position on Revolution

Local church members were not asked for their opinion or input on the 1993 apology by their national office and many Hawai'i members of the church still are upset that the office took the position it did. They resent the attempt to rewrite history to make it appear that the church played a role in the overthrow. And they resent the transfer to Hawaiian organizations of endowment monies and land contributed to the Hawai'i branch of the church over the years by its members. It was an inappropriate apology, not based on any facts offered in evidence, the result of lopsided research at best.

Church apology inappropriate

Senator Akaka sounded a theme much exploited by sovereignists but bearing little relationship to fact; namely, that the overthrow somehow had an adverse effect on the welfare of Native Hawaiians. Arguably, the overthrow created conditions that five years later *helped* rather than hindered Hawaiian welfare because it brought into play the support of the U.S. government. What Senator Akaka said was:

Revolution not to blame for Hawaiian status

> "The deprivation of Hawaiian sovereignty, which began a century ago, has had devastating effects on the health, culture and social conditions of Native Hawaiians, with consequences that are evident throughout the Islands today."

The idea that somehow the Revolution is to

blame for the health, cultural and social status of Hawaiians from 1893 until today is hard to fathom. Remember, too, that Native Hawaiians controlled the elective and appointed government offices up to World War II. If one is to hold any government responsible for the welfare of the Hawaiian people in the earlier part of the 19th Century, it should be the Monarchy. The Monarchy did its best to prepare its people for the inevitability of living with Western culture but it wasn't equipped financially to bear the burden and costs.

O.A. Bushnell, in his provocative 1993 book, *The Gifts of Civilization*, attributes the breakdown in Hawaiian civilization in large part to the unsavory characters who were Hawai'i's visitors during the four decades after Western contact and before the missionaries arrived. Many of the men who went to sea in those days and thus ended up in Hawai'i could well be generalized as being of the lowest character. Social welfare was not their game and they certainly evinced little consideration for their fellow man. In their viewpoint, Hawaiian natives were fair game for every kind of exploitation.

Monarchy tried to prepare people for Western culture

Further, at the time of the Revolution, expenditures of the royal government on welfare and assistance to its people of necessity were virtually nil. The Kingdom often was near bankruptcy. After Annexation, Hawaiians became eligible for the benefits of the United States, a huge step forward. No one argues that Hawaiian problems do not exist today, but they certainly shouldn't be blamed on the Revolution.

Royal government spent little on welfare

The entire Akaka-Inouye resolution needs to be examined in detail to demonstrate how one-sided and distorted the campaign for sovereignty has become. Even our good elected officials, who should have recognized the bias, accepted many of the claims without question. The resolution's thirty-seven whereas clauses are six times longer than the operative body of the resolution and contain numerous errors of fact and distortions of the truth, beginning with the very first clause, discussed in detail below. In no way can passage of the resolution by Congress be considered an affirmation of these errors as the "new truth."

Sovereignty campaign distorted

As Senators Gorton and Brown pointed out during the brief debate, the congressional resolution is not clear as to what it implies or means when it comes to "acknowledging the ramifications of the overthrow...[or]...the proper foundation for reconciliation" mentioned in its brief operating text. The committee report contained no additional information nor any explanation of what the resolution sought by way of reconciliation or compensation. The questioning senators tried to get more information and asked for time to get it. Senator Inouye, without answering their questions in detail, denied their request for an additional half-hour of debate "because a schedule has been established for the rest of the afternoon." Senate rules require unanimous consent for an extension of time.

Resolution unclear on compensation

The mischief this congressional resolution can cause is evident by actions already taken by sovereignty groups. One, the "Nation of Hawai'i" headed by Pu'uhonua "Bumpy" Kanahele, has published an interpretation by its consultant on international law, Francis A. Boyle, that maintains this so-called simple resolution entitles "the native people of Hawaii . . . to a restoration of their independent status as a sovereign nation state." Boyle suggests Kanahele's group take its case to the United Nations and the International Court of Justice. It seems obvious

A Timeline through Hawai'i's History
Western Contact to Statehood
1778-1959

1778

British Captain James Cook opens Hawai'i to Western world, exposing Islands to devastating diseases and colonial ambitions.

1798

Kamehameha I discusses cession to Britain with Captain James Vancouver, but the negotiations go nowhere.

1810

Kaua'i chief yields to Kamehameha I, who had conquered in bloody warfare all other competing chiefs in Hawai'i, uniting the Islands in one Kingdom for the first time in recorded history.

1819

Kamehameha I dies. He is succeeded by his son, Liholiho (Kamehameha II), but the power lies with regent Ka'ahumanu. At her urging, Kamehameha II eats with the women of his court, ending the *kapu* (taboo) system and the old religion, which also had included infanticide and human sacrifice.

1820

Brig *Thaddeus* brings first missionaries. They teach almost entire nation to read and write, preserve the language in a written form, translate the Bible and other literature into Hawaiian. They continue to preach in Hawaiian after the natives learn English. Hawai'i becomes one of most literate nations in the world, surpassing the United States by mid-century.

1840

Kamehameha III, who became King in 1824 after brother's death, establishes a constitutional form of monarchy.

1848

Kamehameha III seeks Annexation with the United States but Washington is against it.

King proclaims Great *Mahele* (land distribution), gives about one-third of his land to Native Hawaiians, one-third to government and retains one-third as "King's lands," later "crown lands."

1849

Kamehameha III signs treaty of "friendship, commerce and navigation" with United States.

1851

U.S. Secretary of State Daniel Webster declares Americans who settle in Hawaiian Islands "have ceased to be American citizens." Most had become subjects of Kingdom, but many believed they were still U.S. citizens. Status of "denizen" allows Kingdom voting rights without need to become a subject.

Kamehameha III, United States begin negotiating Annexation treaty despite objections from Britain and France. Treaty, with lack of enthusiasm in Washington, takes three years to negotiate and King dies before it can be signed.

1854

Kamehameha III dies, is succeeded by *hānai* (adopted) son, Alexander Liholiho (Kamehameha IV), who withdraws treaty of Annexation with United States, favors tie with Britain.

1851-1863

American Board of Missions winds down, then severs its relationship with the Hawai'i missionaries, who either go on missions elsewhere or continue their work with the support of local congregations. The Revolution of 1893 thus occurs thirty years after the last of the missionaries are active in Hawai'i.

Kamehameha IV

1862

Kamehameha IV dies, is succeeded by his natural brother, Lot Kamehameha (Kamehameha V), who favors more absolute Monarchy, continued ties to Britain.

Kamehameha III

Kamehameha V

View of Honolulu

1864

Kamehameha V abrogates the Constitution of 1852 after Legislature refuses to act on proposed amendments, replaces it with a new Constitution that returns certain powers to the Monarchy and introduces property ownership requirements for voting.

The Kingdom's Supreme Court denies claim by Queen Emma, widow of Kamehameha IV, to private ownership of the King's lands. The court rules the lands are owned by the King as a sovereign and not as an individual.

1872

Kamehameha V dies, ending Kamehameha dynasty. Constitution provides for election by the Legislature and Lunalilo becomes first elected king, defeating Kalākaua.

1874

Lunalilo dies, is succeeded in tumultuous election by Kalākaua, who wins legislative vote over the more popular Queen Emma, widow of Kamehameha IV. Riots break out at the courthouse where Legislature is assembled, at Fort and Queen Streets. U.S. troops are landed to preserve order.

1875

United States and Hawai'i sign a Treaty of Reciprocity, establishing an exclusive trade link between the two nations.

1887

"Pearl Harbor Clause" added to Treaty of Reciprocity as part of agreement for further extension, granting exclusive rights to the United States for the use and development of Pearl Harbor.

July 6:
Community-wide distress over years of mismanagement of the Kingdom and dissolute excesses by Kalākaua culminates in mass meeting that imposes Reform Constitution on King, diminishes powers of Monarchy by putting control into hands of Cabinet. Opponents label it "Bayonet Constitution." King's armed forces do not challenge the volunteer riflemen, mostly *haole*, who are part of the mass meeting and who later lead 1893 Revolution.

1889

Charles B. Wilson, later to be Lili'uokalani's marshal, and a group of his supporters face Kalākaua and demand abdication in favor of his sister. Kalākaua declines, effort is dropped.

Later, Robert W. Wilcox, a European-trained half-Hawaiian artilleryman, launches an insurrection against Kalākaua. Lili'uokalani, aware of the move, plans to succeed her brother if Wilcox forces him to abdicate. U.S. troops again are landed to protect American lives and property, but, as in 1893, do not take an active role. The rebellion is put down by same men who saved Kalākaua in 1887 and who in 1893 oust Lili'uokalani, in all three cases without asking for prior surrender of Monarchy's forces.

January:
Kalākaua dies. His sister, Lili'-
uokalani, named by him as his
successor, takes the throne
after swearing to uphold the
1887 Constitution.

April:
The McKinley tariff on Hawaiian sugar entering the United
States has serious effect on Isle
economy until its repeal in
1894.

Wilcox forms *Hui Kalai'āina*, a
Native Hawaiian political group
dissatisfied with Lili'uokalani's
regime because of her association with Marshal Wilson.

January:
Secret Annexation Club is formed, sends
L.A. Thurston to Washington to sound out
possibilities of Annexation. He finds it
cannot be accomplished without a request
from the Hawai'i government. By July
1893, 18 percent of club members are
Native Hawaiians.

February:
Hui Aloha'āina, a Native Hawaiian political
club with several hundred members, is
formed to oppose
Queen Lili'-
uokalani and
favor Annexation.

Lili'uokalani

The 1893 Revolution Begins

Thursday, January 12:
The Kingdom's Legislature, at the
Queen's behest and after much pressure and bribery, removes the Jones-
Wilcox Cabinet, which opposed her
opium and lottery bills. Under the
Constitution, all bills must have the
approval of the Cabinet. She appoints
a new Cabinet. The bills are approved
and the Queen signs them over community objections.

Saturday, January 14:
　　Morning:
After getting the opium and lottery
bills signed, the Queen tells her newly
appointed Cabinet that she is promulgating a new Constitution, in defiance
of her oath to uphold the 1887 Constitution, which calls for legislative initia-
tion and approval of amendments.

Hers would return the Kingdom to a
more absolute Monarchy, disenfranchising the foreign community and
allowing her appointment of the upper
house and the Cabinet. Her action is
the catalyst that gets the Revolution
underway. The four-man Cabinet
refuses to approve her proposal, calls
it unconstitutional.
The Cabinet members, all Royalists,
ask *haole* community leaders for support to depose Queen. All four members meet with Lorrin A. Thurston and
W.O. Smith in Attorney General A.P.
Peterson's office, prepare and sign
notice to Queen of her ouster and sign
request to U.S. Minister John Stevens
seeking support of U.S. troops if they
proceed. Neither document is delivered as Queen changes her mind the
next day.

Saturday, January 14 (continued)

Afternoon:

Meeting at the office of W.O. Smith follows, expands to several hundred people. John Colburn, the Queen's minister of the interior, makes plea for armed community support, backed by Peterson and her personal attorney, Paul Neumann; a hundred men sign up as armed resistance and a counter-revolution against the Queen are openly advocated. The thirteen-member Committee of Safety is then named to carry it out.

Meanwhile, the U.S.S. *Boston* returns to Honolulu with U.S. Minister Stevens aboard. The warship had been on a ten-day trip to Hilo.

Night:

Committee of Safety meets into the evening; Delegation calls on Minister Stevens to apprise him of what has transpired, asks what he would do if Cabinet tried to oust the Queen. He says because Queen's proposed action was revolutionary, he would recognize Cabinet as government and support them as he has supported Hawai'i's government in past.

Sunday January 15:

Morning:

Thurston wakes up Colburn and they wake up Peterson. Thurston tells them the citizens are prepared to join them, follow their lead in declaring the Queen in revolution against the government, the throne vacant and the Monarchy abrogated. He says the Committee of Safety is prepared to move against the Queen whether the Cabinet acts or not. The Cabinet says it is not ready to act.

At a 10 a.m. meeting of the Committee of Safety at the home of member W.R. Castle, Thurston reports the Cabinet position. The Committee meets most of the day as several of the Queen's police keep watch, reiterates its intention to go ahead without the Cabinet and calls a mass meeting for Monday afternoon. The Queen calls her own mass meeting for the same time.

Afternoon:

Queen's Cabinet members meet with Minister Stevens, seeking support for her in the event of insurrection, and are told that U.S. troops will not take sides.

Monday, January 16:

Morning:

The Committee of Safety meets at 9 a.m. in Thurston's office, learns of Queen's mass meeting, reviews formal request from Cabinet for conference. The Queen's marshal, Charles Wilson, stops by, calls Thurston out and tells him Committee must stop its revolutionary plans. Committee declines. Subcommittee sent to meet with Cabinet, finds it has gained promise from Queen not to promulgate the new Constitution, members have changed their minds about deposing her. Wilson goes to Cabinet, asks permission to arrest entire Committee, which still is in Thurston's office. The Cabinet, which has kept Queen informed about Committee's plans, denies permission. Queen takes no action either, though U.S. troops are not yet ashore.

Monday, January 16 (continued)
Committee decides to pursue action against Queen in view of her statements that she is withdrawing new Constitution only until a more opportune moment, and in view of quotes from her in the Hawaiian language newspapers that she will do it "soon."

Afternoon:
A 2 p.m. mass meeting of 3,000 unarmed residents is held within a block of 'Iolani Palace. The meeting hears fiery speeches, cheers, unanimously adopts a resolution calling for freedom, continuation of the right to vote and for a strong and stable government, all of which they believe would be lost under the Queen's new Constitution. The meeting also adopts resolution declaring the Queen to be in revolt and authorizing the Committee of Safety to do whatever is necessary. Committee makes its first request to Stevens for landing of U.S. troops, delivering written request signed by entire Committee to him after the afternoon mass meeting.

About 5 p.m., Capt. G.C. Wiltse, commanding officer of the U.S.S. *Boston*, lands U.S. troops "...for the purpose of protecting our legation, consulate, and the lives and property of American citizens, and to assist in preserving public order."

Tuesday, January 17:
Early Afternoon:
Lt. Cmdr. W.T. Swinburne, the senior U.S. military officer on shore, tells Committee of Safety member Charles Carter about 1 p.m.: "If the Queen calls upon me to preserve order, I am going to do it."

On the front steps of the government building, Henry Cooper reads proclamation of Committee of Safety declaring throne vacant and establishing Provisional Government. A single volunteer is with him besides Committee members and soon-to-be-president, Sanford B. Dole, as he starts, but additional armed volunteers, responding to the call, gather as he reads. Charles Carter goes across the street and asks U.S. commanding officer Swinburne for protection for the Revolutionists. "I remain passive," Swinburne responds.

Late Afternoon:
Provisional Government takes over former Monarchy responsibilities, is recognized as successor government by U.S. Minister Stevens about 4:30 to 5 p.m., accepts surrender of Queen's troops, receives letter of protest from the Queen (who states she is surrendering to U.S. and seeking arbitration by Washington), advises foreign legations of new government and gains their recognition over next 48 hours. Dole later points out Queen's arbitration claim was not negotiated or agreed to by Revolutionists.

Thursday, January 19:
Provisional Government charters ship to send five envoys to Washington, D.C., to confirm recognition by Minister Stevens, seek Annexation. They allow ship to carry letter from the Queen to President Harrison but deny passage to Queen's envoys, who come at a later date. In her letter to the president, the Queen fails to mention anything about arbitration by the U.S. of her surrender.

1893 Revolution Aftermath

March-July:
Former Rep. James H. Blount, on assignment from President Cleveland, conducts secret investigation of the Revolution without telling Provisional Government of his purpose. He fails to interview key Revolutionists, members of Committee of Safety or leaders of Provisional Government, blames U.S. troops for inappropriate action, recommends censure of U.S. Minister Stevens and return of Monarchy to the Queen. Hawai'i government doesn't get copy of his report until late December, weeks after public charges have been made by U.S. Secretary of State Walter Q. Gresham and the president.

November 16:
New U.S. minister to Hawai'i, Albert Willis, meets in secret with Queen to present President Cleveland's request that she grant amnesty to Revolutionists in return for her reinstatement. She replies she will have them beheaded.

December 18:
Lili'uokalani, on third visit by Willis, changes mind on vow to have Revolutionists beheaded, but unknown to the two of them, it is too late. President Cleveland has turned the matter over to Congress on advice of his attorney general, and U.S. Senate has called hearing by its Committee on Foreign Affairs, as one-sided nature, borderline diplomatic ethics of Blount Report become apparent.

December 23:
Minister Willis, unaware Cleveland has dropped the ball, presents Provisional Government with president's demand that it restore Queen to throne. The demand is rejected. In letter written by Dole a few days later, Cleveland learns of Provisional Government's viewpoint on revolt, remains silent on Hawai'i matter for the rest of his term.

Sanford Dole

Lorrin Thurston

1894

January, February:
U.S. Sen. John T. Morgan conducts hearing by Committee on Foreign Relations into Hawaiian Revolution that exonerates Minister Stevens and U.S. troops, repudiates Blount finding and efforts by Cleveland administration to restore ex-Queen to throne.

July 4:
The Provisional Government declares itself the Republic of Hawai'i, includes Annexation goal in its Constitution, is recognized by the Cleveland administration and all countries with Pacific interests.

1895

January:
Royalists organize an unsuccessful counter-revolution under the leadership of Wilcox. Hundreds are captured and convicted of treason. Lili'uokalani is convicted of misprision—the knowledge of treason—and is confined to 'Iolani Palace for eight months. All other sentences are commuted by year-end.

January 24:
Lili'uokalani signs abdication document, swears allegiance to the Republic.

1910

U.S. Court of Claims denies appeal by Lili'uokalani of a territorial Supreme Court ruling that denies the former Queen's claim to private ownership of the crown lands, formerly the King's lands. No individual has claimed ownership since, until the recent claims by sovereignty activists.

1898

August 12, 1898:
Congress adopts joint resolution approving Annexation. The day is known as Annexation Day. Government lands known as "ceded lands" that were transferred successively from the Monarchy to the Provisional Government to the Republic are ceded to the United States to be held in trust for the benefit of all Hawai'i residents.

1900

April 30:
Organic Act is passed by Congress, making Annexation official and creating the Territory of Hawai'i. In first election, Wilcox wins highest elective office, Native Hawaiians dominate Legislature, other offices.

1959

Hawai'i becomes the 50th state of the United States. Title of the ceded lands is transferred back to Hawai'i control.

he is stretching the ambiguous language of the resolution, but as an attorney he knows ambiguity is ready fodder for minds set on creating legal entanglements. Other activist attorneys, like Keppeler, say Boyle is simply wrong.

Sovereignty groups stretch ambiguous language

Senator Gorton questioned the ambiguities and omissions. He said:

> "It is clear the resolution accomplishes one goal. It divides the citizens of the State of Hawaii . . ."

With MacGregor's newly articulated position that it clears away the fog of history, the resolution would wipe out existing history books except those written recently by sovereignty activists.

Let us look at the resolution point by point. Senators Akaka and Inouye claimed its thirty-seven whereas clauses accurately reflect the history of Hawai'i. They do not. The language is based on a one-sided approach that comes from incomplete and inadequate research. Hawai'i-based activists worked up the document in Honolulu, where it was written apparently by MacGregor and sent to Senator Akaka's office. That office appears to have taken the language of sovereignty activists as gospel. The failure to hold any public hearings on the matter or seek input from other historians prevented opposing viewpoints from being considered.

MacGregor's position would erase history

The whereas clauses unfairly portray a Hawai'i far from the Hawai'i that existed at the time of the Revolution. The clauses never acknowledge that authorities disagree on many matters for that period of Hawaiian history. (MacGregor says its passage overrides these disagreements.) Sixty-five senators accepted the clauses as fully fair and correct since our senators said they were, and no one was

Opposing viewpoints not considered

there to argue about errors in the so-called historical facts. The haste of the action precluded anyone from investigating, including the three senators who actively opposed the resolution.

The first whereas clause, for example, states that prior to the arrival of the first Europeans in 1778, the Native Hawaiians lived in a "highly organized, self-sufficient, subsistent social system based on communal land tenure with a sophisticated language, culture, and religion." What actually was going on in pre-contact Hawai'i instead of high and sophisticated social organization was constant warfare among chiefs on each island and constant efforts by the winners to move off-island and conquer other chiefs. The lands were not communally *owned*; they were controlled entirely by whichever chief currently was on top. Queen Lili'uokalani in her writings speaks of the land as being owned by the monarch under a feudal system. The lands were communally *used* because each chief needed the common people to work the soil so he—and they—could subsist.

Pre-contact Hawai'i not sophisticated society

Because of the lack of metal, technologies were necessarily primitive. The language was entirely oral until the missionaries came along forty-two years after Western contact. They put together a written language and taught the natives to read and write. Communication had been limited in scope as it is with any purely oral language. Hawaiians and the early whalers and merchants developed a form of pidgin that bastardized the Hawaiian language but worked for business transactions.

Native language was purely oral

Hawaiian religion before 1778 was built around idols and sacrifices and *kapu* (taboos) that if broken were punishable by death. While the system did not give individuals the personal freedoms we take for granted today, it worked in its day to provide a basis for personal conduct. The very strictness of its rules and punishments meant that the natives observed the system without question. Though intelligent, Native Hawaiians before 1778 realistically cannot be called a "sophisticated" people by any definition of that word.

Hawaiian religion pre-1778 was very strict

The second clause states that a "unified monarchical government . . . was established in 1810 by Kamehameha I, the first King of Hawai'i." It would be more accurate to say that this first king in Hawai'i's recorded history established an absolute Monarchy by making good use of European advisers to conquer in bloody warfare the people of every island except Kaua'i.

The fifth clause contains a horrendous misstatement that distorts the basis for considering an apology when it states that U.S. Minister John L. Stevens "conspired with a small group of non-Hawaiian residents of the Kingdom of Hawai'i . . . to overthrow" the government. Not even the one-sided Blount Report proves Stevens conspired with the Revolutionists. He was not even on O'ahu when planning for the Revolution began and the Committee of Safety was appointed to work out its details, though he arrived later that day. We do know, and he always admitted, that he was pro-Annexation, as were his predecessor U.S. ministers, but there is no evidence he conspired to bring it about. The fifth clause also implies the Revolutionists had no vested interest in the welfare of the Kingdom. It fails to point out that the thirteen members of the Committee (the "small group" mentioned by the clause) all were residents of Hawai'i, all taxpayers, with more than half being subjects of the Monarchy as well. The hundreds of other Hawai'i residents who were present at the mass meeting that had appointed the Com-

Kamehameha established absolute Monarchy

U.S. minister pro-Annexation but did not conspire

mittee, also all taxpayers, were rebelling against what they considered unconscionable acts of their own government. They were not acting as a foreign takeover group. As subjects they had the same standing versus Queen Lili'uokalani as the American colonists did who rebelled against King George III: they felt a change in government was necessary to preserve their country and their welfare.

The sixth clause continues the erroneous conspiracy charge and obscures the truth by stating that Stevens caused "armed naval forces of the United States to invade . . . to intimidate Queen Lili'uokalani and her government." This is clearly argumentative and not a fact for the "education of my colleagues," as Senator Akaka described his resolution three times in his remarks. It is stretching things a bit to call landing of the troops an "invasion." Webster defines "invade" as "to enter for conquest or plunder," as in raid or assault. Stevens' and Wiltse's orders clearly stated the troops were landed to protect American lives and property. They were in the harbor as guests of the Monarchy through the Reciprocity Treaty. When they came ashore, they did *Landing of* not point their weapons at anyone. They respectfully *troops not an* saluted the Queen. They did not fire a shot—they *"invasion"* were ready but their rifles were stacked nearby—nor did they enter any government buildings. They made no effort to seize control, and once the Revolutionists, 24 hours later, announced they had taken control from the Queen, the troops went back to their ship, a procedure they had followed on other occasions during the reigns of earlier monarchs. Their mission on each of those occasions and on this one was one of standing by to protect Americans and *Mission: to pro-* their interests. Admittedly this point falls into a dis- *tect Americans* puted, gray, politicized area of Hawaiian history, and

284

if he had wanted to be fair to his colleagues, Senator Akaka might better have described it in those terms.

The seventh clause perpetuates a myth by stating that the 1893 Committee of Safety "represented . . . sugar planters, descendants of missionaries and financiers" as if those separate groups had banded together and selected individuals to act for them in the Revolution. The most powerful sugar planters in fact were against the Revolution and Annexation, fearing Annexation would change the rules under which they brought in labor. Claus Spreckels, for example, the major sugar baron of the 19th Century, was an ardent supporter of both King Kalākaua and Queen Lili'uokalani. British planters such as Theo H. Davies also strongly supported the Monarchy and opposed Annexation. The descendants of missionaries at the time were no more a cohesive group on the question of Annexation than the descendants of Hawaiians are today when it comes to defining the goals of sovereignty.

Spreckels, sugar interests backed Monarchy

The eighth clause is a semantic exercise that imputes evil to the Provisional Government put in place by the Revolutionists because it was formed "without the consent of the Native Hawaiian people or the lawful government of Hawai'i and in violation of treaties between the two nations and of international law." That argument, of course, would negate the American Revolution. From Queen Lili'uokalani's point of view, of course, the Revolutionists were acting illegally when they removed her from the throne. But they were acting as revolutionaries always do, with the moral justification of believing their cause was right. They certainly did not represent another nation. When they took control of the country, the Provisional Government they proclaimed became the lawful government of

Hawai'i. They did not ask anyone to approve the Revolution, nor was that required.

The Monarchy had no treaties with the United States or any other government ruling out revolutions, nor does international law oppose such reforms.

The ninth clause sets forth the masterful protest statement issued by Lili'uokalani when she said she was surrendering on the day of the Revolution. She said she was surrendering to the United States, although it was the Revolutionists who were asking her to give up without a fight. She submitted her protest to them, not the United States. Her protest was delivered to Provisional Government President Sanford Dole about 7 p.m. as the brief Revolution was running its course. Minutes earlier he and his supporters had completed the detailed steps involved in making clear to foreign diplomats, including Stevens, that the Revolutionists had indeed taken over the government of Hawai'i. They had occupied the seat of government, had proclaimed the Provisional Government and were preparing to take over the Queen's army and the city police force.

It had been a long day and Dole knew the Queen was surrendering to his new government and not some foreign power such as the United States. He did not represent the United States and the United States was not present while the Queen was discussing surrender with her Cabinet and other advisers. The Provisional Government had a representative there, S.M. Damon, but he was not there to negotiate for the Provisional Government. Dole accepted her letter, as he explained later, as if it had come through the mails. Accepting it was a means of bringing about a bloodless and peaceful end to the Revolution, and neither side wanted a drawn-out, bloody

Monarchy had no treaties barring revolutions

Queen's protest delivered to Provisional Government

battle. The Queen's statement has served as a confusing point, however, in subsequent analyses of the Revolution. It became the basis for an after-the-fact negotiating point for the Queen's supporters, but not the definitive argument implied by this clause.

Queen's statement confused the issue

The congressional resolution gets argumentative again in its tenth clause, which states that without "active support and intervention" by U.S. diplomatic and military personnel the "insurrection" would have failed. There is no evidence or factual way to determine this. It is not a factual matter. The Queen had a few more troops at an early moment, but they were not as motivated as the Revolutionists and failed to put up any kind of defense. Indeed, many Native Hawaiians, including those in her own Cabinet, wanted her deposed if she persisted in attempting to promulgate a new Constitution in violation of terms of the existing Constitution she had sworn to uphold. Key leaders of the Revolution were not questioned by Blount about the impact of the troops. They testified before the Morgan Committee, however, that they did not need the support of the U.S. troops to accomplish their mission and pointed to two previous occasions, in 1887 and 1889, when they, the same men, had prevailed over troops of the Monarchy.

Many Native Hawaiians wanted Queen deposed

The twelfth clause demonstrates the half-truths that plague efforts to ensure a balanced understanding of what happened in 1893. The clause states that President Cleveland sent former Congressman James H. Blount, a fellow Democrat, to Hawai'i in 1893 to conduct an investigation of the overthrow and that Blount concluded that "U.S. diplomatic and military representatives had abused their authority and were responsible for the change in government." As Dole pointed out later, if this

Revolutionists did not need U.S. troops to help them win

were the case, it was a matter for resolution between the United States and its representatives, and not the Provisional Government. The clause fails to point out the acknowledged criticism of Blount's investigation: that he interviewed sixty Royalists including all of their acknowledged leaders but only twenty Annexationists, none of whom were leaders of the Revolution. It also fails to point out that a subsequent investigation by Senator John T. Morgan, a Democrat from Alabama, using only sworn testimony, vindicated Stevens by a margin of 5 to 4 in the committee.

No fault of Revolutionists if Queen felt U.S. would help

Morgan's Committee vindicated Stevens

The fourteenth clause has President Cleveland reporting "fully and accurately" on the overthrow without acknowledging his remarks were based only on Blount's one-sided investigation and therefore could be neither full nor accurate. It was a report based on half the evidence laced with the inaccuracies one would expect from reliance on lopsided research.

The nineteenth clause erroneously states that while the Provisional Government "was able to obscure the role of the U.S. in the illegal overthrow of the Hawaiian Monarchy, it was unable to rally the support from two-thirds of the Senate needed to ratify a treaty of annexation." There are two errors here, a small one of fact, the other a distortion of history. The error of fact: the Provisional Government had been replaced five years earlier by the Republic of Hawai'i so it wasn't the Provisional Government that was dealing with the Congress in 1898 but a sovereign nation, the Republic, recognized around the world. The distortion: U.S. Senate supporters in 1898 did fail to adopt a treaty but instead simply and successfully went the route of adopting a joint resolution of Annexation in lieu of the treaty. The same

Treaty not required for annexations

procedure had been followed in annexing the Republic of Texas. The Annexation of Hawai'i was legal.

Senate supporters adopt joint resolution instead of treaty

The twenty-first clause says that Queen Lili'uokalani was imprisoned in 'Iolani Palace and forced by the Republic to officially abdicate her throne. True as far as it goes, but to be informative to the senators, it should have added that she was imprisoned for being part of an unsuccessful counter-revolution. Incidentally, it was supported sub rosa by the United States, which allowed the shipment of arms from California to the Queen's forces. Allowing the shipment of arms was a clear violation of U.S. and international law. The proposed smuggling of arms and the counter-revolution plot were smoked out by the Republic's Marshal, E. Hitchcock. His sleuthing efforts reached the Republic before the Queen's forces were ready to attack and her forces were quickly suppressed when they had to move prematurely. Subsequently, additional arms were found buried on the grounds of the Queen's home, now Washington Place.

Shipment of arms clear violation

The twenty-fifth and twenty-sixth clauses say that with Annexation the Republic of Hawai'i ceded public lands to the United States "without the consent of or compensation to the native Hawaiian people or their sovereign government." The sovereign government of Hawai'i at the time of Annexation, recognized by the United States and every other foreign nation involved, was the Republic. Treaties were the province of its Senate, and that body, with a number of Native Hawaiian members, voted unanimously in favor of Annexation. The Republic controlled public lands as had its predecessor governments, and with the approval of its elected Senate, consented to the transfer. Neither Native Hawaiians nor any residents of the Islands as individuals con-

Government did approve Annexation

trolled government lands. Not mentioned is the master stroke of Republic negotiators who got the United States to agree to put the ceded lands in a sort of trust for the people of Hawai'i, with the income to be spent only in Hawai'i, a benefit not achieved by any other annexed territory and which opened the way for the current 20 percent distribution to OHA.

National lands never owned by individuals

The twenty-ninth clause reiterates that the "indigenous Hawaiian people never directly relinquished their claims to their inherent sovereignty or over their national lands to the U.S." Again the resolution fails to point out that the "national" lands were government lands, public lands that never had been owned by individual Native Hawaiians. They were set aside in 1848 by King Kamehameha III as lands for the government to use for support of **all the residents of Hawai'i**—public lands. The "indigenous Hawaiian people" had never tried to gain title to these lands until the sovereignty movement surfaced.

Hawaiians voted for Statehood

The thirty-first clause records that on August 21, 1959, Hawai'i became the 50th state without adding that Hawaiians and part-Hawaiians voted overwhelmingly, along with everyone else, in favor of that action. This is a pointed omission in view of erroneous claims in earlier clauses that Native Hawaiian peoples had not voted in favor of any association with the United States.

The thirty-second clause states that the "health and well-being of the Native Hawaiian people is intrinsically tied to their deep feelings and attachment to the land." A statement such as this in the context of an apology resolution carries implications beyond that of a simple apology. It has become an accepted part of the Hawaiian mystique that Hawaiians, through religion and tradition, have an unusual and special affinity for the land as a living thing. The language along these lines wouldn't be part of the resolution unless those who wrote the resolution planned to use that clause later to seek title. To tie the apology in with current claims for ownership of the land misuses the non-ownership, spiritual relationship of early Hawaiians with the land.

In pre-contact Hawai'i, and in fact until the Great *Mahele* in 1848, all land was under the direct and absolute control of the monarch, and anyone who preached otherwise wasn't long for this world. Neither early religion nor traditions gave the Hawaiian commoner anything more than the opportunity—often the obligation—to work the land. The idea of now parceling ownership out to descendants of those early subjects because Hawaiians have "deep feelings and attachment" to land will be hard to sell. Most Americans, regardless of race, have deep feelings for land. Imagine the feelings of the other 80 percent of Hawai'i's people if public lands were somehow taken from their government, where they benefit all of the residents of Hawai'i, and turned over to members of the part-Hawaiian population!

Until Mahele, Monarchy controlled all land

That clause and the thirty-third say "the long-range economic and social changes in Hawai'i over the nineteenth and twentieth centuries have been devastating to the population and to the health and well-being of the Hawaiian people." There is no mention of any benefits from the multitude of federal welfare and other national monies and agencies that have assisted the residents of Hawai'i in the 20th Century. Responsibility for problems of the 19th Century might more appropriately be directed to the Monarchy. Remarks like this go to a point well-made by Senator Danforth during the debate when he described what he called an annoying tactic of

Who is to blame for ills of Hawaiians?

sovereignists, that of portraying Hawaiians as victims.

He testified first that the great challenge of this country has always been the challenge of attempting to hold together diverse peoples:

> "It is a challenge which is tested constantly. It is tested by bigots and by hateful people; by mean people; by people who like to lord over others and discriminate against other people.

> ". . . it is possible to divide not only by being mean, but by making ourselves victims . . . and if we have not been victims ourselves, then somebody else has been a victim, some ancestor has been a victim, so please apologize.

> ". . . by making ourselves a nation of victims, it is possible to emphasize what divides us and separates us, rather than what keeps us glued together."

Sovereignists portray Hawaiians as victims

Senator Gorton earlier had spoken eloquently to the same point, from a different direction. He referred to an experience in 1989 when he was part of a Senate visit to a conference on Eastern Europe in Dubrovnik, Yugoslavia. It marked the 600th anniversary of the Battle of Kossovo, a battle in which Turkish Moslems slaughtered the Serbian Christian army and ended the independence of Serbia for the better part of half a millennium. He noted that a short two years later and continuing today, many of those Serbs were in the process of killing Bosnian Moslems in significant measure to revenge their loss at Kossovo in 1389.

That combination of ethnic politics and claims to particular pieces of land is literally lethal across stretches of Eastern Europe, throughout much of Africa, and in many nations in Asia, Senator Gorton said. "It is an evil which we as Americans have largely avoided. And with all of the respect that I can possibly muster for my two friends and colleagues from Hawai'i and for all of the evident goodwill in the world which they show, this resolution is a signpost pointing toward that dark and bitter road," he said in remarks quoted in the Congressional Record.

Emphasizing division, not togetherness

"In guidebooks about the State of Hawai'i, and it is mentioned in our own history, that State is given as an example of how people from different backgrounds can live together happily and peacefully. Yet here we begin that process of division.

"At the time of the commemoration of this coup, or this overthrow, last January (1993) the Governor of Hawai'i caused the flag of the United States to be removed from the capitol for five days. I must hasten to add he was denounced by the two Senators from Hawai'i for having done so. But it was symbolic of the divisive nature of this kind of proposal."

Noting that Senator Akaka had not mentioned monetary compensation in his opening remarks, Senator Gorton quoted from an article in the *Los Angeles Times* regarding the aims of various sovereignty groups that include compensation, independence, lands, etc.

The *Times* article said:

". . . these demands for compensation differ profoundly from those offered to Japanese-Americans . . . . Those reparations were given to individuals who were greatly wronged by their Government, who were deprived of their homes and of their liveli-

Ethnic politics and claims to land lethal

hoods solely by reason of their race and ethnic origin, and who were alive to receive reparations granted to them . . ."

The senator continued:

"This [revolution] took place more than 100 years ago. No one is alive who played any role in it . . . . This is a different time and a different generation . . . . every square inch of the United States was acquired in a manner which bears certain similarities to the acquisition by the United States of America of what is now the State of Hawai'i . . .

"In fact, we are no different than any other society in the world today. I doubt that there is a square mile of the world which is occupied by exactly the same people who were the original human beings on the spot. But it is the genius of us as Americans, it seems to me, that this does not count in America. What counts is that we are all citizens, and that we are all equal.

"In no realistic way did we apologize for the acts by people over whom we had no responsibility and with whom we shared no life whatsoever. As a consequence . . . we must look toward the consequences not only of what we do here but the consequences of that coup. The consequences of that overthrow are the fact that Hawai'i [has become a] State of the United States. The fact that it has more than one million inhabitants living together in peace and harmony in an extremely prosperous society, the fact that all except for aliens are citizens not only of the State of Hawai'i but of the United States of America.

"Are these adverse or unhappy consequences? Are these consequences or

Gorton: We are no different from any other society today

Consequence of the overthrow: Statehood

ramifications of that overthrow which we wish to undo?

"This Senator intensely regrets the fact that we are in this process creating a division which does not exist . . ."

After quoting former University of Hawai'i President Harlan Cleveland that in his judgment the ". . . diffusion of American democracy and enterprise with Hawaiian culture mixed now by immigration and intermarriage with Japanese, Chinese, Korean, Filipino, and other workways and mindsets has produced one of the world's most intriguing experiments in the building of a multicultural society," Senator Gorton notes this is the "actual real world consequence of something which took place more than a century ago."

Multicultural society a real-world consequence

He quotes Harlan Cleveland as saying that "sovereignty, which . . . many of the Native Hawaiian groups wish, is unlikely to be the answer. . . ."

Senator Danforth added to the theme:

". . . warfare and divisions are not things to be emphasized constantly . . . the past is not something to be constantly relived with a view toward how to get other people to apologize.

Ex-UH boss: Sovereignty unlikely to be answer

"There comes a time to put warfare behind us and divisiveness behind us and to dedicate ourselves to a common purpose, because we are all Americans, and because it is challenging enough to live together in this one country as one people without constantly fighting the battles of the past."

The operative language of the resolution following the thirty-seven whereas clauses is contained in five short paragraphs, and change may be beyond our control as individuals. But it is proper to point out that the language is specious in part.

Resolution language is specious in part

The first paragraph "acknowledges the historical significance of the [overthrow]," without saying what that means, and then goes on to say it "resulted in the suppression of the inherent sovereignty of the Native Hawaiian people." The Queen was the sovereign. The Hawaiian people were her subjects. Perhaps in the language of international diplomacy they had an "inherent sovereignty," but as a practical matter in 19th-Century Hawai'i they had no power, no sovereignty. The people are sovereign in a democracy, but certainly not in a Monarchy like the one Queen Lili'uokalani sought to reimpose with her proposed new Constitution.

People are sovereign only in a democracy

The third paragraph similarly goes beyond the facts. It says the Congress apologizes "for the overthrow . . . with the participation of agents and citizens of the United States." Was the Congress apologizing for the fact that some of America's citizens, as residents and subjects of Hawai'i, were overthrowing a monarchy in favor of a democratic form of government?

The resolution then goes on to include an apology for "the deprivation of the rights of native Hawaiians to self-determination." Since the Native Hawaiian people had no rights to self-determination under the Queen's rule and would have been even more tightly ruled under the new Constitution she proposed, this makes no sense. There is no logic in our Congress apologizing for the loss of something that never existed and certainly wasn't taken away by the overthrow. Again, failing to hold a public hearing resulted in the Senate acting without knowledge of the facts.

Native Hawaiians had no self-determination rights under Queen's rule

The last two paragraphs contain the language

that mystified Senators Gorton, Brown and Danforth: The Congress (in the fourth paragraph) "expresses its commitment to acknowledge the ramifications of the overthrow . . . in order to provide a proper foundation for reconciliation between the United States and the Native Hawaiian people," and in the fifth paragraph urges the president to do the same.

Language mystifies senators

What those ramifications are, Senator Gorton points out, is "nowhere mentioned in the course of the resolution or in the modest committee report on that resolution." In fact, the committee report contains little more than the remarks of Senator Akaka that he repeated on the floor of the Senate.

Senator Gorton went on to say:

"Is this a purely self-executing resolution which has no meaning other than its own passage, or is this, in their minds (Senators Akaka and Inouye), some form of claim, some form of different or distinct treatment for those who can trace a single ancestor back to 1778 in Hawai'i which is now to be provided for this group of citizens, separating them from other citizens of the State of Hawai'i or the United States?

Gorton: Resolution has no meaning

"At the very least, before we vote on their resolution, we ought to understand what the two Senators from Hawai'i mean those ramifications and consequences to be."

As the song says, he got no satisfaction. The debate ended.

Perhaps the resolution is as Senator Inouye explained when he made his final argument in reply to Senator Gorton:

". . . this is a simple resolution of apology, to recognize the facts as they were 100 years

Inouye: "A simple resolution of apology"

ago. As to the matter of the status of Native Hawaiians . . . are Native Hawaiians Native Americans? This resolution has nothing to do with that. This resolution does not touch upon the Hawaiian homelands. I can assure my colleague of that. It is a simple apology."

Apology to whom?

But an apology to whom? To the hundreds of Native Hawaiians who formed the *Hui Hawai'i Aloha'āina* the year before the Revolution, calling for the overthrow of the Queen? To the Native Hawaiian Cabinet members who sought to depose her before the Committee of Safety was formed? To the Native Hawaiians in the Republic's Senate who unanimously favored Annexation to the United States? Or perhaps the overwhelming numbers of Hawai'i's citizens, including Native Hawaiians, who embraced Statehood?

In due time, the resolution will lapse. It is the nature of resolutions to do that. They do not have the force of law. But perhaps the best thing to do is repeal it and start over.

$\mathcal{F}$act or Fiction?

he proponents of Hawaiian sovereignty have mounted a much more effective public information campaign than those who question the movement. Much of it is masterminded from within the taxpayer-supported Center for Hawaiian Studies at the University of Hawai'i. The campaign has included wide use of UH professors as a speakers' bureau and the writing of countless letters and articles to the editors of Hawai'i's newspapers.

Hawaiian Studies Center masterminding campaign for sovereignty

This effective campaign has taken place in spite of the failure of the various advocates of Hawaiian sovereignty to agree on common goals. On the other hand, those who question the notion of Hawaiian sovereignty have no formal structure at all. Theirs is not an organized movement, and arguments tend to relate to narrow issues. Many specialists writing in the newspapers on Hawaiian land, for example, believe that sovereignty positions on this subject are irrational and based on misinterpretation or misunderstanding of historical data. Articles to correct perceived misstatements on land issues have appeared from time to time, but writers on this subject seldom get into the broader aspects of sovereign-

Sovereignty doubters have no central core

ty. The overall result is that pro-sovereignty letters and articles in general outnumber their opponents' efforts by ten to one.

While many good answers and major points have been made by writers who are opposed or concerned about sovereignty, the preponderance of information is flowing mostly in the other direction. We need to take a look at the erroneous claims by sovereignty proponents that are made most often and are generally left unanswered. This chapter will attempt to separate fact from fiction.

Trying to separate fact from fiction

Newspaper editors usually seek to balance "opinion pieces"—the longer articles that generally appear opposite the editorial page—with pieces containing opposing views, either on the same day or on following days. With the subject of sovereignty, however, the sheer volume of articles offered by pro-sovereignty writers has made this difficult and the balance is tilted.

With Letters to the Editor, the possibility of the public being provided with balancing viewpoints is even less. As a matter of newspaper policy, letters run unanswered. They often carry innuendoes that deftly chisel away at the facts. It's a surreptitious way to rewrite history, and if the revisionism is repeated often enough, it becomes difficult to set straight the fiction.

Letters to the Editor often rewrite history

An example ran in *The Advertiser* on December 2, 1995, over the signature of Kamal Kapoor. "Nation status won't free Hawaiians from U.S. rule," the headline states, catching the key point of the letter writer. But what is the reader to make of this? That Hawaiians want to be free of "U.S. rule" and becoming a nation won't do it?

Sophisticated readers know that the headline above a letter, while looking very positive, is not necessarily a factual statement in itself; it is written merely to call attention to the writer's main point. Unfortunately some readers, skimming through the letters page, take the headlines as statements of fact.

Readers take headlines as fact

In this case, the writer states that the "nation-within-a-nation" advocated by Ka Lāhui and other Hawaiian sovereignty advocates "is not sovereignty at all. It is merely another form of dependence." The writer says that under this model the Hawaiian people "must still get permission from the U.S. government to use their 'independent' land . . ." He restates the myth: "Congress can also take away the 'sovereign' people's land whenever it sees fit . . . without permission from the Hawaiian people.

"The only way *kanaka maoli* can get what is rightfully theirs and be truly independent is to achieve full secession from the United States," the writer concludes.

On the surface the statements may sound rather logical, but there are several problems:

Many problems with pro-sovereignty statements

Problem 1: The writer assumes that some form of sovereignty will be achieved; he admits to no gray area. But realistically, sovereignty is far from being a sure thing.

Problem 2: The implication is made over and over that land has been taken from the Hawaiian people. Buzz words are oft-repeated in sovereignty letters, such as those in Kapoor's letter: "their independent land," "the sovereign people's land," "reclaiming without permission of the Hawaiian people," "what is rightfully theirs." Phrases like these obviously are designed to give the impression of theft. There is little opportunity for this to be questioned, or for expert opinion to point out that in the first place the Hawaiian people did not own the land being discussed; it has been government land

Assumption is land was stolen

since King Kamehameha III set it up that way. Before he gave a portion to the government, it was all his, not the people's.

Problem 3: A naive reader of a letter like this could easily assume that secession from the United States is an option. Amazingly, not everyone remembers that this point was settled for Americans in the Civil War. "Full secession" is not an option and sovereignty leaders are engaging in a disservice to their followers to imply that it is. Some, including Kapoor, think it is. They should heed the words of Senator Inouye on this point, on February 16, 1997, in an article in *The Advertiser*: "We had a Civil War over that. I think that was very clearly articulated with blood."

Inouye's words: Full secession not an option

The confusion cuts many ways. Some descendants of the *ali'i* claim it is they and not the common Hawaiians who have rights to the land. A letter in the *Star-Bulletin* on July 18, 1996, for example, over the signature of Monica Wilcox Hatori, tells the *kanaka maoli* to back off: "We, who can prove our unbroken continuity relationship to King Kamehameha and his father Keoua, are the true owners of these lands.

Government land not owned by ali'i or commoners

"If we, the descendants of the *ali'i*, cannot receive justice then what are the hopes for the descendants of the people?"

That's the fiction. The fact is the land isn't owned by the *ali'i* descendants either, and never was. Once Kamehameha III turned over the lands to his and future governments in 1848, those lands became government lands. Interestingly, until the current claims on the part of *kanaka maoli*, which no one as yet has taken to court, no commoners had tried to gain title. Queens Emma and Lili'uokalani, as mentioned earlier, had tried unsuccessfully to do so.

Another side to the land question is the payment by the state government to OHA of 20 percent of the revenues earned by the ceded lands. This relatively recent development is covered in depth in Chapter Nine, "Land Is the Key." Letter writers are all over the place on this one. A letter in the *Star-Bulletin* on May 13, 1996, over the signature of Lance L. Luke, starts off erroneously by saying that the ceded lands "are actually lands stolen by the state government and used by the state and federal government and other parties for free or for a small fraction of the actual rental value."

Letter incorrectly defines ceded lands payments

Luke adds that the "Hawaiian people are still getting ripped off because although they are entitled to it, they do not receive 100 percent . . ." These last two statements are the fiction.

The fact is the 1959 Congress-approved Admission Act, which made Hawaiʻi a state and returned the ceded lands to our control, provided how those lands and the income from them could be used. The language limited their use to five areas, one of which was the welfare of Native Hawaiians with 50 percent or more Hawaiian blood. That's why the Legislature allocated one-fifth—20 percent—to Hawaiian welfare to be administered through OHA, which on its face introduces another layer of bureaucracy before the monies reach *kanaka maoli*. The hope is OHA will be more responsive than government agencies as a whole. Use of those ceded land funds still is limited to those with 50 percent or more Hawaiian blood and this needs to be broadened by congressional action. The Admission Act significantly broadened the language of the Annexation Act sixty-one years earlier, in 1898, which had admitted Hawaiʻi as a Territory. The earlier act transferred the ceded lands to the United States but provided that

Admission Act told how lands could be used

revenues from them "shall be used solely for the benefit of the inhabitants of the Hawaiian Islands for educational and other public purposes."

On the general subject of commentary on sovereignty issues, there are a few Native Hawaiian letter writers who buck the tide. One of the more prolific is a Waimānalo resident named Benny Olepau, 80 years old in 1997, who describes himself as a "100 percent Hawaiian." Among his more than seventy published letters since 1980, he comments on a wide spectrum of community events and has often written brief notes that attempt to bring sovereignty activists back to reality. One, dated July 9, 1996, is headed "Hawaiians should stop blaming others." That statement is made in general tones on occasion by other writers, but this particular letter relates to the alleged loss of language and culture. "The educated Hawaiians blame the foreigners for the loss of their language and culture," Olepau writes. He adds: "They are wrong. The Hawaiians themselves lost their language and culture because they became '*haole*-fied'."

Many Hawaiians proud to be American citizens

He reasons that "There were many foreigners of many races in Hawaii. England had the influence . . . . When the United States took over Hawaii, the Hawaiian flag became part of the United States."

Emphasizing what may well be the unexpressed feeling of many Hawaiians, he continues: "I am proud to be an American citizen of Hawaiian ancestry. I volunteered in World War II and completed my education under the G.I. Bill. I am a resident on Hawaiian Home Lands in Waimānalo as a 100 percent Hawaiian."

Here are a few other words of counsel for Hawaiians from Benny Olepau:

In a letter appearing September 19, 1995:

"I agree with Walter F. Judd, who said, 'No land was stolen' as the sovereignty movement claims and 'to describe the overthrow as non-Hawaiians stealing from Hawaiians is to distort history beyond recognition.'

"Hawaiians must bury the past and look ahead for the good of all who make Hawai'i their home. Only then can Hawai'i be the Aloha State."

On October 6, 1995, another of his letters states: "Hawaiians are better off under the U.S. government. Hawaiians cannot stand on their two feet without government assistance. Can a self-government assure better benefits for the Hawaiian race? My answer is loud and clear: No.

"Time will tell whether I am wrong," he adds. "Regardless of the outcome, I shall forever be a citizen of the United States because no other government can replace what I have."

Finally, on September 6, 1997, he told his "fellow Hawaiians" that "A sovereign government for Hawaiians is not for me . . . Non-Hawaiians born in the . . . Islands are children of Hawai'i and Hawai'i is also their land."

A major factor in the creation of revisionist confusion is the congressional apology resolution adopted in 1993. Typical of the problems it creates appeared in a letter in *The Advertiser* on October 21, 1994, over the signature of Sondra-Field Grace of Anahola, Kaua'i. She says, "In your Oct. 15 article, 'OHA to buy ceded land from state,' Clayton Hee 'acknowledged that some Hawaiians might question having to pay for land they say already belongs to the Hawaiian people.'

"In fact," Grace continues, "U.S. Public Law 103-150 states: 'Whereas, the indigenous Hawaiian people never directly relinquished their claims to

Apology resolution created confusion

their inherent sovereignty as a people or *over their national lands* (Ed.—emphasis by Ms. Grace) to the U.S., either through their monarchy or through a plebiscite or referendum...'

"Thus," she adds, "it is not just 'some Hawaiians,' but the U.S. Congress and President Clinton who acknowledge this fact."

Revisionists hail the apology resolution as "U.S. Public Law 103-150" as discussed in Chapter Ten of this book. In actuality, it is not a coded part of U.S. law. Its operative clauses express no point of law and as a resolution would not be law anyway. Sovereignists, however, describe the whereas clauses themselves as having the force of law. Citations of claims set forth in the whereas clauses have appeared already in law articles and court opinions. To compound the problem, many of these clauses are in error. There appears to be no recognition that whereas clauses in general do not have the force of law. As Senator Inouye has said, "It is just a resolution."

An opinion piece on Mākua Valley in *The Advertiser* on June 21, 1996, over the byline of Samuel L. Kealoha Jr., is another example of the difficulties in resolving the question of ceded lands. Kealoha, a trustee of OHA at the time, said in the article, "What many ignorant souls, including *The Honolulu Advertiser*, do not understand is that the land on both sides of the highway at Mākua . . . belongs to the Hawaiian people. It is part of the 1.4 million acres that was ceded to this crooked state, via Statehood, in 1959."

His letter adds, "In a recent court decision, Judge Daniel Heely ruled that lands were illegally taken without compensation or consent from the Kingdom of Hawai'i [by] the illegal overthrow. . . ."

Fact or fiction? What Kealoha is doing is continuing the fiction. Keep saying the ceded lands belong to the Hawaiian people even though as an OHA trustee he knows it is government land and that by legislative action, 20 percent of its revenues go to OHA to administer. Keep saying that the courts have said the lands were illegally taken when that is not what they have said. No court has ever said the ceded lands are anything but government lands. The Monarchy's own Supreme Court twice ruled they are government lands. The highly controversial Heely decision itself is under appeal.

Heely decision was appealed

Articles appearing in the national press also confuse the issue, hampered by space and the complexity of the problem. An article in *The New York Times* on July 23, 1996, about Hawai'i's 1996 plebiscite on a sovereignty convention is an example. It explains very well the idea behind the vote and where it could lead, and presents a reasonably balanced report on what sovereignty could mean.

But there are problems in three areas of *The Times* report:

1. The article states:

". . . the vote itself represents the crest of a powerful swell of native Hawaiian revival that began in the 1970s and could, decades down the road, bring about the restoration of independence the island Kingdom lost when American businessmen, backed by marines, overthrew Queen Lili'uokalani in 1893."

New York Times swallows party line on sovereignty

There are three problems with this sentence, one being repetition of the continuing myth that the United States somehow was responsible for the overthrow and that therefore independence for Hawai'i is an option. An objective review of the testimony of those on the scene during the Revolution makes it clear that U.S. marines did not physically assist the Revolutionists. The marines themselves, only about one-fifth of the U.S. forces that were landed, were assigned to the U.S. consulate and the U.S. legation. They and the rest of the troops were landed, as they had been on three tumultuous occasions in earlier years, to protect American interests. Their experience with the political necessity that they remain neutral led their officers to keep them out of sight, never on the offensive, never pointing their weapons. But they were caught in a political reversal in Washington when the pro-Annexation Republican administration of President Harrison was replaced by the anti-Annexation Democratic administration of President Cleveland. The false message that U.S. marines were backing the Revolutionists has been repeated so often it is accepted by many as the shortcut version of what happened. It is simply not true.

False: U.S. marines backed Revolutionists

Secondly, the Revolutionists were not acting as "American businessmen." Some *were* businessmen and many of those businessmen were Americans. But as Revolutionists they were acting as residents of Hawai'i and community leaders, most of them subjects of the Kingdom, revolting against a Queen who days earlier had attempted a revolution of her own. She had announced plans to promulgate a new Constitution that soon would have disenfranchised foreign-born residents and given new powers to the Monarch, all in violation of the Constitution she had sworn to uphold when she took office. Her action came about two years after she had tried unsuccessfully to take the Kingdom from her brother by force and just days after she had betrayed many of her supporters by signing lottery and opium bills she had earlier disavowed. Not even her own appointed

Cabinet backed her on her attempts to rewrite the Constitution.

In the third place, the Revolutionists successfully toppled a decaying Monarchy as a governing force. They substituted a new and independent government that opened citizenship to all, albeit with temporary conditions that controlled voting rights, and openly sought Annexation to the United States. They knew this eventually would bring full citizenship and voting rights to all male members of the community (women's suffrage had not yet come into being).

This government was independent for five years. To attempt now to disenfranchise today's Hawai'i residents and turn the Islands over to a new form of government (surely no one thinks of a return to monarchy?) is mind-boggling. Constitutional lawyers would have lifetime careers ahead of them on this one.

2. *The Times* article continues:

"In 1978, a state constitutional convention created the Office of Hawaiian Affairs to administer to the needs of native Hawaiians and get them a share of the proceeds from the use of 1.7 million acres of public land that once belonged to the kingdom of Hawaii."

This sentence, seemingly innocuous, implies two conditions that give erroneous impressions. One, OHA was not designed to "get [Native Hawaiians] a share of the proceeds from the use of 1.7 million acres of public land that once belonged to the kingdom of Hawaii." Native Hawaiians already were guaranteed a share in the proceeds from the ceded lands under terms of the Admission Act that brought Statehood. Secondly, by stating that the lands "once belonged to the kingdom," the implication is left that the lands and their benefits were taken from that Kingdom. In actuality, the transfer of administration of the government lands from Lili'uokalani's Monarchy to the new Provisional Government was as simple an administrative act as was the transfer of them from Kalākaua's Monarchy to Lili'uokalani's. These lands were government lands under the Monarchy, the Provisional Government and the Republic before they went to the United States in a form of trust and were returned at Statehood. The people of Hawai'i enjoyed the income from them at the beginning, and still do.

Transfer of lands a simple administrative act

3. And finally the article says:

"There is consensus, even among the haole, as whites are called here, that the native Hawaiians are owed something from the United States for what American rule has cost them, from their threatened culture to their lost lands."

Hawai'i's people enjoy income from government lands

This is apparently based on a subsequent statement in the article, that an *Advertiser* poll in 1995 showed that "83 percent [of Hawai'i residents] said they did think Hawaiians deserved some kind of reparations or redress." No specifics were presented in that poll, nor had there been any educational process in preparation for the asking of such a question of people who have had little background in Hawaiian history. What most people know about sovereignty is what they read or hear on TV and this has been heavily weighted with stories sympathetic to Hawaiians as victims of some kind. But to say reparations would be in return for "what American rule has cost them" goes well beyond the poll's question. What has American rule cost the Hawaiian? It is hard to see how it has cost them anything, the benefits seeming to far outweigh any psychological losses that have been claimed. Becoming a part of America, gaining citizenship and the benefits of association with the world's most stable nation are positive measures, not negative "costs." American rule did not "cost them their lands." The lands were held separately in trust for all of us, not added to the federal land bank as were American Indian lands. They certainly have not been "lost."

American rule: What has it cost Hawaiians?

A letter in *The Advertiser* over the signature of Dene Edens in July 1993 is an early example of the moves to maintain that not only were the lands stolen, but so was the nation. "Hawaiian nation was stolen," reads the headline on the letter. The letter erroneously implies it was U.S. policy to overthrow the Hawaiian Monarchy. In fact, as soon as President Cleveland decided to call the successful Revolution an American venture, he ordered those involved to return the Monarchy to Queen Lili'uokalani. Had it been U.S. policy to take over Hawai'i, he certainly would not have done that. Neither his administration nor the previous Harrison administration advocated that the United States take over Hawai'i.

Not U.S. policy to take over Hawai'i

A point made by Senator Inouye in a July 25, 1993, article in *The Advertiser* exemplifies the power of revisionist history. He states: "The United States owes to the Hawaiian people that which Hawaiian people were wrongly deprived of in 1893—the fundamental right to govern themselves." The assumption obviously is that in 1893 they were possessed of a government that they had selected for themselves, a point sovereignty enthusiasts also attempt to make. The fact is that Queen Lili'uokalani, like most queens, was not elected. She was appointed by her brother to be his successor. The power of the people

Revisionist history powerful but not true

of Hawai'i actually was used in 1893 to *remove* her after she tried to promulgate a new Constitution in violation of the existing Constitution of Hawai'i she had sworn to uphold.

Earlier in his article, Senator Inouye stated that the Revolution of 1893 was "an action not supported by the people of Hawaii, nor approved by the elected members of the legislature of the Kingdom . . . and most certainly not approved by the queen herself." The Revolution certainly wasn't approved by the Queen, but the outcome presents the possibility it *did* have the support of the people. Although outnumbering the Revolutionists by 10 to 1, Hawaiians did not rise to support the Queen. People were voting with the force of their emotions, and the sweep of the Revolution was clearly a test of wills. The Queen's did not prevail.

Queen's Legislature did not approve Revolution, wasn't asked

The Legislature of the Kingdom, of course, was not asked to approve the Revolution, though some of its members took part. The Legislature of the Republic, however, which was the next elected body representative of the people of Hawai'i, did approve Annexation and by extension the Revolution itself.[66] As noted earlier, many Native Hawaiians were among its members, including the speaker of the House. Perhaps the most telling indication of the quality of support for the Queen at the time of the Revolution lies in the actions of her Cabinet members, who, as detailed in Chapter Four, had come close to deposing her themselves.

Republic's Legislature approved Annexation

Senator Inouye also said: "It would be difficult to contend that the overthrow and the resultant change in the status of the government of Hawai'i were carried out in a manner that was consistent with the standards that were then recognized in the world community." His phrasing indicates he is open to argument on the matter and it well *can* be argued that revolution was and always will be a well-established means of overthrowing an undesirable government. The fact that the new government was quickly recognized by every nation interested in the Pacific, including the United States, is evidence there was nothing in the action that inhibited other governments from welcoming this new member into the fraternity of nations.

Revolution a means of overthrowing unwanted government

In the same article, Senator Inouye said that at that point in 1993 he believed Native Hawaiian people should enjoy the same political status afforded Alaska natives and American Indians. He has often said this is a point that has been argued since Statehood. In June 1996, in a letter to *The Advertiser* concerning the impending plebiscite, he noted the issue still is not settled. He said: ". . . the sponsors of legislation to reform the federal acknowledgment process affecting Native American tribes have advised me that any reference to Native Hawaiians that may have erroneously been included in federal Indian legislation either has been or will be deleted from those legislative proposals."

No legislative efforts to make Native Hawaiians Native Americans

He went on to imply that until Native Hawaiians themselves are in agreement on whether they want that status, nothing will happen. There are sovereignty proponents, including Senator Akaka, who already speak of Native Hawaiians as Native Americans. Senator Inouye, long associated with the Native American movement, makes it clear that Native Hawaiians are not considered Native Americans and that in 1997 there were no legislative efforts headed in that direction.

On a minor note, Sol Kahoʻohalahala, chairman of the Hawaiian Sovereignty Elections Council for the 1996 plebiscite, was quoted in a September

1996 report of the election, commenting on the Revolution: "The conspirators sneaked back to the back
steps of this building [the seat of Hawaiian government at the time], intentionally avoiding the general
Hawaiian public."

The opposite is true: The proclamation
announcing the new Provisional Government was
read from the *front* steps of the building in full view
of 'Iolani Palace, with officers of the new government
in attendance and the "general Hawaiian public"
welcome.[67] Every history of the event, based on testimony in the Blount Report and sworn statements
and testimony in the Morgan Report from men who
were there at the time, is in agreement on this point.
Kaho'ohalahala's misstatement is typical revisionism; sovereignists frequently try to belittle actions of
the Revolutionists.

In the same article, Representative Quentin
Kawananakoa, a rational voice on the side of sovereignty, is quoted as saying: "My great-grandfather
was inside this building at the time of the overthrow
. . ." The senior Kawananakoa was a high official of
the Queen's government and was among those who
elected to stay on during the transition to the new
government. He was instrumental that first night in
getting notice of the change in governments off to
foreign governments represented in Honolulu, all of
whom recognized the new government immediately.
The Provisional Government removed only six people from administration of the government: the
Queen, her marshal and the four members of her
Cabinet. All others were asked to stay on. Some, like
Kawananakoa, stayed on for awhile, then left to
become part of an opposition party and joined the
Queen's unsuccessful attempt at a counter-revolution. With the defeat of that effort and her subse-

*Proclamation
read from
palace-side
front steps*

*Kawananakoa
rational voice
on sovereignty*

314

quent abdication, many became supporters of Annexation. Many also remained active in politics under the Republic and, of course, the Territory.[68]

Many supported Annexation

Here's a summary of erroneous statements that appear frequently in current efforts to rewrite Hawai'ian history:

Fiction: Lili'uokalani was chosen by the people of Hawai'i to be their Queen.

Fact: She was named by Kalākaua, her brother, to be his successor. Kalākaua, a man with lesser chiefly lineage himself, had been elected by the Legislature in 1874 by a narrow margin over Queen Emma. The election was so controversial it culminated in an all-out riot that had to be quelled by U.S. troops, landed, as in 1893, for the purpose of protecting American interests. Queen Lili'uokalani was never approved by the vote of her people.

Queen never approved by vote

Fiction: Queen Lili'uokalani was removed from her throne by U.S. marines.

Fact: A force consisting of one-fifth U.S. marines and four-fifths U.S. bluejackets was landed in Honolulu to protect Americans and their property, as had similar forces on three occasions during the reign of King Kalākaua. In 1893, the troops never came face to face with the Queen or her forces and did not participate in the Revolution.

Fiction: American missionaries and sugar interests led the Revolution that unseated Lili'uokalani. (Sometimes the phrase "American businessmen" is also used to describe, erroneously, the makeup of the leadership Committee. In other cases, the Revolutionists are referred to as "foreigners.")

Missionaries and sugar interests did not unseat Lili'uokalani

Fact: The thirteen-member Committee of Safety included nine with American connections and four Europeans, all of whom were qualified voting residents of Hawai'i. The chairman, Henry Cooper, a relative newcomer to the Islands, had qualified the year before the Revolution. Only three of the thirteen were missionary descendants; one a second generation and two, third generation. Of the thirteen, seven were subjects of the Kingdom, having sworn allegiance to the crown (including five of the former Americans and two of the Europeans), four were American citizens and two were European nationals. Five were attorneys; none were sugar plantation owners or operators. Three had been elected by the largely Hawaiian electorate as legislators in the Monarchy's House of Representatives. None worked for any of the handful of missionary-dominated businesses in Honolulu.

Fiction: Lands of the Hawaiian people were stolen from them.

Fact: Lands gained in fee simple by the chiefs or commoners as a result of the Great *Mahele* in 1848 were held by them until sold or otherwise transferred. None were stolen. Lands held by the government, later called the "ceded lands," were government lands when they were so designated that same year by Kamehameha III. They were transferred, virtually intact, from monarch to monarch to the Provisional Government, to the Republic, to the United States when Hawai'i became annexed as a territory, and back to Hawai'i as a state in 1959. The income from them was used for the benefit of the residents of Hawai'i when they were set aside as government lands, and still is to this date. Neither the lands nor their income were stolen. Individual Hawaiians never owned any of the ceded lands.

Lands, income not stolen

Fiction: The missionaries sought to kill the Hawaiian language and stifle the culture.

Fact: The missionaries saved the Hawaiian

language when they arrived forty-two years after Captain Cook by translating it into a written language and teaching almost the entire Kingdom to read and write Hawaiian and, in most cases, English, too. They thought, in the strictness of their own early 19th-Century upbringing, that the hula was not compatible with turning Hawaiians into Christians, and opposed it. But they taught music and harmony to the Hawaiians, recorded history, fought disease, advocated temperance, struggled to prepare Hawaiians for their inevitable exposure to the Western world, left the mission when requested to do so by Hawai'i kings to serve as advisers and consultants to the government, though in total they constituted only 4 percent of the foreigners who served the various Hawaiian monarchs in the 19th Century. The missionaries, probably more than any other element of the community, worked to implement Kamehameha III's decision to put fee simple ownership of the lands into the hands of Hawaiian natives.

Missionaries translated Hawaiian into written language

Missionaries worked to implement King's land decision

Fiction: The missionaries and the Republic of Hawai'i banned the Hawaiian language from schools.

Fact: As reported earlier, far from banning the language, the missionaries *saved* the Hawaiian language by putting it into written form, printing literature, including the Bible, in Hawaiian and preaching in Hawaiian throughout the 19th Century. Regarding actions of the Republic, A. Grove Day notes in his 1955 history, *Hawai'i and Its People*, "A decade before Annexation, a steady advance was begun toward achieving the American ideal of universal, compulsory, nonsectarian, and tax-supported education. All English-language government schools were by 1888 free to students . . . . Under the Republic, education was restored to its early important

Missionaries saved Hawaiian language, did not ban it

place under a separate Department of Public Instruction, and English was made the classroom language." The latter clause may have given rise to the interpretation that there was a ban on use of the Hawaiian language. The author could find no record of a law, ruling or ordinance banning use of the language, though anecdotally many Hawaiian grandmothers recall their use of the language being banned. It is not clear whether this was a result of government action or parental action. By the mid-1920s the Legislature had passed a bill requiring that Hawaiian language courses be made available to anyone who wished them. But that does not indicate there ever was a ban on use of the language itself.

Fiction: The congressional apology resolution has the force of law and its whereas clauses have become factual by act of Congress as U.S. Public Law 103-150.

Resolution called a simple apology

Fact: Resolutions do not create public law. They are not codified as part of the laws of the land. The whereas clauses in particular are not part of the law nor did adoption of the resolution make them factual accounts of history. No hearings were held to verify their accuracy. This resolution was called a "simple resolution of apology" by one of its two sponsors, Senator Inouye.

Fiction: Hawaiians voted overwhelmingly to hold a constitutional convention to provide for a Native Hawaiian government in the 1996 plebiscite.

Small percent of Hawaiians voted for plebiscite

Fact: Of the 79,400 ballots sent to eligible Hawaiian voters, 46,377 were not returned or were returned blank, indicating 58 percent chose not to vote for the convention. Of the balance of 33,023, there were 22,294 votes in favor of the convention, or 67.5 percent of the ballots returned. Opponents point out, however, that the 22,294 "yes" votes also mean only about 28 percent of those eligible to vote said "yes" to the proposal.

Fiction: The 1997 Public Television video, *Hawai'i's Last Queen*, included an emotional episode that said the Hawaiian Flag taken down at Annexation was "cut up into little ribbons by the missionaries and given to their children as souvenirs of what they had done to the Hawaiians."

Fact: There is no historical record of any such incident. The producers of the video knew no Hawaiian historian had ever mentioned such an act and knew this fable first appeared in the 1950s as an item written by a newspaper columnist known for her often fictitious tales of old Hawai'i. They used it anyway, telling this writer that it captured the spirit of the Annexation period. H.J. Bartels, curator of 'Iolani Palace and sympathetic in a rational way to sovereignty issues, believes this flag incident is fictional. He suggests it may have sprung from an item in the August 5, 1898, *Pacific Commercial Advertiser*, page 1, column 3. The item related that a commercial firm had approached President Dole with the idea of raising and lowering the flags on a colorful ribbon-like lanyard that then could be cut into pieces and sold as souvenirs. There is no report this was ever done but the Dole family in the 1970s sold to antique dealer Robert Van Dyke a piece of cloth resembling this description, which may have been the lanyard sample shown to President Dole. At any rate, there were no missionaries alive at the time of Annexation and the four missionary descendants who were involved in leadership of the Revolution and the Provisional Government—Castle, Dole, Smith and Thurston, all attorneys—certainly didn't spend their time cutting up Hawaiian flags.

Fiction: All Hawaiians shut their windows

No historical record of missionaries cutting up Hawaiian Flag

No missionaries alive at the time of Annexation

and stayed home during the Annexation Day ceremonies at 'Iolani Palace, August 12, 1898.

Fact: Photographs of the day show Hawaiian
leaders seated or standing with the dignitaries on a
platform at the *makai* entrance to the Palace, while
other Hawaiians are visible on the grounds. A much
publicized picture shows Queen Lili'uokalani and a
handful of her retinue seated in her home at the time
of the ceremonies, but not all Hawaiians, by any
means, were opposed to Annexation.

*Not all Hawai-
ians opposed
Annexation*

Fiction: "Queen [Lili'uokalani] was living,
on February 12, 1897, in Washington, D.C., at the
Shoreham Hotel. Three days later she would move to
the Cairo Hotel after becoming alarmed over rumors
that assassins had been hired by Lorrin Thurston to
kill her at the Shoreham"—extract from the President's Remarks, front page of the 'Iolani Palace
Quarterly, Spring 1997, under a photo of President
Abigail K. Kawananakoa.

Fact: In her book, *Hawai'i's Story by
Hawai'i's Queen*, Lili'uokalani has this to say about
her 1897 visit to Washington:

> "One day in February, the proprietor of
> the Shoreham notified me, that, as I had
> failed to engage my apartments for inaugura-
> tion week, he had rented them to others, and
> that every room in the hotel would then be
> occupied . . . . Rather than await the arrival of
> the future occupants of those rooms . . . it
> seemed best to me to move at once....[So] on
> or about the 14th of February, I moved with
> my party to the large thirteen-story building
> on Q Street, N.W., known as 'The Cairo'....Its
> newness and immaculate cleanliness
> impressed me favorably at once...[and] there
> we remained until about the 9th of July, at
> which time I removed to New York City...."

*Queen said
nothing about
assassination
concerns*

You will note the Queen, who rarely had a good word to say about Thurston, also says nothing about any assassination concerns at the Shoreham, although she often brought up such worries in her Honolulu diaries of the 1894 period (not that she ever mentioned Thurston in connection with them!). "It was just a rumor," notes Bartels. "We left it in because it caught the state of mind of the times." Interestingly, that's about what the producer of *Hawai'i's Last Queen* said to me in a letter about the flag-cutting incident: "It may not be true, but we think it catches the flavor of the period." In other words, what's wrong with a little baloney if it makes the stew taste better?

Producer admits show contained possible untruth

Chapter Twelve

*W*here Do We Go From Here?

he Hawaiian Kingdom existed—even thrived—in isolation for centuries, but sovereignty advocates generally acknowledge the Monarchy days are gone forever. Beating the opposition into submission worked for Kamehameha I, who was dealing with other Hawaiians under their own 18th-Century rules of warfare. It can't work in the 20th Century in a complex society governed by a Constitution and the rule of law.

Problems can be solved with mutual trust and support

The problems that face Hawaiians today can be solved only in an atmosphere of mutual trust and support among all of the races and viewpoints now in place in these Islands. We must work toward togetherness and avoid actions that could be divisive.

The majority of Hawai'i's people are not likely to vote for independence or even an independent Hawaiian "nation-within-a-nation." These basic changes in our structure would have to be decided at the federal level anyway.

Majority unlikely to approve transfer of ownership to minority

Hawai'i's majority is not likely to approve ownership transfer of any significant measure of the state's ceded lands to the part-Hawaiian minority except possibly as part of negotiated settlements resolving monies due OHA and the Hawaiian Homes Commission from disputes of past mismanagement.

The majority, however, already does appear to accept the idea of special allocations of tax monies being controlled by Native Hawaiians. It has accepted the earmarking of 20 percent of the income from ceded lands directly for Hawaiian welfare under the direction of the state Office of Hawaiian Affairs. In today's environment of concern over anti-discriminatory actions, that allocation may be challenged. It was accepted, however, by the majority at the time of Statehood and, if killed, should be rescued somehow. It provides the funding for a wide and potentially productive variety of Hawaiian-based programs despite the extra layer of bureaucracy involved in getting this money from the land revenues to the ultimate beneficiaries. And, it could help hold the state and its people together instead of further dividing them.

Majority accepts earmarked income from ceded lands for Hawaiians

In their enthusiasm, sovereignty leaders have led thousands of Hawaiians and part-Hawaiians to believe the major goals of independence and control of all of the ceded lands are achievable. The failure to achieve these major objectives will lead to inevitable disappointment.

Sovereignty needs new direction

New directions for the sovereignty effort are needed. These seem not only possible but their foundations are already in place, waiting for cohesive leadership. The enthusiasm of sovereignty activists could play a major role in making sure that leadership is provided and is productive. To be most effective, this new leadership should recognize that some goals are beyond reach and viable alternatives must be developed. Developing alternatives is in the interest of us all. There could be disastrous effects if nothing were to happen, leaving the Hawaiian community with only lost expectations after these many years of pursuing sovereignty. Unfulfilled expectations could translate into more cultural or socio-economic problems.

Many aspects of sovereignty already have wide approval. These accepted aspects should be pursued by both Hawaiians and non-Hawaiians as goals and activities to fill the emotional gap that could otherwise come about with the failure of the more publicized sovereignty goals to be achieved.

Pursuit of Hawaiian culture supported

The most obvious widely supported goal is the pursuit of Hawaiian culture. Progress is being made in this area with the resurgence of interest in Hawaiian language and the teaching of other cultural aspects in elementary and higher schools. The *kumu hula* are doing a great job in the further revival and development of interest in dance. But we should move beyond the argument that foreigners in the 19th Century sought to destroy Hawaiian culture or sought to ban the language. Teaching of the language, saved originally by the missionaries who put it in a written form, fell by the wayside in the Republic's struggling years when English was proclaimed to be the language of the classroom, but it is widely supported again today. To continue the argument over when or whether it was banned, for how long, by whom and why, is needlessly divisive.

Language ban argument is unnecessary

We should back off also from the erroneous thought that Hawaiian culture is something only Hawaiians can appreciate. Immersion language schools and classes in culture should be open to all students. Such an approach would lessen the danger that students of Hawaiian ancestry begin to think learning the language, for instance, is an end-all achievement. For our youngsters to become successful in today's world, English is still essential and we are shortchanging young Hawaiians to preach otherwise. Long the international language of business,

English is essential for success

325

English has replaced French as the international language of diplomacy. It is not a thoughtful act to allow an American citizen to grow up without a good command of English.

Hawaiian as a second language could be as valuable and satisfying to Islanders as the pursuit of other languages is in schools throughout the country, and it should be encouraged. Hawaiian language courses have been mandatory under Hawaiian law since 1925 and need to be made available in fact as well as law wherever there are students or families interested.

Hawaiian as a second language valuable

The effort to set aside Kahoʻolawe as an exclusive Hawaiian preserve is an example of an unnecessarily divisive approach to the preservation of Hawaiian culture. Why isolate Hawaiian culture? Why should a significant portion of the state be set aside for the benefit of just one segment of the population? No lands of the Kingdom ever were set aside for use by one race only. Development of Kahoʻolawe will take significant monies beyond expected initial help from the federal government in clearing remaining armed bombs. It would be unfair enough to set aside lands for use by only one segment of the population, much less compound the unfairness by using general tax revenues to pay for their upkeep.

Historically important places found on all islands

Labeling Kahoʻolawe as a revered and special Hawaiian place is an unnecessary stretch of fact and credibility in the first place. All of the Islands contain places that were important in Hawaiian history. Sites on the other islands, however, far exceed in importance those that exist on Kahoʻolawe. Physical features of the island itself—its lack of water and forests and very limited agricultural potential—kept it from playing an important role in early Hawaiian history. The Hawaiian hierarchy had its choice of places to live and enjoy and certainly would not have opted for a near-barren island when garden spots existed on nearby islands. Fishermen of course visited it from time to time. Kamehameha I, who often visited the south shore of Lanai, may even have stopped by. House or shelter platforms do exist.

Kahoʻolawe bleak in 1800s

The Treaty of Reciprocity between the United States and Hawaiʻi of 1855 contained a bleak description of Kahoʻolawe in the mid-19th Century:

"Separated from East Maui by ʻAlalākeiki Channel, 6 miles wide, [the island] is about 11 miles in length and 8 miles wide.

"It is low and almost destitute of every kind of shrub or verdure (vegetation), excepting a species of coarse grass. The rocks of which it is formed are volcanic, but nothing is known of any active or extinct craters on the island.

"At one time this island was used as a penal settlement; but it is now chiefly used as a sheep run, the soil of decomposed lava being too poor a quality for cultivation.

"No towns noted; probably none exist."

Its value today lies in its virtually untouched availability. This value is negated to a large extent by the damage inflicted on it by its early use as grazing lands and later as a target island, useful though the latter may have been to U.S. security over the years.

By legend, Kahoʻolawe was the starting point for voyages to Tahiti, though voyaging canoes would have been built, stocked and loaded with people elsewhere. With this background, there is logic in having the island developed and administered as a Hawaiian project by Hawaiians and Hawaiian organizations. As indicated earlier, however, doing so as an exclusive arrangement for a single ethnic group is divisive, discriminatory and unnecessary. Kahoʻolawe should

Exclusive arrangement for Hawaiians is divisive

be accessible to everyone either as potential participants or as visitors. The sovereignty movement
would benefit from the support of others than
Hawaiians.

The massive compensation for past mismanagement of the Hawaiian Homes Administration
land program has stretched tolerance for further
compensation at the expense of non-Hawaiian racial
groups about as far as it can be stretched. Most of the
monetary values for so-called injuries to Hawaiians
by misconduct of the program were determined arbitrarily by the Waihee administration. There was no
public process, just a swirl of action that was enact-
ed by a Legislature under pressure to do something
for Hawaiians. In the case of the Hawaiian Homes
Commission, it was an overdue corrective process
and justification for the correction existed. But continuing to pay off past injuries or mistakes with tax
monies from people who had nothing to do with the
original problems is too divisive. We must get the
potential for divisiveness behind us. Our combined
efforts and monies should go to developing and carrying out new projects that will bring the community together.

*Compensation
for Hawaiian
injuries arbi-
trary*

It is unfortunate that many sovereignty advocates continue to claim that Hawaiians have been
badly treated in their homeland and are not getting a
fair share of benefits from the land that was once
owned by their leaders. The record shows otherwise.

*Record shows
Hawaiians have
not been treated
badly in their
homeland*

The Statehood Admission Act was the first
time Native Hawaiians were designated as beneficiaries of the ceded lands. The act tied the definition of
Native Hawaiian to the Hawaiian Homes Commission Act, however, which meant that only people
with 50 percent Hawaiian blood are among those
specifically designated as beneficiaries by the Admis-

sion Act. OHA has resolved this problem somewhat by agreement with the state Attorney General's Office to segregate OHA revenues, using the Admission Act definition when it dispenses ceded land revenues, and using the broader definition set by the 1978 Constitutional Convention when it uses other state revenues, or revenues from other sources. Congress, of course, could amend the Admission Act definition, but today's concern with enacting special rules and privileges for minorities will make this difficult.

Native Hawaiians receive special dispensation

Native Hawaiians, as broadly defined, already receive significant special dispensation. In addition to the Hawaiian Homes Commission Act (HHCA), there are now some 10 other state and federal acts whose benefits go to Native Hawaiians.

At the state level, recent amendments and rulings have tightened provisions of the HHCA to preclude non-Hawaiians from using those lands, and Kaho'olawe was set aside for the practice of Native Hawaiian traditions. At the federal level, Native Hawaiians benefit from the Older Americans Act of 1965, the National Historic Preservation Act of 1966, the Rehabilitation Act of 1973, the Native American Programs Act of 1974, the Developmental Disabilities Assistance and Bill of Rights Act Amendments of 1987, the Indian Health Care Amendments of 1988, the Disadvantaged Minority Health Improvement Act of 1990, the Native Hawaiian Health Care Improvement Act of 1992 and the Native Hawaiian Education Act of 1994. As Stuart Minor notes in his comprehensive *Yale Law Journal* article published in December 1996, some of these single out Hawaiians of 50 percent native blood.

Non-Hawaiians prevented from using lands

Singling out Hawaiians of 50 percent native blood

Most, however, he says, use the recent expanded definition, which is more in keeping with the treatment of Native American Indians. Many Hawaiians hope to become defined as Native Americans and thus gain benefits given Native Americans under that designation, including the right to build and operate casinos. OHA leadership has already discussed the casino potential with its Washington contacts, though in 1996, Patton Boggs, one of the top-level law firms and leading lobbyists in the capital, urged then-OHA Chairman Clayton Hee to downplay the issue for the time being. Hee lost his chairmanship in October 1997.

OHA chairman urged to downplay casino discussions

Hawaiians, as members of the general public, share along with everyone else in the 80 percent of ceded land revenues that go toward generic public purposes such as schools, parks, roads, agricultural infrastructure, etc. Since Native Hawaiians constitute about 20 percent of the population, they share to the extent of about 20 percent in those general benefits. Twenty percent of 80 percent is 16 percent. Adding this 16 percent to the 20 percent of overall ceded land revenues that is set aside exclusively for Native Hawaiians, we find that 36 percent of ceded land revenues are being used today for the benefit of persons of Hawaiian descent. No one is complaining about this percentage at the moment. Sovereignty activists and others who claim erroneously that the ceded lands were stolen from the Hawaiians might do well to pause and perhaps deal with this distribution in a positive manner instead of inviting attack by seeking more.

Thirty-six percent of ceded land revenues used to benefit Hawaiians

A.A. Smyser, contributing editor of the *Honolulu Star-Bulletin*, in an article dated November 6, 1996, looked in depth at the question "Are Hawaiians Being Treated Fairly," and concluded the answer is a "qualified yes."

He noted they share like everyone else, as

mentioned above, in facilities and lands that are public, including public schools, and in addition benefit from the monies of six landed trusts and various funded programs. He listed these as:

"(1) the Princess Bernice Pauahi Bishop Estate, which educates Hawaiian children through its Kamehameha Schools,

"(2) the Hawaiian Homes program, which is finally picking up steam because of land and cash infusion and has about 6,250 families on lots,

"(3) the Queen Lili'uokalani Trust, which helps needy Hawaiian children,

"(4) the King Lunalilo Trust, which maintains a home for aged Hawaiians,

"(5) the Office of Hawaiian Affairs, with assets well above $200 million and current annual income from the state—which Governor Cayetano wants to reduce sharply—of about $15 million,

"(6) numerous federal grants (listed above), many of them administered by Alu Like and

"(7) the Queen Emma Foundation, which includes the Queen's Medical Center. The medical center serves all Hawai'i's people but the estate focuses its investment spending on Hawaiians."

Smyser goes on to note that more than 100 part-Hawaiian heirs of the James Campbell Estate, four of the Mark Robinson Estate and many part-Hawaiian holders of private land holdings ranging in size from the 225,000 acres of Parker Ranch to single-family homes are benefiting from the lands.

What could be done to make all of these programs for the support of Native Hawaiians more effective? For one thing, they could be better publicized. But in the main, they would benefit from Hawaiian organizations themselves getting behind them and making them work.

These and other programs should be supported more strongly by the major Hawaiian trusts and estates. Bishop Estate trustees could take a broader look at their mandate as custodians of Hawai'i's largest trust. Taking refuge today in a supposed fiduciary mandate that they maximize the return from trust assets, they have invested hundreds of millions of dollars from the proceeds of land sales in business deals. But they have done so largely outside of Hawai'i—where the business climate and potential dollar returns arguably are better. They point out they are charged with preserving and increasing the return from the assets left by Princess Pauahi in order to further the education of Hawai'i's children and hence must look for safety and the highest rate of return. In 1996, they canceled a key program that was serving 10,000 preschool Hawaiian children and they consistently ignore the implied challenge of Pauahi that they use her assets to benefit Hawaiian children. Imagine the benefits that could accrue to Hawaiians (and everyone else, incidentally) if the Bishop Estate invested those hundreds of millions of dollars in Hawai'i—in housing projects, hotels pointed toward the Hawaiian experience, or other programs. These might or might not produce fewer dollars in returns for the estate but would boost the economy and provide work for part-Hawaiians. If they fear a charge of malfeasance for neglecting the highest possible dollar returns, perhaps the Legislature could take them off the hook by confirming as prudent, if not mandating, a more sensitive and local approach to the use of income from Hawai'i's lands. In the latter part of 1997, estate trustees were under-

Programs need more support from Hawaiian trusts and estates

Bishop Estate should invest in Hawai'i

going scrutiny by the state Attorney General's Office as the result of a general outcry over their handling of the estate.

The same mandate for a more Hawai'i-sensitive approach could be applied to other landed estates, even the private ones such as Campbell and Robinson, and probably would be well-received by trustees sensitive to the source of the estates' wealth. The other *ali'i* trusts—Queen's Hospital Foundation, Lili'uokalani and Lunalilo—already are looking for ways to better serve their Hawaiian constituents.

Ali'i trusts looking to better serve Hawaiians

Jeremy Rifkin, in his provocative 1995 book, *The End of Work,* raises issues and offers solutions that have direct application to the future of our part-Hawaiian population. Rifkin examines the impact of information age technologies on the job market and his title summarizes the direction he believes we are heading: Human beings in every sector are being replaced with computers, robotics and other technologies. In his discussion of solutions, he suggests the increased development of a social economy, a community services sector, to balance the traditional government and business sectors of our economy and provide job opportunities for the millions of displaced workers. Job opportunities for the part-Hawaiian population already are limited. Unemployment rates among them are the highest for any ethnic segment in these Islands. Rifkin's suggestions for expansion of the social sector are cast in a global context and advocate compensation for community service. He calls for examination of innovative ways to finance expanded community service through such means as a value-added tax, reduction of the workweek, a government-guaranteed annual income, etc.

Job opportunities for Hawaiians are limited

Hawaiian unemployment rate highest in the state

This kind of thinking suggests an opportunity for OHA and other Hawaiian organizations to pull the Hawaiian community together. OHA could, for example, use some of its revenues to provide direct support for unemployed part-Hawaiian workers in return for their working together on housing programs—such as those conducted by Alu Like, the Hawaiian Homes Commission and the OHA Habitat project. There are other activities that would benefit both the workers and their community. The development of Hawaiian culture parks, the rehabilitation and perpetuation of *heiau*, beaches, streams, trails and taro patches are examples of other projects that could become community service applications funded by OHA monies. They would make Hawai'i more interesting for visitors and more productive for residents.

OHA should continue with community service projects

OHA already is studying the idea of using some of its settlement monies to invest in business ventures in Hawai'i, as Maori organizations have done in New Zealand; this seems like a wise move.

Certain of the ceded lands could well provide the environment for high-tech development. To entice that kind of investment the land usage would necessarily have to be combined with justifiable government subsidies and changes in the present state attitude toward business. Revenues from the increased value of ceded lands used for such development could be earmarked for the training of Native Hawaiians who may not have the necessary high-tech skills as well as for the community service compensation described above.

Earmark money to train Native Hawaiians

The high-tech industry seeks out places to work that would appeal to its skilled workers as good places to live. Hawai'i, if its favorable climate and beauty were supplemented with a supportive attitude by the government and its people, would be hard to beat in the world market.

The climate of developing a better relationship with Hawaiians would benefit simply by a community-wide backing off of the ongoing efforts to paint Hawaiians as "victims." One outspoken Hawaiian, Benny Olepau of Waimānalo, thinks Hawaiians should stop trying to take advantage of their relationship to the Island culture and their feeling that as victims they deserve better treatment.

Stop painting Hawaiians as victims

"We Hawaiians cannot turn back the clock and expect to live in the past with modern materials. We cannot favor only Hawaiians; we must include all residents in Hawai'i.

"We are responsible for our misfortunes," he wrote.

In connection with analyzing the problems and progress of Hawaiians, much thought needs to be given to a workable and realistic definition of "Hawaiian." Intermarriage with foreigners began at the moment of Western contact and descendants of such early marriages often have minimal amounts of Hawaiian blood. It barely makes sense to call those descendants "Hawaiians" forever.

Realistic definition for Hawaiian

The determination to label one's self "part-Hawaiian" seems sometimes like a business decision—what's going to be most effective economically. And it could lead to abuse. In future years, some part-Hawaiians with minimal levels of native blood might be tempted to call themselves Hawaiian only for some financial consideration—entitlements, land awards, participation in the ownership of a casino, etc.—but desire to be like everyone else when it comes to voting, schooling, working, receiving benefits and the like.

Part-Hawaiian label a business decision

Defining a Hawaiian as one with an eighth native blood may be far enough down the line to go for formal recognition. Further dilution could lose recognition of the effect, value and influence of the Hawaiian gene.

Even formalizing the "Hawaiian" designation at the one-eighth measure would mean a significantly smaller number of persons calling themselves Hawaiian. It would have a much more realistic impact on the statistics measuring the status of Hawaiians. At the moment these statistics must be viewed with suspicion because of the vast mix of blood and genes. There's no realistic way to determine which gene is responsible for a social condition.

A smaller number of people calling themselves Hawaiian

If one needed an eighth share of Hawaiian blood to be called Hawaiian, the Hawaiians as a racial grouping might no longer find themselves at the bottom of the scale in so many measures of social welfare. The value to self-esteem of those calling themselves "Hawaiian" could be considerable.

Hawaiian culture has much to offer in many other areas, such as medicine, ocean navigation and interracial relationships.

Hawaiians have long history of using herbs for maladies

Early Hawaiians, with no contact with the Western world, had a long history of the use of herbs for various maladies. Uses they developed over the centuries are becoming known, but concentrated and extensive study and replanting probably could expand significantly what is known of these ancient practices. Who knows what the blending of knowledge and experiments with the healing powers of the various herbs could develop?

The March 1997 issue of OHA's monthly publication, *Ka Wai Ola o OHA*, reports on the recognition of Hawaiian herbal healer "Papa" Henry Auwae as a "living treasure." The Hongpa Hongwanji Buddhist Temple of Honolulu in making the award noted his outstanding contributions.

Ka Wai Ola notes:

"'Papa' Auwae, 91, is a native of Kokoiki, Kohala, and now lives in Keaukaha, Hawai'i. He is noted for helping to bridge the gap between traditional Hawaiian la'au lapa'au herbal healing and western medical methods. He has shared his knowledge of Hawaiian herbal healing with Queen's Health Systems, National Cancer Institute and North Hawai'i Community Hospital, with Native Americans, and at many community gatherings throughout Hawai'i. He is a seventh-generation la'au lapa'au healer and was trained from the age of seven by his great-great-grandmother. He is recognized as a master kahuna la'au lapa'au with knowledge of the use of 2,500 medicinal herbs. His students not only learn about use of the plants but also about preservation of the environment in which they grow, and the spiritual basis of true healing, which he believes comes from God."

Bridging the gap between Hawai'i and the West

Students learn to preserve environment

They also learn much about the values of early Hawaiian lore and culture.

The astonishing recovery of ancient navigational methods pioneered by the first Hōkūle'a voyage is another area of great pride for Hawaiians. Expanded experiences with these skills will further develop pride and self-esteem and as a practical matter could cast new light on where the early visitors to these Islands came from.

Archeological studies have been going on for decades, but new skills and equipment are available and can be developed more fully. Better-financed studies and research on migration routes going all the way back to Sulawese and other possible South-

New skills and equipment improve studies of archeology

east Asian jumping-off places for the original migrations could be expanded to include Hawaiian scholars. The potential is enormous.

Studies such as these, of course, are ongoing on a limited basis, but they could benefit from a concerted and expanded OHA or state-funded program to enlist scholars with Hawaiian ancestry and broadened goals.

The state-wide sovereignty conference voted on in 1996 and sure to be the subject of continued discussion in the years to come might productively focus, if it ever convenes, on formulating a program that would include these notions and others. Both private and public sources of financing programs like these exist and could be enlisted.

Master plan needed to bring about new Hawaiian renaissance

The key, of course, is the coming together of Hawaiians to create a master plan for sovereignty goals. Right now the focus seems to be on power. Each sovereignty group has its own agenda and sees itself as the central corps for a renewed Hawaiian outlook. It will take a new Kamehameha with the vision of the historic leader to put aside the romantic but futile notion of a new nation, and build upon what is already available and achievable. Properly organized and explained, the master plan could gain wide public support. It could become the basis for a new Hawaiian renaissance.

Historical Figures

A List of Historical Figures Appearing in this Book

Akaka, Daniel—junior U.S. senator from Hawai'i in late 20th Century. With Senator Daniel Inouye, introduced the congressional apology resolution in 1993, the hundredth anniversary of the 1893 Revolution.

Alexander, William De Witt—early Western historian of Hawai'i, born in 1833 of missionary parents, testified at length before Morgan Committee after Blount rejected him.

Armstrong, Samuel Chapman—missionary descendant who became a general in the Union Army at the age of 26, commanded an African-American regiment; later founded Hampton Institute in Virginia for African-Americans.

Ashford, Volney V.—Canadian turned Hawaiian Royalist who with his brother, C.W. Ashford, led abortive 1889 revolution against Kalākaua, opposed successful 1893 Revolution against Lili'uokalani, and was involved in her unsuccessful 1895 counter-revolution. Throughout, felt Annexation to U.S. was best overall solution for Hawai'i.

Bayard, Thomas F.—U.S. secretary of state in Kalākaua period.

Bishop, Charles Reed—philanthropic businessman, traveling to Oregon with William L. Lee, arrived by accident in Honolulu from Boston on October 12, 1846; married Bernice Pauahi, great granddaughter of Kamehameha I. She created Bishop Estate; he created Bishop Museum and founded predecessor of First Hawaiian Bank.

Hawaiian Historical Society

Blount, James H.—former Georgia congressman sent to Hawai'i in 1893 by President Cleveland to investigate the overthrow of the Hawaiian Monarchy, recommended censure of U.S. Minister John L. Stevens and reinstatement of Lili'uokalani.

Bolte, Crister—German national, Hawaiian subject, member of the Committee of Safety, was sent to contact Dole about his taking presidency of Provisional Government.

Brown, Andrew—Scottish national, member of Committee of

Safety. Fairly obscure man, coppersmith with the Honolulu Iron Works at time of Revolution.

Bush, J.E.—sent by Kalākaua to take over Samoa during King's abortive effort to unite Polynesia. Later a Native Hawaiian backer on occasion of Lili'uokalani, but, as editor of Hawaiian newspaper and leader of liberal party, generally opposed her. Favored Annexation over continuation of Monarchy.

Carter, Charles L.—American, naturalized Hawaiian, member of Committee of Safety and one of five ministers sent to Washington to negotiate Annexation. Law partner of L.A. Thurston. Only Provisional Government fatality in the counter-revolution. Oldest son of H.A.P. Carter, minister of foreign affairs for Kalākaua, and Sybil A. Carter; nephew of Queen's adviser, J.O. Carter.

Carter, Henry A.P.—called by Historian Ralph Kuykendall "perhaps the ablest diplomat ever to serve the Hawaiian Kingdom," Carter was born in Honolulu of non-missionary American parents and married missionary daughter Sybil Judd. Served Kalākaua and Lili'uokalani as minister to the United States and Europe from 1875 until his death in 1891.

Carter, Joseph O.—brother of H.A.P. Carter and uncle of Charles Carter, but on the opposite side of the fence politically to his nephew, Charles. J.O. Carter was president of C. Brewer and a close adviser to Lili'uokalani, was with her when she surrendered in 1893, got her to finally agree to amnesty for the Revolutionists during her three meetings with Minister Willis, then was forced by his Annexation-minded stockholders to resign as Brewer president when his role was revealed. In his earlier years, he was a reporter on *The Pacific Commercial Advertiser* when it was founded in 1856.

Castle, William R.—member of Committee of Safety born in Honolulu in 1849, graduate of Harvard and Columbia law schools, worked in New York until he returned to Hawai'i as attorney general in 1876 at request of King Kalākaua; served in the Legislature in 1878, '86, '87, '88, turning against Kalākaua in 1887. In 1887 and 1888 he was president of the Legislature. Appointed Hawai'i minister to Washington after U.S. Secretary of State Gresham forced L.A. Thurston to withdraw in 1895.

Cleghorn, Archibald S.—appointed governor of O'ahu by his sister-in-law, Lili'uokalani; father of Princess Ka'iulani, who was designated successor to the throne had Monarchy continued. Advised Queen strongly against the lottery bill.

Bishop Museum

Cleveland, Grover—president of United States 1893-97. Sent Blount to Hawai'i to investigate Revolution. Tried to restore Lili'uokalani to throne, but dropped the idea when she would not agree to grant amnesty to rebels.

Colburn, John F.—Native Hawaiian minister of interior at time of overthrow. With Peterson went to business community for support to oust Queen if she continued effort to promulgate new Constitution. Became supporter of Annexation in 1895 after abortive counter-revolution, Queen's abdication.

Cook, Capt. James—his landing in the Hawaiian Islands in 1778 was its first recognized contact with the Western world.

Cooke, Charles M.—son of missionaries Amos Starr and Juliette M. Cooke, born in 1849 at the Chiefs' Children's School. Cofounder of Bank of Hawaii. Involved in development of sugar plantations. One of the original trustees of Bishop Estate, appointed by Bernice P. Bishop herself.

Cooper, Henry—arrived in 1890 from Indiana, named chairman of the Committee of Safety at mass meeting on January 14, 1893, appointed its other twelve members. Circuit court judge in 1893-95, served four years as minister of foreign affairs for the Republic among other duties. Acting president when Dole went to Washington in 1897, became first secretary of the territory after Annexation.

Cornwell, W. H.—Royalist, minister of finance for the Queen in 1893; with Colburn sought community backing to oust her if she persisted in promulgating new Constitution.

Damon, Samuel Mills—born in 1845 of missionary parents, close adviser and friend of Lili'uokalani, sent by Dole to seek her surrender to avoid bloodshed. Finance minister and consultant for Kalākaua in 1887, for the queen from 1889-1890, for the Republic, 1893 to 1900. Member of Kingdom's privy council 1884 to 1889. Pioneer banker with Bishop in founding what is now First Hawaiian Bank. An original trustee of Bishop Estate. Creator of Moanalua Gardens on land left him by Pauahi Bishop. Died 1924.

Dole, Sanford Ballard—president of the Provisional Government. Had been justice of Monarchy's Supreme Court. Became president of the Republic and first governor of the Territory, serving until 1903. Appointed a federal judge in Hawai'i, 1903-1916. Son of Punahou School's first principal, he was born in 1844 on the campus. Died 1926.

Dominis, John—husband of Lili'uokalani. His father built Washington Place, her home until her death in 1917 when it became home to Hawai'i's governors.

Emma Rooke, Queen—granddaughter of John Young, widow of Kamehameha IV, contender for the crown against Kalākaua but lost to him in bitter election by Legislature in 1874, which resulted in riot that had to be quelled by U.S. troops. Strong British leanings. With her husband founded

Queen's Hospital and St. Andrew's Priory School.

Emmeluth, John—businessman, had two stores in the 1890s. Held American citizenship, member of Committee of Safety. Became one of the "Extreme Annexationists"; to push cause, helped create the evening *Hawaiian Star* in 1893.

Foster, John W.—U.S. secretary of state in Harrison administration, to whom Stevens wrote two weeks after the Revolution his famous despatch: "The Hawaiian pear is fully ripe and now is the golden hour for the United States to pluck it."

Gibson, Walter Murray—adviser to Kalākaua, gained lands, special favors from the King. Ordered out of Kingdom as an unsavory character at time of 1887 Reform Constitution.

Gregg, David L.—U.S. minister to Hawai'i who completed three-year negotiation of a formal treaty of Annexation in 1854 at request of the Hawaiian government. Kamehameha III, who had started the proceedings in 1851, died before the treaty could be signed and his successor withdrew the agreement.

Gresham, Walter Q.—U.S. secretary of state under Cleveland, opposed Annexation, strongly favored restoration of Lili'uokalani as Queen, advised Minister Willis in ill-fated effort to get Provisional Government to return control to her. Demanded recall of L.A. Thurston as minister in 1895 after heated argument over diplomatic protocol.

Harrison, Benjamin—president of the United States at the time of the Revolution, recognized new government, sympathetic to Annexation but unable to gain passage of treaty before his successor, Grover Cleveland, took office and withdrew it.

Hartwell, A.S.—respected jurist who with L.A. Thurston was approached by Queen's Cabinet members on January 14, 1893, for support from the community to oust her; drew up proclamation for them to carry it out, which became moot in their minds when she agreed to withdraw temporarily her effort to promulgate her new Constitution.

Inouye, Daniel—powerful late-20th-Century U.S. senator for Hawai'i. Introduced the congressional apology resolution with Senator Akaka, explained it did not seek special treatment for Hawaiians and did not have the force of law—"It's just a simple [resolution of] apology," he told the Senate during hour-long debate on the matter in 1993.

Jones, Peter Cushman—businessman born in Boston in 1837, came to Hawai'i in 1857 with 16 cents in pocket. Became partner in C. Brewer in 1871, president in 1883. Founding president of Bank of Hawai'i and Hawaiian Trust Co. Built Palāma Chapel, out of which grew Palāma Settlement. Chairman of mass meeting that forced Kalākaua to accept the 1887 Reform Constitution; served as minister of finance in Cabinet that Lili'uokalani dumped two days before 1893 Revolution.

Ka'ahumanu—favorite wife of Kamehameha I. At his direction, became regent after his death, guiding young Liholiho, Kamehameha II. Responsible for ending *kapu* system and banning Hawaiian religion before arrival of missionaries. Advised Liholiho to let them come ashore for trial year.

Ka'iulani, Princess—daughter of the Cleghorns, niece of Queen Lili'uokalani, named by her as successor if the 1895 counter-revolution had succeeded, schooled in England for four years, returned to Hawai'i after Revolution, died at age 24.

Kalākaua, King David—second of the elected kings of Hawai'i, served from his tumultuous election in 1874 after the death of Lunalilo until his own death in 1891 in San Francisco. Known as the "Merrie Monarch," did wonders for the Hawaiian psyche, but effectively ruined the economy of the

Kingdom with wild schemes and profligate spending, leading to mass meeting forcing Reform Constitution on him in 1887. Built 'Iolani Palace in 1882. Attempt to oust him in 1889, which had approval of his ambitious sister, Lili'uokalani, led to battle on Palace Grounds that killed seven, was quelled by same men who overthrew Queen in 1893.

Kalaniana'ole, Jonah Kūhiō—would have been third in line for the throne in 1895 had counter-revolution succeeded, elected in 1902 as Hawai'i's second delegate to Congress, served two decades, gained passage of Hawaiian Homes Act.

Kamehameha I, King—most powerful chief in Hawai'i history, born about 1736, according to early Hawaiian historian Samuel Kamakau; by 1795 had conquered in bloody battles all of the Islands except Kaua'i, making use of Western arms, ships, advisers. By 1810 unified all Islands into Hawaiian Kingdom when Kaua'i chief surrendered without a fight. Died in Kailua, Kona on May 8, 1819 as missionaries were preparing to leave for Hawai'i.

Kamehameha II, King—'Iolani Liholiho, son of Kamehameha I and Keopuolani. Born 1797. Ruled 1819-1824 before he and his Queen died of the measles during a visit to London. Under the influence of Ka'ahumanu, appointed *kuhina nui* (regent) by Kamehameha I, ended the ancient religious system of the islands. Allowed the first missionaries to land, fill the religious vacuum with Christianity.

Kamehameha III, King—Kauikeaouli, born 1814, longest-term Hawai'i ruler in recorded history, 1825-1854. Son of Kamehameha I and Keopuolani, was named successor by Liholiho, became King at age 9 with Ka'ahumanu continuing as *kuhina nui* until her death. Became King on his own at age 18 in 1833. In 1840, promulgated first written laws of Islands, instituting constitutional Monarchy. In 1848, promulgated Great *Mahele*, division of lands. In 1852, promulgated new Constitution after constitutional convention, Legislature agreed on terms. Actively sought Annexation to United States in 1851 when he could see Hawai'i was going to be taken over by one colonial power or another, died before treaty of Annexation could be signed.

Kamehameha IV, King—Alexander Liholiho, born 1834, ruled 1854-1863 under Constitution of 1852, grandson of Kamehameha I; adopted and named as heir in 1835 by Kauikeaouli as a favor to his cousin and successor *kuhinanui*, Kina'u, by way of reconciliation for her ouster as *kuhina nui* when he, Kauikeaouli, became 18. Son of Kina'u (a daughter of Kamehameha I and Kaheiheimalie) and Mataio Kekūanaōa, a high chief and governor of O'ahu. Favored Britain slightly over United States so withdrew unsigned treaty of Annexation worked out by his predecessor. With his wife, Queen Emma, a great-granddaughter of a younger brother of Kamehameha I, founded Queen's Hospital, and brought in Episcopal Church.

Kamehameha V, King—Lot Kamehameha, born 1830, ruled 1864-1872, promulgated new Constitution on his own in 1864 after Legislature rejected constitutional convention—same illegal move tried by Lili'uokalani but he got away with it. He added property ownership as requirement for voting for House. Never married. Died without naming successor, thus ending Kamehameha dynasty, prompting in 1873 first election of a Hawaiian king, by popular vote with confirmation by the Legislature.

Kaulukou, John L.—Native Hawaiian speaker of the House of

Representatives under the Republic at time of Annexation.
Had been a strong Royalist political and legal figure in days
of Kalākaua and Lili'uokalani—marshal, legislator, judge.
Publicly called Annexation to the U.S. the best thing possible for Hawai'i and its people.

Kawānanakoa, Prince David—would have been second
in line for succession to throne if Monarchy had
been reinstated in 1895. Helped Provisional Government keep things running after 1893 Revolution but soon left government. Was involved in
attempted counter-revolution.

King, Capt. James A.—pioneer inter-island shipping magnate
appointed by Dole as minister of interior of Provisional Government and then of Republic. Married to Hawaiian. Parents
of Delegate to Congress and later Governor Samuel Wilder
King and grandparents of Federal Judge Samuel P. King.

Kinney, W.A.—Hawai'i-born subject of the Kingdom, member of
House of Representatives in 1887, 1888 sessions, played role
in writing and adoption of Reform Constitution. Early law
partner of L.A. Thurston and W.O. Smith.

Kuykendall, Ralph S.—early-20th-Century historian, wrote
definitive three-volume history of Hawai'i covering period
1778-1893. Died in May 1963 just before completion of
third volume of *The Hawaiian Kingdom*, which was completed from his notes by a fellow University of Hawai'i historian, Dr. Charles H. Hunter.

Lansing, Theodore F.—American member of Committee of Safety. Came to Honolulu to join M. Phillip & Co. and with that
firm organized Pioneer Building and Loan Co. in 1890 to
provide financing for home building. In 1898 formed Gear,
Lansing & Co., residential land developers involved in subdi-
visions in Makiki and Kaimukī on land acquired from David
Kawānanakoa and Kūhiō Kalaniana'ole.

Lee, William L.—arrived by accident in 1846 with close friend
Charles Bishop, became chief justice of Supreme
Court in his 20s, wrote 1852 Constitution. Worked
tirelessly for Kamehameha III after Great *Mahele*
in 1848 to get lands into hands of Hawaiian
natives. Most important American adviser to
Kamehameha IV. Died in 1857 at age 36.

Liliʻuokalani, Queen Lydia Kamakaeha Dominis—born
1838, last of the Hawaiʻi monarchs, overthrown in
1893 after she tried to promulgate new Constitu-
tion without following procedures she had sworn
to uphold in 1891 when she took office as designated successor to her brother, Kalākaua. New
Constitution would have expanded powers of
Monarchy beyond those of Kalākaua before the
Reform Constitution of 1887. Died November 11, 1917.

Lunalilo, King William C.—first of the elected kings, topping
Kalākaua in legislative vote in 1873. A very popular figure,
he died without naming a successor. Created Lunalilo Trust
with gift of more land than was in Bishop Estate, but his
trustees sold most of the land to build home for aged Hawaiians and the trust now barely is able to maintain it.

Macfarlane, E.C.—close adviser of Queen Liliʻuokalani who
went on her behalf at Blount's suggestion to Washington in
1893, conferred with Secretary of State Gresham, Minister
Willis and Minister Mills, bringing back word that Blount's
goal and recommendation would be for her reinstatement.

McCandless, John A.—entrepreneur, businessman, American,
arrived 1881, naturalized Hawaiian member of Committee
of Safety. Member of Provisional Government Advisory
Council; elected to Senate of Provisional Government and
Republic, 1894-98. Held no sugar stock at time of Revolution
but later became vice president of Pioneer Mill, Oʻahu Sugar,

president of Home Insurance, director of Bank of Hawaii,
president of McCandless Bldg. Co. and director of Waialua
Plantation.

McChesney, F.W.—American member of Committee of Safety,
came to Hawai'i from Iowa in 1855, formed wholesale grocery and feed store. Blount declined to interview him, but
McChesney told Morgan Committee that contrary to Blount,
Revolution would have succeeded without U.S. troops coming ashore and that he "never expected U.S. troops to fight
our battle."

McKinley, William A.— U.S. president following Cleveland.
McKinley was more sympathetic to Annexation, which
passed in 1898 during his term.

Mills, Ellis—U.S. consul general in Hawai'i appointed by Cleveland to succeed Stevens after Blount turned down the job.
Had taken notes for Blount during his interviews and later
was man behind the screen recording Lili'uokalani interview
with Willis, when she said she would behead the Revolutionists if she were reinstated, causing Cleveland to back off
his effort to put her back on throne.

Moreno, Celso Caesar—controversial figure in Honolulu for
about a year, 1879-1880, who endeared himself to Kalākaua,
the Legislature and a number of Native Hawaiian leaders
with various schemes for opium licenses, a $10 million loan,
etc. Appointed minister of foreign affairs by the King on
August 14, 1880, and removed within days after an uproar
in the diplomatic corps. He left Honolulu, taking Robert W.
Wilcox with him for military training in his native Italy.

Morgan, James Francis—born in New York City, 1862. Came to
Hawai'i at age three. Started working at 12 at EP Adams
Auction Co., eventually becoming sole owner. Helped organize Honolulu Stock and Bond Exchange, served as its president. Member Provisional Government Advisory Council.

Morgan, John T.—Democratic U.S. senator from Alabama whose Committee on Foreign Relations took sworn testimony about the 1893 Revolution; in 5-4 decision exonerated Stevens, U.S. troops from blame for Revolution.

Neumann, Paul—attorney and adviser to Lili'uokalani, with J.O. Carter wrote letter claiming her surrender was to the "superior forces of the United States" instead of the Provisional Government that had demanded it. Dole noted receipt of the document, unintentionally opening door to charges U.S. had played key role in success of the Revolution.

Nordhoff, Charles — Reporter with New York *Herald*. Staunch supporter of the Royalists, wrote inaccurately about Provisional Government, which sought to expel him from Hawai'i but yielded to protest by his good friend, Blount, and let him stay.

Opukahaia, Henry (known back east as Obookiah)—Young Hawaiian runaway from enemies in Kealakekua Bay who ended up in Yale Divinity School and whose death in 1818 was largely responsible for the first missionaries deciding to come to Hawai'i to carry on the work he had planned to do.

Parker, Samuel—Native Hawaiian minister of foreign affairs in the Cabinet appointed by close friend, Lili'uokalani, just before Revolution. After 1895 failure of counter-revolution, he joined his fellow former Cabinet member, John Colburn, in coming out in favor of Annexation. Grandson of founder of Parker Ranch where Ka'iulani died.

Pauahi, Bernice Bishop—daughter of High Chief Pākī and his wife Konia; great-granddaughter of Kamehameha I. Married Charles Reed Bishop. Resisted attempts to name her successor to Kamehameha V though she was of Kamehameha line and had gone to Chiefs' Children's School with other royal children. Parents adopted Lili'uokalani and at one

Hawaiian Historical Society

time, after she and Bishop were married, they all lived together in *Haleakalā*, Bishop house on King Street between Fort and Alakea. House torn down to construct Bishop Street at turn of century. Pauahi probably Hawai'i's ultimate benefactress—her will established Kamehameha Schools and multibillion-dollar Bishop Estate.

Pierce, Henry—U.S. minister to Hawai'i in early 1870s. Like his predecessors was in favor of Annexation. Brought troops ashore to help quell 1874 riot when Kalākaua was elected.

Peterson, A.P.—Caucasian Royalist who was attorney general in Lili'uokalani's last Cabinet at time of Revolution. Sought support of business community against Queen's proposed Constitution. Had cast deciding vote for opium and lottery bills in 1892 legislature, earning scorn of community.

Pua, S.K.—member of Monarchy's House of Representatives, long-time supporter of Queen, but concerned about Marshal Charles Wilson's influence and tried to get a resolution through 1892 Legislature to have him removed.

Smith, W.O.—attorney, member of Committee of Safety. Born on Kaua'i, 1838, son of missionaries James Williams and Millicent Smith. Highly regarded by royal family, asked by Lili'uokalani to handle her estate despite his involvement in 1893 Revolution and subsequent governments. Before the Revolution, served as sheriff on Kaua'i and then Maui, was deputy attorney general of Monarchy for nearly seven years while serving intermittently in Legislature from 1878 to 1892. Attorney general of Republic, 1893-1898. One of original trustees of Bishop Estate. Died 1929.

Bishop Museum

Spreckels, Claus—sugar baron from California, manipulator, supporter of Kalākaua and Lili'uokalani. Loaned Monarchy money in exchange for influence. Queen's diaries show she thought he would be means to restore her to the throne.

Stevens, John L.—United States minister to Hawai'i in 1893 whose Annexation leanings put him at the center of the controversy after the Revolution, but whose role has probably been vastly overstated.

Tenney, Edward Davies—Arrived in 1877 at 18. Member of Provisional Government Advisory Council. Started in sugar at Hilo and by 1880 was a junior clerk at Castle and Cooke, eventually becoming president. In 1942 was president of Matson Navigation while still president of C&C.

Thurston, Asa—with wife, Lucy Goodale, member of the pioneer missionary group. Born in Fitchburg, Mass., in 1787, stayed in church service his whole life, dying in Honolulu in 1868. Graduated from Yale in 1816 and Yale Divinity School in 1819. Came to Hawai'i in 1820.

Hawaiian Mission Children's Society

Thurston, Asa Goodale—son of Asa and Lucy Thurston, born 1827 in Kona; father of Lorrin A. Thurston. Left in 1840 to school for ten years; prep school, Yale, and in 1849 became Hawai'i's first graduate from Williams College. Elected to Legislature in 1853. Married missionary daughter Sarah Andrews in 1853. Speaker of the House during last year of reign of Kamehameha III in 1854. Founding president of Mission Children's Society formed to send missionaries to South Seas. Died at 32 when Lorrin was a little over one year old, daughter Helen not yet born.

Thurston, Lorrin A.—born in Honolulu in 1858, grandson of four missionaries; grandfather of this author. Spoke Hawaiian fluently as had his father and grandfather. Lawyer; elected to House of Representatives in 1886 at age 28, House of Nobles in 1892, served Hawaiian government as minister of interior, 1887-1890, under Kalākaua, became his prime minister, wrote Reform Constitution and was

Bishop Museum • Post

instrumental in 1893 Revolution. After Revolution, worked ardently for Annexation. Married Clara Shipman in 1886. She died in childbirth in 1891 and he married Harriet Potter in 1894. In 1898, became owner/publisher of *The Pacific Commercial Advertiser,* later *The Honolulu Advertiser,* helped set aside Haleakalā and Kīlauea as federal preserves, fostered Kīlauea Observatory. Died in 1931.

Thurston, Lorrin Potter—son of Lorrin and Harriet, born 1900. Was publisher of *The Honolulu Advertiser* 1931-1960, founder of Pacific Area Travel Association, chairman of Statehood Commission at time Hawai'i became state.

Thurston, Lucy Goodale—grandmother of Lorrin A., she came with the first company of missionaries in 1820, was last survivor of that group when she died in 1876. Wrote *The Life and Times of Lucy G. Thurston*, detailed record of the rigors of missionary life, including account of her radical mastectomy without anaesthesia in 1855.

Thurston, Sarah Andrews—mother of Lorrin A., raised three children after husband's death at age 32 by teaching at schools on O'ahu and Maui. Daughter of missionaries Lorrin and Sarah Andrews. Her father wrote first Hawaiian dictionary, founded Lahainaluna School, taught engraving to natives.

Waterhouse, Henry—Hawaiian subject of Tasmanian birth, came to Hawai'i in 1851. Member of Committee of Safety. Pressed for and helped draft the Reform Constitution in 1887. One of the two members of the Committee of Safety to be interviewed by Blount, who took statement from him trying to determine time of recognition of new government by U.S. Minister Stevens, called Waterhouse a liar when his recollection didn't parallel that of Queen's witnesses.

Wilcox, Robert W.—Hawaiian activist, called "chronic revolutionist" by boyhood friend, L.A. Thurston. Thurston said he called him that because it didn't seem to make much difference to him which side he was on as long as he was engaged in a fight. Led attempted revolution against Kalākaua in 1889, abortive revolution in 1892, sat out 1893 Revolution but was leader of the unsuccessful counter-revolution in 1895. Sentenced to death but sentence was commuted. After Annexation, got back into politics and with new Hawaiian majority, was elected Hawai'i's first delegate to Congress in 1900. Defeated in 1902, he ran for sheriff of O'ahu in the off-year county election of 1903 and died on Oct. 23, 1903, during the campaign.

Wilder, William C.—American, Hawaiian subject member of Committee of Safety. Wealthy shipping magnate, arranged for himself and other four Annexation ministers from Provisional Government to leave for Washington two days after Revolution. President of the Republic Senate, 1897. Editor of *Pacific Commercial Advertiser* in 1890s.

Willis, Albert S.—special U.S. minister sent to Hawai'i by President Cleveland to reinstate Lili'uokalani, depending on whether she would grant amnesty to Revolutionists. When the ex-Queen refused, Cleveland's plot, a violation of international diplomatic codes, fell apart. Queen later recanted her non-amnesty position, Willis asked Dole administration to turn government back to her but his request was denied.

Wilson, Charles B.—marshal of Kingdom, chief of police at time of Revolution. Strong supporter of Queen. His influence opposed by many, including Hawaiian political leaders, but if he had arrested Committee of Safety when he wanted to on Sunday, January 15, Revolution might not have succeeded. Son John, later mayor of Honolulu, built Pali Road.

Wiltse, G.C.—captain of U.S.S. *Boston* who gave order for troops to go ashore to protect American lives and property after his officers reported great unrest developing January 16 at two mass meetings, one native, one the rest of community.

Wodehouse, James H.—British minister to Hawai'i at time of Revolution, a great friend and supporter of Lili'uokalani. Strongly opposed Annexation of Hawai'i to United States.

Wolf, Fraulein—Lili'uokalani's German teacher-turned-seer who provided questionable psychic readings for the Queen, particularly concerning the lottery bill and Cabinet appointees.

Young, Alexander—mechanical engineer, arrived in 1865; set up foundry and machine shop in Hilo. Bought interest in Honolulu Iron Works and invested in sugar. An interior minister after the Revolution. Member of House of Nobles, 1889; member of Advisory Council of Provisional Government. Built the Alexander Young Hotel, acquired the Moana and later the Royal Hawaiian.

Young, John—boatswain of the British ship Eleanora who jumped ship on the Kona coast of the Big Island in 1790, proved invaluable advisor to Kamehameha I in trade negotiations and in his conquest of the other islands. Married daughter of chief, served on king's advisory council until his death. His granddaughter, Emma Rooke, married Kamehameha IV and became Queen Emma.

Young, Lucien—U.S. naval lieutenant, second in command of the U.S.S. *Boston* in 1893 who testified decision to land troops was made by Capt. Wiltse, not Minister Stevens. Also testified troops ordered to remain neutral, were located so as to avoid siding with either government or rebels.

Bibliography

Adler, Jacob, *Claus Spreckels: The Sugar King in Hawaii*, (Mutual Publishing, Honolulu 1966)

Adler, Jacob and Robert M. Kamins, *The Fantastic Life of Walter Murray Gibson: Hawaii's Minister of Everything*, (University of Hawaii Press, Honolulu 1986)

Alexander, Elizabeth, et al., ed., *Missionary Album, Portraits and Biographical Sketches of the American Protestant Missionaries to the Hawaiian Islands*, Sesquicentennial Edition, (Hawaiian Mission Children's Society, Honolulu 1969)

Alexander, William De Witt, *Two Weeks of Hawaiian History*, (Hawaiian Gazette Co., Honolulu 1893)

Alexander, William De Witt, *History of Later Years of the Hawaiian Monarchy ... and the Revolution of 1893*, (Hawaiian Gazette Co., Honolulu 1896)

Allen, Helena G., *The Betrayal of Liliuokalani: Last Queen of Hawaii 1838-1917*, (The Arthur H. Clark Company, Glendale, CA 1982)

Allen, Helena G., *Sanford Ballard Dole: Hawaii's Only President*, (The Arthur H. Clark Company, Glendale, CA 1988)

Andrade, Ernest, Jr., *Unconquerable Rebel: Robert W. Wilcox and Hawaiian Politics*, 1880-1903, (University Press of Colorado, Niwot, CO 1996)

Bailey, Paul, *Hawaii's Royal Prime Minister: The Life & Times of Walter Murray Gibson*, (Hastings House, New York 1980)

Benjamin, Stuart Minor, *Equal Protection and the Special Relationship: The Case of Native Hawaiians*, (The Yale Law Journal, Vol. 106, No. 3, Dec. 1996)

Bingham, Hiram, *A Residence of Twenty-One Years in the Sandwich Islands; or the Civil, Religious and Political History of those Islands*, (Hezekiah Huntington, Hartford 1847)

Bushnell, O.A., *The Gifts of Civilization: Germs and Genocide in Hawai'i*, (University of Hawaii Press, Honolulu 1993)

Campbell, Archibald, *Voyage Round the World: From 1806 to 1812,* edited by James Smith, (Archibald Constable and Company, et al., Edinburgh 1816)

Cahill, Emmett, *The Shipmans of East Hawai'i,* (University of Hawaii Press, Honolulu 1996)

Chapin, Helen Geracimos, *The Role of Newspapers in Hawai'i,* (University of Hawaii Press, Honolulu 1996)

Chinen, Jon J., *Original Land Titles In Hawaii,* (Honolulu 1961)

Chinen, Jon J., *The Great Mahele,* (University of Hawaii Press 1958)

Cooper, George, and Gavan Daws, *Land and Power in Hawaii,* (University of Hawaii Press, Honolulu 1990)

Day, A. Grove, *Hawaii and Its People,* (Mutual Publishing, Honolulu 1955)

Day, A. Grove, *History Makers of Hawaii,* (Mutual Publishing, Honolulu 1984)

Damon, Ethel M., *Sanford Ballard Dole and His Hawaii,* (Hawaiian Historical Society by Pacific Books, Palo Alto 1957)

Daws, Gavan, *Shoal of Time: A History of the Hawaiian Islands,* (University of Hawaii Press, Honolulu 1974)

De Varigny, Charles, *Fourteen Years in the Sandwich Islands,* translated by Alfons L. Korn, (University of Hawaii Press & The Hawaiian Historical Society, Honolulu 1981)

Dole, Sanford B., *Letter to Minister Willis* (Star Electric Presses, Honolulu 1894)

Dole, Sanford B., *Memoirs of the Hawaiian Revolution,* Andrew Farrell, editor (Honolulu Advertiser Publishing Co., Ltd., Honolulu 1936)

Dwight, Edwin, *Memoirs of Henry Obookiah,* (Woman's Board of Missions for the Pacific Islands 1968)

Fitzpatrick, Gary L. and Riley M. Moffat, *Surveying the Mahele,* Editions Ltd., Honolulu 1995)

Frye, Senator William P., *Speech before the Senate,* Feb. 28 & Mar. 1, 1894

Frear, Walter F., *Anti-Missionary Criticism: With Reference to Hawaii,* Paper to Honolulu Social Science Association, Jan. 7, 1935.

Fuchs, Lawrence H., *Hawaii Pono: A Social History,* (Harcourt, Brace & World, Inc., New York 1961)

Gray, Francine Du Plessix, *Hawaii: The Sugar-Coated Fortress,* (Random House, New York 1972)

Harris, Edwin A., *A Hero of Fitchburg: Asa Thurston,* (Sentinel Printing Company, Fitchburg 1878)

Hobbs, Jean, *Hawaii: A Pageant of the Soil,* (Stanford University Press, Stanford 1935)

Ii, John Papa, *Fragments of Hawaiian History*, translated by Mary Kawena Pukui, (Bishop Museum Press, Honolulu 1959)

Irwin, Jeffrey, *The Prehistoric Exploration and Colonization of the Pacific* (Cambridge University Press, Cambridge 1992)

Judd, Walter F., *American Missionaries in Hawaii*, unpublished papers (Honolulu 1996)

Kameʻeleihiwa, Lilikalā, *Native Land and Foreign Desires • Pehea Lā E Pono Ai?*, (Bishop Museum Press, Honolulu 1992)

Kent, Harold Winfield, *Charles Reed Bishop, Man of Hawaii* (Pacific Books, Palo Alto 1965)

Kirch, Patrick Vinton, *Legacy of the Landscape*, (University of Hawaii Press, Honolulu 1996)

Kotzebue, Otto Von, *A New Voyage Round the World, In the Years 1823, 24, 25 and 26*, (Henry Colburn and Richard Bentley, London 1830)

Kuykendall, Ralph S. and A. Grove Day, *Hawaii: A History*, (Prentice-Hall, Inc., Englewood Cliffs, NJ 1961)

Kuykendall, Ralph S., *The Hawaiian Kingdom*, three volumes, (University of Hawaii Press, Honolulu 1938, 1953, 1967)

Levy, Neil M., *Native Hawaiian Land Rights*, (California Law Review 1975)

Liliʻuokalani, *Diaries*, Hawaiʻi Archives, Bishop Museum

Liliʻuokalani, *Hawaii's Story by Hawaii's Queen* (Mutual Publishing, Honolulu 1990)

Lydecker, Robert C., compiled from records in the Archives of Hawaiʻi, *Roster, Legislatures of Hawaii, 1841-1918,* (The Hawaiian Gazette Co., Ltd., Honolulu 1918)

MacKenzie, Melody K., ed., *Native Hawaiian Rights Handbook*, (Native Hawaiian Legal Corp. & Office of Hawaiian Affairs, Honolulu 1991)

Morgan, William M., *Strategic Factors in Hawaiian Annexation*, (Claremont Graduate School 1980)

Nellist, George F., ed., *The Story of Hawaii and Its Builders*, (Honolulu Star Bulletin, Ltd., Honolulu 1925)

Piercy, LaRue W., *Hawaii's Missionary Saga: Sacrifice and Godliness in Paradise*, (Mutual Publishing, Honolulu 1992)

Rifkin, Jeremy, *The End of Work,* (G.P. Putnam's Sons, New York 1996)

Russ, William A. Jr., *The Hawaiian Revolution 1893-94*, (Susquehanna University Press, Selinsgrove 1959)

Russ, William A. Jr., *The Hawaiian Republic 1894-98*, (Susquehanna University Press, Selinsgrove 1961)

Siddall, John W., ed., *Men of Hawaii*, Vol II, (Honolulu Star-Bulletin,

Ltd. 1921)

Spaulding, Thomas Marshall, *The Crown Lands of Hawaii,* (University of Hawaii Press, Occasional Papers No. 1, Honolulu 1923)

Thurston, Lorrin A., editor, *The Fundamental Law of Hawaii,* (The Hawaiian Gazette Co., Ltd., Honolulu 1904)

Thurston, Lorrin A., *A Handbook on the Annexation of Hawaii*

Thurston, Lorrin A., *Memoirs of the Hawaiian Revolution*, edited by Andrew Farrell, (Honolulu Advertiser Publishing Co., Ltd., Honolulu 1936)

Thurston, Lucy G., *Life and Times of Mrs. Lucy G. Thurston,* (S.C. Andrews, Ann Arbor 1882)

Unknown, *A Narrative of Five Youth from the Sandwich Islands,* (J. Seymour, New York 1816)

Whitney, Caspar, *Hawaiian America: Something of its History, Resources and Prospects,* (Harper & Brothers, New York 1899)

Zambucka, Kristin, *Princess Kaiulani: The Last Hope of Hawaii's Monarchy,* (Mana Publishing Co., Honolulu 1984)

Hawaii, Fact and Fiction, Hawaiian Mission Children's Society, (Honolulu 1967)

Hawaii, Handbook No. 85, Bureau of the American Republic, (Washington, D.C. 1897)

Hawaiian Hansard: A complete Verbatim Report of the Proceedings and Speeches of the Hawaiian Legislative Assembly of 1886, (Daily Bulletin Steam Printing Office, Honolulu 1886)

Hawaiian Journal of History, Volumes 26-30, (Hawaiian Historical Society, Honolulu 1992-96)

Hawaiian Laws 1841-1842, Translation of the Constitution and Laws of the Hawaiian Islands, Established in the Reign of Kamehameha III, (Lahainaluna 1842, Reprinted by Ted Adameck, Green Valley, NV 1994)

House Ex. Document No. 48, 53rd Congress, second session, 1893.

San Francisco Chronicle, July 28, 1898

Senate Executive Documents No. 45, 52nd Congress, Second Session to No. 60, 53rd Congress, Third Session. (1893-1895)

Reports of Committee on Foreign Relations, United States Senate, 1789-1901, 1st Congress, First Session, to 56th Congress, Second Session, Diplomatic Relations with Foreign Nations–Hawaiian Islands, Vol. VI, (Government Printing Office, Washington 1901)

University of Hawaii Law Review, Vol. 17, No. 2, Fall 1995

United States Court of Claims decision, May 16, 1910.

*F*ootnotes

Chapter One

1. Russ, William A. Jr., *The Hawaiian Revolution 1893-94*, (Susquehanna University Press 1959) 351.

2. Ibid, 169.

3. Russ, William A. Jr., *The Hawaiian Republic 1894-98*, (Susquehanna University Press 1961) 53; and Thurston, Lorrin A., *Memoirs of the Hawaiian Revolution*, edited by Andrew Farrell, (Honolulu Advertiser Publishing Co., Ltd. 1936) 535-537.

Chapter Two

4. Congressional Record, 52nd Congress, Second Session, Senate Ex. Document 45.

5. Ibid.

6. Ibid.

7. Bushnell, O.A., *The Gifts of Civilization: Germs and Genocide in Hawai'i*, (University of Hawaii Press, Honolulu 1993) 107.

8. Alexander, Elizabeth, et al., *Missionary Album, Portraits and Biographical Sketches of the American Protestant Missionaries to the Hawaiian Islands*, Sesquicentennial Edition, (Hawaiian Mission Children's Society 1969) 17.

9. Ibid, 33.

10. Ibid, 31, 112, 128, 162.

11. Blount Report, contained in House Ex. Doc. No. 48, 53rd Congress, second session, 1893.

Chapter Three

12. Official correspondence Pierce to Fish, Sept. 2, 1973.

13. Thurston, *Memoirs . . .*, 23-4.

14. Hartwell correspondence.

Chapter Four

15. Morgan Report, Reports of Committee on Foreign Relations, United States Senate, 1789-1901, 1st Congress, First Session, to 56th Congress, Sec-

ond Session, Diplomatic Relations with Foreign Nations–Hawaiian Islands, Vol. VI, (Government Printing Office, Washington 1901) *Blount's report is 180 degrees from this sworn testimony. Blount alleged Thurston approached the Cabinet members, but he did not interview him or his colleagues.*

16. Ibid, 963-98.
17. Ibid, 817-19.
18. Ibid, 807-10.
19. Thurston to Foster, Feb. 21, 1893, USDS notes from Hawaiian Legation Vol. 4.

Chapter Five

20. Fuchs, Lawrence H., *Hawaii Pono: A Social History*, (Harcourt, Brace & World, Inc., New York 1961).
21. Kuykendall, Vol. II, 115-118.
22. Kuykendall, Vol. III, 344.
23. Ibid, 578.
24. Morgan Report, McCandless testimony 967-975; Thurston, *Memoirs . . .* and others.
25. Alexander, William De Witt, *Two Weeks of Hawaiian History*, (Hawaiian Gazette Co. 1893) and Blount Report.
26. Ibid.
27. Ibid.
28. Morgan Report, Thurston statement.
29. Blount Report, Parker to Blount.
30. Ibid, Stevens.
31. Morgan Report, Swinburne testimony.
32. Ibid.
33. Proclamation Abrogating Monarchy, Archives of Hawai'i.
34. Senate Report No. 227, Morgan Report findings, Feb. 26, 1894.
35. Russ, *The Hawaiian Republic*, 95.
36. Ibid, 205.
37. Fuchs, 158.
38. Ibid, 406 and *Honolulu Star-Bulletin*.
39. Fuchs, 161.
40. Fuchs, 162.

Chapter Six

41. Russ, *The Hawaiian Revolution*, 71.
42. Kuykendall, Vol. 1, 420.
43. Ibid, 420-428.
44. Morgan Report, 563.

Chapter Seven

45. Russ, Morgan Report, Thurston.
46. Russ, *The Hawaiian Revolution*, 205-8.
47. Senate Executive Doc. 13, Gresham to Willis Dec. 3, 1893.

48. Russ, 243.

49. Morgan Report, 812-13.

50. Ibid, 946.

Chapter Eight

51. Blount Report, J.W. Jones to Blount.

52. Blount Report, 673, Ashford statement.

53. Kent, Harold Winfield, *Charles Reed Bishop: Man of Hawaii*, (Pacific Books, Palo Alto 1965) 90.

54. Morgan, William M., *Strategic Factors in Hawaiian Annexation*, (Claremont Graduate School 1980) 85.

55. Ibid.

Chapter Nine

56. Irwin, Jeffrey, *The Prehistoric Exploration and Colonization of the Pacific*, (Cambridge University Press, Cambridge 1992).

57. Kotzebue, Otto Von, *A New Voyage Round the World, in the Years 1823, 24, 25, and 26*, Vol. II, (Henry Colburn & Richard Bentley, London 1830) 153.

58. Bushnell, 6.

59. Senate Executive Doc. No. 13, 53rd Congress, Second Session, Blaine to Comly June 30, 1881.

60. Kuykendall, Vol. I, 69.

61. Ibid, 41.

62. Correspondence, Persis Collection of the Stamps and Postal History of Hawai'i.

63. Kuykendall, Vol. I, 286-287.

64. Ibid, 289.

65. Hobbs, Jean, *Hawaii: A Pageant of the Soil*, (Stanford University Press 1935) 118.

Chapter Eleven

66. *The Honolulu Advertiser*, Sept. 10, 1897.

67. Morgan Report, McCandless testimony, 985; Alexander, *History of the Later Years . . .* , 58.

68. Thurston, *Memoirs . . .* , Colburn to Thurston, letter dated Jan. 30, 1895; Archives of Hawai'i.